Early praise for
Rapid Android Development

I highly recommend this book; there is no other text on Processing and Android quite like it on the market. It is extremely exhaustive and well structured, and it avoids the pitfalls of preaching to the converted or assuming too much prior knowledge. It is not a small thing to write for experienced creative coders and n00bs alike. Daniel Sauter clearly knows his stuff.

➤ **Jesse Scott**
Adjunct Faculty, Interaction Design and Smartphone Development, Emily Carr University of Art + Design and Langara College

Rapid Android Development successfully aims at a wide audience—from beginners to experienced developers. I recommend it to anyone who wants to use Processing to develop Android apps, especially creative coders who will be inspired by the diverse techniques for mobile development that fill this book.

➤ **Andrés Colubri**
Computational Researcher, Harvard University and Fathom Information Design

Even if you think you know Processing for Android, this book will still teach you something new, be it 3D, data storage methods, or networking techniques. It provides a solid framework from which aspiring Android developers can launch into developing apps, all while being enjoyable to read.

➤ **William Smith**
Moderator, Processing Forum

Daniel Sauter's *Rapid Android Development* provides a serious guide to using the platform for creative coding that Processing provides for leveraging the full potential of Android devices. Advanced graphics, gestures and sensors are only the tip of the iceberg, and you will find yourself diving into sophisticated sensor-based applications, games and art-ware, learning a host of techniques for coding and even publishing them in Google's Play market. This book is invaluable!

➤ **Jesus Duran**
    Artist, educator, and CTO of Ketai LLC

Whether used for education, application prototyping or just plain fun, Processing for Android is easy to learn and can produce truly stunning visual results. If you don't have time or interest to learn the intricacies of Android OpenGL, radios and sensor programming, but want to benefit from all the magic that these technologies have to offer, this book provides the shortest and most informative path toward achieving that goal.

➤ **Mike Riley**
    Author, *Programming Your Home*

Rapid Android Development

Build Rich, Sensor-Based Applications with Processing

Daniel Sauter

The Pragmatic Bookshelf

Dallas, Texas • Raleigh, North Carolina

Many of the designations used by manufacturers and sellers to distinguish their products are claimed as trademarks. Where those designations appear in this book, and The Pragmatic Programmers, LLC was aware of a trademark claim, the designations have been printed in initial capital letters or in all capitals. The Pragmatic Starter Kit, The Pragmatic Programmer, Pragmatic Programming, Pragmatic Bookshelf, PragProg and the linking *g* device are trademarks of The Pragmatic Programmers, LLC.

Every precaution was taken in the preparation of this book. However, the publisher assumes no responsibility for errors or omissions, or for damages that may result from the use of information (including program listings) contained herein.

Our Pragmatic courses, workshops, and other products can help you and your team create better software and have more fun. For more information, as well as the latest Pragmatic titles, please visit us at *http://pragprog.com*.

The Android robot is reproduced from work created and shared by Google and is used according to terms described in the Creative Commons 3.0 Attribution License (*http://creativecommons.org/licenses/by/3.0/us/legalcode*).

The team that produced this book includes:

John Osborn (editor)
Potomac Indexing, LLC (indexer)
Molly McBeath (copyeditor)
David J Kelly (typesetter)
Janet Furlow (producer)
Juliet Benda (rights)
Ellie Callahan (support)

Printed in the United States of America.
ISBN-13: 978-1-93778-506-2
Printed on acid-free paper.
Book version: P2.0—November 2013

Contents

Part I — Getting Started with
the Touch Screen and Android Sensors

Part II — Working with Camera and Location Devices

Part III — Using Peer-to-Peer Networking

Part V — Creating 3D Graphics and Cross-Platform Apps

Foreword

Processing was hand-rolled at MIT 12 years ago, by Ben Fry and Casey Reas, conceived originally as a programming environment for media artists. Really, it had two purposes. First, it was supposed to be quick and painless to create and compile a program. Second, it was built to be teachable—the commands and structures made sense, and (most of) the things that usually make programming painful were tucked away so that the user didn't have to think about them. In the years that have passed since its birth, Processing has been used for a dizzying array of projects, from robotics to architecture to dance to science to gaming and beyond. But these two core principles, ease-of-use and ease-of-learning, still guide the project and how it is developed.

With Processing for Android, and with Daniel's work on KETAI, these core philosophies are alive and breathing in the world of mobile devices. In a matter of minutes (really!), we can create real working applications on Android. Instead of being limited by the offerings in online "app marketplaces," we can build our own tools, focused on markets as large or as small as we want them to be. Want to make an app to track the time you spend with your kids? Build it in Android. Want to sample colors on your trip to the botanical gardens? Make an app, in minutes. Have an idea for the next big mobile game? Sketch it in Processing, and test it on your phone and tablet, with a single click.

Casey Reas has said that Processing was built to have a very low floor and a very high ceiling. It is meant to be both easy to use, and extremely functional. This core principle applies neatly to Processing for Android, which is at the same time very easy to learn, and extraordinarily powerful. With Daniel's book, readers will be quickly building and deploying simple projects to their Android devices. By working through the well-crafted examples and taking advantage of the code samples and libraries, they will easily be able to progress toward building more advanced apps, incorporating sensors and databases and all sorts of other useful and amazing things.

The central metaphor for Processing has for years been the sketchbook. Now this computational sketchbook is no longer tethered to our desks in an unwieldy box. We can take it with us into the world. A digital sketchbook, in our pocket. What an amazing idea.

Jer Thorp, Co-founder, The Office for Creative Research
March 2013

Acknowledgments

I'd like to acknowledge the following individuals who have contributed to this project and thank them deeply for their support:

First and foremost, Jesus Duran, CTO of Ketai LLC, without whom the Ketai library used in this book would neither have come to existence nor contain the comprehensive list of features that it has today—his talent and rigor have been essential to bringing Android features within Processing's reach in a timely and reliable way;

John Osborn, my editor, whose valuable feedback and recommendations were always right on target and instrumental to completing a book that could be useful and clear to diverse audiences;

Casey Reas, Processing cofounder, whose guidance and friendship are what brought me to Processing in the first place—I consider Processing to be not only one of the most versatile teaching and production tools available to solve problems but also the subject of the most generous community of creative coders out there;

Ben Fry, Processing cofounder, who has relentlessly guided Processing through its countless updates while maintaining a particular sense of humor that helped form the popular multimodal development environment into what it is today;

Andres Colubri, whose four-dimensional genius has produced a significant OpenGL and video overhaul for Processing and who has made major contributions to the Android mode;

Joshua Albers, Jon Buckley, Andres Colubri, Stephen Mendez, Michael Riley, Andreas Schlegel, Jesse Scott, and William Smith for their thorough technical reviews of the book and their valuable feedback;

The University of Illinois at the Chicago School of Art and Design, my institutional home that has always supported my efforts and also made it possible for me to launch the Mobile Processing Conference http://mobileProcessing.org in Chicago in 2010; and

Irena Knezevic, my partner, on whom I rely for the critical judgment and daily joy that is required to write a book.

Preface

Processing is a favorite among artists and designers and widely popular among developers who look for a productivity edge.[1] The programming language and environment has developed from a sketching tool to a production environment for a range of operating systems and platforms. The *Android mode*, introduced to Processing with the release of version 2.0, now makes it as easy to develop Processing apps for the Android as for the desktop.

Initiators Ben Fry and Casey Reas have promoted software literacy since 2001 using Processing, a free open source tool that can be used by individuals at any level of programming experience. The Processing project thrives on the support of its generous online community, whose members encourage collaboration and code sharing and are responsible for one of Processing's most important features: its libraries.

Libraries have made Processing the versatile and capable coding environment that it is today. Members have contributed more than 130 libraries to Processing over the last decade. I have extensively used Processing in the classroom during the past eight years and have realized various projects with it, sometimes in conjunction with Processing's sister project, Arduino.[2] In 2010, I started the *Ketai* (the Japanese term for cell phone culture) library with Jesus Duran,[3] which brings Android hardware features to Processing and makes it possible to work with sensors and hardware devices using simple and easy-to-read code.

In comparison, developing Android apps in Java using the standard Eclipse IDE entails a much steeper learning curve,[4] one that requires a programmer to master both the syntax of a modern object-oriented language and the features of a complex development environment. In Processing, we can see results

---

1.   http://processing.org/
2.   http://arduino.cc/
3.   http://code.google.com/p/ketai/
4.   http://developer.android.com/sdk/eclipse-adt.html

immediately because we are working with a straightforward syntax and a wide range of libraries and tools designed specifically to support visually lavish and highly interactive applications.

Android users expect a rich, interactive mobile user experience from their phones and tablets, one that takes full advantage of their touch screens, networking hardware, sensors for geolocation and device orientation, built-in cameras, and more. In this book, we'll learn how to create apps for Android devices that take full advantage of their many built-in hardware affordances.

Introducing Processing for the Android

Android is based on the Java programming language. Processing is also based on Java, making it the perfect platform for developing Android apps using Processing's straightforward syntax. The addition of the Android mode was a natural progression for Processing in order to streamline application development while targeting a broad range of operating systems and devices with one comprehensive programming language. In fact, Processing's software architecture allows us to mix in Java statements and packages, Android statements and packages, and Processing sketches and libraries wherever we feel like it.

This book focuses on Android apps developed in Processing. There are no differences between the Android mode and Processing's Java mode for desktop applications when it comes to the basic programming structure and syntax. Android-specific features that require device sensors and hardware are not available on the desktop and therefore are not usable in Processing's Java mode. They are available, however, as soon as we switch to Android mode.

In the last chapter of the book we'll discuss cross-platform challenges for mobile apps and introduce Processing's JavaScript mode. HTML5 web apps developed in Processing run on all modern browsers found on smart phones, tablets, and desktops today. While interoperability is an important factor, we will limit our discussion of web apps to the last chapter, as we can't access many of the hardware sensors and devices that make for exciting apps.

All core Processing methods are identical across modes, so when we develop Android apps we can also consider and use code examples written for Java mode. The Processing website contains a complete reference for all Processing methods.[5] So does the IDE, which ships with a packaged reference that we can use without a connection to the Web; it's available from the Processing menu by selecting Help → Reference.

---

5.   http://processing.org/reference/

Let's take a look at some of the main advantages to developing Android apps in Processing:

- If you are new to programming, Processing for Android is much easier to learn than Java. If you are an experienced Java programmer already, Processing is a great programming environment for rapid prototyping of graphics and sensor-heavy apps.

- Processing uses straightforward syntax. In comparison to Java, it is more concise.[6] Processing doesn't require you to understand advanced concepts such as classes or screen buffering to get started, yet it makes them accessible to any advanced users who want to use them. This makes Processing programs shorter and easier to read.

- The lightweight programming environment installs quickly and is easy to use. Processing is available for GNU/Linux, Mac OS X, and Windows. If you work with multiple computers or want to help someone else get started quickly, being up and running in a few minutes can make all the difference.

- Processing for Android supports OpenGL. When working with GPU-accelerated 2D and 3D graphics and geometry, lights, or textures, comprehensive OpenGL support is essential to ensure reasonably high frame rates and a fluid user experience.

- The latest version of Processing supports three application environments, or modes. Applications written in Java mode will run on Linux, Mac, or Windows systems. Programs written in Android mode will run on Android devices, and those written in JavaScript mode will run in any HTML5 browser. The Android mode is designed for creating native Android apps.

- Once your sketch prototyping is done, you can easily move your work to Eclipse for debugging and deployment. Processing lets you export your sketches as Android projects in the File → Export Android Project menu, creating an android directory with all the necessary files in it.

- Though currently deactivated and still under development, Processing will also facilitate the process of publishing to Google Play using a built-in dialog that guides you through the signing and releasing process (File → Export Signed Package).[7]

---

6. http://wiki.processing.org/w/Java_Comparison
7. https://play.google.com/store

This list of advantages should provide you all the evidence you need to conclude that Processing is a great environment for developing Android apps. Your projects can scale in scope and context: from sketch to prototype and from prototype to market-ready application, from CPU-focused graphics rendering to hardware-accelerated GPU-focused rendering, from Processing statements and libraries to Android and Java statements and packages, and from a particular operating system and device to other operating systems and devices. You won't need to worry about a different last-minute route or an alternative solution for your software projects. Projects can grow with you and will let you enjoy the iterative process of design and development.

Who This Book Is For

The book is written for the following readers:

- *Readers with some programming experience*: Readers with a basic understanding of programming concepts can quickly learn the Processing language as they work their way through the examples. Processing is that easy to learn.

- *Intermediate Processing users*: Readers looking to create Android apps from within the Processing IDE can maintain a good balance between simplicity and versatility.

- *Educators who teach courses on mobile technologies*: Teachers often navigate the academic triangle of limited time, limited budget, and classes without prerequisites. This book brings advanced mobile features within the reach of students with little or no prior programming experience using a free tool that does not require developer licenses or subscriptions.

- *Java and Android developers*: Experienced developers look for a productivity gain. Because Processing builds on Java, developers can use their Java code and knowledge with Processing, leveraging a host of libraries for productivity gains.

- *JavaScript and web developers*: Processing.js syntax is identical to standard Processing syntax, making it easy to create JavaScript-powered web applications that can run inside browsers without plugins or other modifications. Processing.js also takes advantage of WebGL hardware acceleration.

- *Arduino users and hobbyists*: Some readers have experience with the Processing language by using it to program the Arduino electronics platform and are interested in adapting Android phones or tablets for use as sensing devices, controllers, or graphics processors.

Prerequisites

If you have never programmed in Processing or any other language before, you can turn to two excellent sources to get you up to speed; I've listed them at the end of this paragraph. You need to have an idea of the basic principles of programming to fully enjoy the book, such as the use of variables, conditionals, and loops. If you feel a little shaky with any of those concepts, I recommend you get one of the two books and keep it close by for frequent consultation. If you have scripted or programmed before, even if only at a basic level, you should be able follow the examples in this book with a close read.

Getting Started with Processing [RF10]
> This casual, inexpensive book is a concise introduction to Processing and interactive computer graphics.[8] Written by Processing's initiators, it takes you through the learning process one step at a time to help you grasp core programming concepts.

Processing: A Programming Handbook for Visual Designers and Artists, Second Edition [RF11]
> This book is an introduction to the ideas of computer programming within the context of the visual arts.[9] It targets an audience of computer-savvy individuals who are interested in creating interactive and visual work through writing software but have little or no prior experience.

What's in This Book

This book will have you developing interactive sensor-based Android apps in no time. The chapters include previews of all the classes and methods used for the chapter projects, as well as a description of the particular sensor or hardware device that we'll be working with. Small projects introduce the basic steps to get a particular feature working, which leads up to a more advanced chapter project.

Part I of the book gets you started with the touch screen and Android sensors and cameras. Chapter 1, *Getting Started*, on page 3, walks you through the steps of installing Processing and the Android SDK. We'll write a simple app and run it in the emulator and on an Android device. Chapter 2, *Working with the Touch Screen Display*, on page 17, will show you how to use mouse position, finger pressure, and multitouch gestures on the touch screen panel while also providing details on the support for color that Processing provides.

---

8. Available at http://shop.oreilly.com/product/0636920000570.do.
9. Available at http://mitpress.mit.edu/catalog/item/default.asp?ttype=2&tid=11251.

Chapter 3, *Using Motion and Position Sensors*, on page 39, introduces us to all the device sensors built into an Android. We'll display accelerometer values on the Android screen, build a motion-based color mixer, and detect a device shake.

In Part II, we'll be working with the camera and location devices found on most Androids. Chapter 4, *Using Geolocation and Compass*, on page 69, shows us how to write location-based apps. We'll determine our location, the distance to a destination and to another mobile device on the move, and calculate the speed and bearing of a device. Chapter 5, *Using Android Cameras*, on page 93, lets us access the Android cameras through Processing. We'll display a camera preview of the front- and back-facing cameras, snap and save pictures to the camera's SD card, and superimpose images.

In Part III, we'll learn about peer-to-peer networking. Chapter 6, *Networking Devices with Wi-Fi*, on page 127, teaches us how to connect the Android with our desktop via Wi-Fi using the Open Sound Control protocol. We'll create a virtual whiteboard app, where you and your friends can doodle collaboratively, and we'll build a marble-balancing game, where two players compete on a shared virtual board. Chapter 7, *Peer-to-Peer Networking Using Bluetooth and Wi-Fi Direct*, on page 151, shows us how to use Android Bluetooth technology to discover, pair, and connect Android devices. We'll create a remote cursor sketch and build a survey app to share questions and answers between devices. Chapter 8, *Using Near Field Communication (NFC)*, on page 189, introduces us to the emerging short-range radio standard designed for zero-click interaction at close proximity and is expected to revolutionize the point-of-sale industry. We'll read and write NFC tags and exchange data between Android devices via NFC and Bluetooth.

Part IV deals with data and storage, as all advanced apps require some sort of data storage and retrieval to keep user data up-to-date. In Chapter 9, *Working with Data*, on page 215, we'll load, parse, and display data from text files and write data to a text file in the Android storage. We'll also connect to a data source hosted online to create an earthquake app that visualizes currently reported earthquakes worldwide. Chapter 10, *Using SQLite Databases*, on page 245, introduces us to the popular SQLite database management system and Structured Query Language. We'll record sensor data into a SQLite database and query it for particular data attributes.

Part V gets us going with 3D graphics and cross-platform apps. Chapter 11, *Introducing 3D Graphics with OpenGL*, on page 265, will show us how to work with 3D primitives, how virtual light sources are used, and how cameras are animated. Chapter 12, *Working with Shapes and 3D Objects*, on page 289, deals with 2D vector shapes and how to load and create 3D objects. Chapter 13, *Sharing and Publishing Applications*, on page 315, opens up our mobile app development to a wide range of devices and platforms using the JavaScript mode in Processing. We'll discuss some of the benefits of web apps being able to run on all modern browsers and the range of limitations using built-in device hardware.

How to Read This Book

The five parts of the book can each be considered self-contained mini-courses that you can jump right into once you have completed Part I, have properly installed all the required software, and are up and running. While the book does progress in a step-by-step fashion from fundamental to advanced subjects, you can jump right into Part II, III, IV, or V if you need to tackle a particular family of sensors or Android features for a current project.

Whenever we undertake a project that builds on prior code, refines an earlier project, or revisits important concepts mentioned earlier in the book, we'll cross-reference those earlier sections accordingly; if you are using the ebook, you can use the link to jump directly to the referenced section.

Throughout our journey in this book, I encourage you to get inspired by the projects in the Processing exhibition (http://processing.org/exhibition/), learn from the Processing community (http://forum.processing.org/), use the code examples included in IDE File → "Examples...," refer to the online tutorials (http://processing.org/learning/), collaborate with peers (http://sketchpad.cc), and learn from public sources, such as http://www.openprocessing.org/.

What You Need to Use This Book

For all the projects in this book, you need the following software tools. The first chapter guides you through installing those tools step by step.

- Processing 2[10]
- Android 4.0 Ice Cream Sandwich or higher[11] (2.3 Gingerbread is sufficient for all projects but Chapter 7, *Peer-to-Peer Networking Using Bluetooth and Wi-Fi Direct*, on page 151, and Chapter 8, *Using Near Field Communication (NFC)*, on page 189).
- Ketai Sensor Library for Processing[12]
- Processing Android installation instructions[13]

---

10. http://processing.org/download/
11. http://developer.android.com/sdk/
12. http://ketaiLibrary.org
13. http://wiki.processing.org/w/Android#Instructions

The projects in this book require at least one Android device. To complete Part III, you need two Android devices. This allows us to run and test the sketches on the actual hardware, use the actual sensors, and get the actual mobile user experience that is the focus of this book.

Tested Android Devices for this Book

The example code for the projects in this book has been tested on the following devices, shown in Figure 1, *Tested Android phones and tablets*, on page xx:

Figure 1—Tested Android phones and tablets. Clockwise from top left: ASUS Transformer Prime, Samsung Galaxy SIII, Samsung Nexus S, and Google Nexus 7

- Asus Transformer Prime Tablet with 32 GB memory (Ice Cream Sandwich, Jelly Bean)
- Samsung Galaxy SIII (Ice Cream Sandwich, Jelly Bean)
- Samsung Nexus S (Ice Cream Sandwich, Jelly Bean)
- Google Nexus 7 with 8 GB memory (Jelly Bean)

All the code is available online. Feel free to comment and drop some feedback!

Online Resources

You can download the complete set of source files from the book's web page at http://pragprog.com/titles/dsproc/source_code. The compressed file available online contains all the media assets you need organized by chapter directories and individual projects. If you're reading the ebook, you can also open the discussed source code just by clicking the file path before the code listings.

The online forum for the book, located at http://forums.pragprog.com/forums/209, provides a place for feedback, discussion, questions, and—I hope—answers as well. In the ebook, you'll find a link to the forum on every page next to a "report erratum" link that points to http://pragprog.com/titles/dsproc/errata, where you can report errors such as typos, technical errors, and suggestions. Your feedback and suggestions are very much appreciated.

Let's get started! Once we're done installing our software tools in Chapter 1, *Getting Started*, on page 3, we are only minutes away from completing our first Android app.

Daniel Sauter
Associate Professor of New Media Art, University of Illinois–Chicago School of Art and Design
daniel@ketaiLibrary.org
Chicago, 2013-03-4

Part I

Getting Started with
the Touch Screen and Android Sensors

Getting Started

This book explores the cutting-edge hardware and software features that are built into Android phones and tablets today. You'll create sophisticated graphics and user interfaces in no time, and you'll develop a range of projects that build on the hardware sensors, cameras, and networking capabilities of your Android device. You'll put them to work creatively to make your Android apps more useful, usable, and exciting. We'll consider Android phones and tablets as universal sensors, processors, and remote controls in the context of this book, and we'll create projects that go beyond the typical app. Along the way, we'll spark new app ideas for you to explore in the future.

You'll learn how to create advanced Android apps using Processing, a widely popular open source programming language and environment that is free to use and was designed for learning the fundamentals of programming. With more than 130 libraries expanding the Processing core, as well as the possibility to extend it with Java and Android classes and methods, it is a simple yet powerful language to work with. Processing comes with three modes that let you create applications for different devices and operating systems: *Java mode* lets us create standalone applications for GNU/Linux, Mac OS X, and Windows. *Android mode* in Processing enables us to create apps for Android phones and tablets—we'll use this mode throughout the book. And finally, *JavaScript mode* enables us to create web apps using Processing.js,[1] and those will run in all HTML5-enabled web browsers installed on smart phones, tablets, and desktop computers.

Processing's simple syntax lets you write apps whose sophisticated displays belie the straightforward, readable code in which they're written. Initially developed to serve as a software sketchbook for artists, designers, and

---

1. http://processingjs.org/

hobbyists and to teach the fundamentals of computer programming in a more visual way, Processing is one of the most versatile production environments on the market today.

In 2010, the case for programming with Processing became even stronger with the addition of the Android mode to the Processing environment, whose intent, in the words of the Processing all-volunteer team, is to make it "foolishly easy to create Android apps using the Processing API."[2]

In this chapter, we'll begin by installing the software tools we'll need, and then we'll take a look at the basic structure of a typical Processing program, known as a *sketch*. We'll write our first Android sketch, one that draws figures on our desktop screen. Then we'll switch to Android mode on page 13 without leaving the Processing IDE and run that same app on the built-in Android emulator. Finally, we'll load the sketch onto an actual Android device and run it there.

With an understanding of the basic development cycle in hand, we'll learn on page 18 how to use the touch screen interface to add some interactivity to our sketch. We'll explore how it differs from a mouse pointer and make use of touch screen values to change the visual properties of the app, first with gradations of gray and then with color.

In addition to the traditional RGB (red, green, and blue) values that most programmers are familiar with, Processing provides additional color modes that provide greater control over hue, saturation, and brightness (HSB). As we work on our first apps, we'll take a closer look in particular at the HSB mode, which delivers all three.

Throughout the chapter we'll work with simple code that uses the Android touch screen sensor interface to change the position, color, and opacity of the 2D graphics it displays. Let's jump right in and install the software we need to develop Android apps in Processing.

1.1   Install the Required Software

Let's get started and download the software we'll need to develop Android apps. The Processing download comes in a pretty small package of approximately 100–120 MB. It consists of free open source software and is available from the Processing website without prior registration. For workshops, in the lab, in an office, or in a teaching environment where multiple machines are in use, the lightweight *Processing development environment* (or "Processing

---

2.   http://wiki.processing.org/w/Android

IDE") is a good alternative to a full-featured *integrated development environment* (IDE) such as Eclipse.[3]

The Processing IDE doesn't include some of the advanced syntax highlighting and autocomplete features for which Eclipse is valued.[4] However, the Debug tool and XQMode live syntax and error checker can be installed separately.[5] Despite that, professional programmers appreciate the Processing IDE for its quick install. It comes with all the necessary tutorials and example sketches that allow us to explore specific programming topics right away. Processing does not require installation; just extract the application file and start.

What You Need

To implement the projects in this book, you'll need the following tools:

- Processing 2.0[6] (current version is 2.0b8)

- Java 1.6 (or "Java 6")[7]

- Android 4.0 Ice Cream Sandwich or higher[8] (2.3 Gingerbread is sufficient for all projects except Chapter 7, *Peer-to-Peer Networking Using Bluetooth and Wi-Fi Direct*, on page 151, and Chapter 8, *Using Near Field Communication (NFC)*, on page 189.)

These are the minimum software requirements. If you have a newer version, you'll be just fine. Later we'll install some additional libraries that give us easier access to the features of an Android device. For now, use the following steps to build the core Processing environment we'll use throughout this book.

Install Processing for Android

Here are the steps to install Processing for the Android.

1. Download Processing 2.0 for your operating system (OS X, Windows, or Linux) at Processing.org/download. The Processing download includes the Processing IDE, a comprehensive set of examples and tutorials, and a language reference. The Processing package does not include the Android software development kit, which you'll need to download separately.

---

3.   http://en.wikipedia.org/wiki/Integrated_development_environment
4.   http://wiki.processing.org/w/Eclipse_Plug_In
5.   http://debug.martinleopold.com/ and https://github.com/downloads/Manindra29/XQMode/XQMode%20v0.4a.zip.
6.   http://processing.org/download/
7.   http://java.com/en/download/
8.   http://developer.android.com/sdk/

2. Extract the Processing application from the .zip file on Windows, .dmg file on Mac OS, or .tar.gz file on Linux, and move it to your preferred program folder (for example, Applications if you are developing on OS X, Program Files on Windows, or your preferred /bin folder on Linux).[9]

Install the Android SDK

1. Find and download the Android SDK by going to http://developer.android.com/sdk/. Choose the package that's right for your operating system and complete the installation of the Android SDK.[10] On Windows, you may wish to download and use the installer that Android provides to guide your setup. If Java JDK is not present on your system, you will be prompted to download and install it.[11]

2. When the Android SDK download is complete, go to the Processing wiki at http://wiki.processing.org/w/Android#Instructions and open the Android installation instructions you'll find there. Follow the instructions for your OS step by step. The wiki lists which components are required to configure Processing for Android on your operating system and tells you how to get Android installed properly. Android may have dependencies that are specific to your operating system, such as additional device drivers. If you are developing on Windows, follow the USB driver installation instructions available at developer.android.com/tools/extras/oem-usb.html. If you are developing on Linux, follow the instructions for setting up your device for development at http://developer.android.com/tools/device.html#setting-up.

Now that you have installed all the necessary components to develop Android apps on your own system, let's jump right into Processing and write our first sketch.

1.2 Write Your First Android Sketch

Go ahead and launch Processing from the applications directory. The Processing IDE launches, opening an empty sketch window, as shown in Figure 2, *The Processing IDE*, on page 7.

Since you've launched the application for the first time, Processing has just created a sketchbook folder for you, which is located in Documents on the hard drive, independent of the OS you are developing on. I recommend you save all your sketches to this location. Then Processing can list them for you

---

9. http://processing.org/learning/gettingstarted/

10. http://developer.android.com/sdk/installing.html

11. http://docs.oracle.com/javase/7/docs/webnotes/install/

Figure 2—The Processing IDE. We edit Processing code directly within the Processing IDE sketch window, as shown here.

within the IDE (click the "Open..." toolbar button). Also, when you update to future versions of Processing, the sketchbook loads up exactly the same way as before.

Explore the Processing IDE

The toolbar on top of the sketch window contains the key features of the IDE, with a Run button to launch and a Stop button to stop your apps. Next to those are the New, Save, Open, and Export buttons, which explain themselves pretty well. You can find a more detailed description of the sketchbook and the IDE in the Processing Development Environment tutorial on the Processing website.[12]

---

12. http://processing.org/reference/environment/

When you start Processing for the first time, it defaults to Java mode, as indicated on the right side of the toolbar. This area also functions as a drop-down menu, allowing us to switch between the different modes the Processing IDE provides. Besides the default Java mode, the drop-down menu in Processing 2.0b8 is already preloaded with the Android and JavaScript mode. In the final release of Processing 2.0, this drop-down will be slightly different. You'll need to add the Android mode, choosing "Add mode..." from the menu. Depending on which mode you've selected, the Run and Export buttons on the toolbar produce different results, which are listed next.

Java mode "Run" displays a program window to view the sketch running on the desktop computer. "Export" produces a standalone application for Mac OS, Windows, and Linux independent of the operating system you are developing on.

Android mode "Run" launches the app on the Android device. "Export" creates a Android package for Google Play, a feature currently under development.

JavaScript mode[13] "Run" launches a web page in the default browser, with a Processing JavaScript canvas showing the sketch. "Export" creates a web package, including all dependent files for uploading to a web server.

A tab below the toolbar shows the current sketch name, which defaults to one containing the current date if the sketch has not been saved yet. Processing prompts us to provide another filename as soon as we save the sketch. The right-arrow button to the right of the tab allows us to add more tabs if we'd like to split the code into separate sections. As sketches grow in scope and complexity, the use of tabs can be a great way to reduce clutter by separating classes and methods for different purposes into distinct tabs. Each tab is saved as a separate Processing source file, or .pde, in the sketch folder.

The text editor, shown in white below the tab on page 7, is the actual area where we write and edit code. The line number of our current cursor location within the code is shown at the very bottom of the sketch window.

The message area and console below the text editor provide us with valuable feedback as we develop and debug.

You can always find more information on the key IDE features discussed here, as well as a summary of the installation, on the Learning page of the Processing website.[14]

---

13. http://processing.org/learning/javascript/
14. http://processing.org/learning/gettingstarted/

Now that you know how to work with the Processing editor, you're almost ready to write your first sketch.

Understand the Structure of a Sketch

Any Processing sketch that will interact with users or make use of animated graphics—as is the case for all the sketches in this book—must include two methods:

- An instance of the setup() method, which initializes key variables and settings the sketch will use and is executed only once when the app starts

- An instance of the draw() method, which continuously updates or redraws the screen to respond to user input and real-time events

If we redraw the screen fast enough, users will perceive individual images, or *frames*, as continuous movement. It's a principle of film and animation we have all experienced.[15]

A typical Processing sketch starts by defining the global variables it uses, followed by both setup() and draw() methods. setup() is called exactly once when you start a sketch to initialize key parameters. For instance, we can set a particular window size() or screen orientation(), or we can load custom fonts and media assets. setup() is responsible for taking care of everything we need to do once to configure a sketch.

The draw() method, in contrast, is called repeatedly to update the screen sixty times per second by default. We can adjust this rate using the frameRate() method. If our drawings are complex or if they require substantial amounts of processor power to compute, Processing might not always be able to keep up with the 60 fps frame rate. We can always get some information on the current playback rate through the frameRate constant Processing provides to us. As a point of reference, cinema film runs at 24 fps and digital video typically at 30 fps.

Neither setup() nor draw() accepts parameters. They are void methods and do not return values. Both are used in virtually every Processing sketch.

Write a Sketch

Let's now say "Hi" to Processing by creating a simple sketch that draws an ellipse repeatedly at the current cursor position. We'll add some complexity to its graphical output by having the ellipse expand or contract along its vertical and horizontal axes, depending on how fast the mouse moves across

---

15. http://en.wikipedia.org/wiki/Persistence_of_vision

the screen. This basic drawing sketch, shown in Figure 3, *A simple sketch*, on page 10, gives us immediate visual feedback and uses your mouse as input. As you move along, experiment and play with parameter values to better understand them.

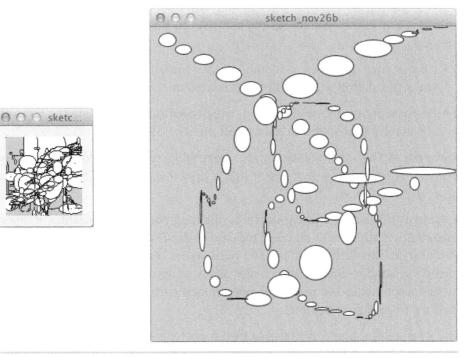

Figure 3—A simple sketch. With the ellipse-drawing primitive, Processing can generate dynamic output. On the left is a 100 x 100 pixel window; on the right, a 400 x 400 pixel window.

We use a single drawing primitive for this sketch, the ellipse(), also used to draw circles by providing equal width and height for the ellipse. In Processing, an ellipse(x, y, width, height) requires four parameters:[16]

- The horizontal x position of the ellipse center
- The vertical y position of the ellipse center
- The ellipse width
- The ellipse height

---

16. http://processing.org/reference/ellipse_.html

The following snippet contains the code we'll need for our sketch. Go ahead and type this into the text editor, as illustrated in Figure 4, *Writing code in the Processing IDE*, on page 12:

```
void setup()
{
}

void draw()
{
        ellipse(mouseX, mouseY, mouseX-pmouseX, mouseY-pmouseY);
}
```

We want the position of the ellipse to follow the mouse, and for this we need to know where it's located at any given moment. Processing stores this information in two constants: mouseX and mouseY. The pair returns the x and y coordinates of the mouse in pixels relative to the origin of the display window, not the computer screen. In Processing, the origin of the display window ([0, 0]) is located at the upper left corner of the device window; [width-1, height-1] is located at the lower right.

We'll use mouseX and mouseY to set the horizontal and vertical position of the ellipse center. For the width and height parameters of the ellipse, we'll use two additional constants: pmouseX and pmouseY. pmouseX and pmouseY store the *previous* mouse position from one frame ago. If we move the mouse, we can calculate the mouse speed by subtracting the previous from the current mouse position. By subtracting mouseX from pmouseX, we determine the horizontal mouse travel distance in pixels within one frame, or for one-sixtieth of a second. We use the same approach for the vertical trajectory by subtracting pmouseY from mouseY for the vertical speed. pmouseX and pmouseY are lesser-known constants and more rarely used than mouseX and mouseY, but they're very useful when we are interested in the speed of the mouse.

Run the Sketch

Go ahead and run the sketch by pressing the Play button. Processing will open a display window whose default size is 100 by 100 pixels, as shown in Figure 3, *A simple sketch*, on page 10. Alternatively, you can select Sketch → Run on the Processing menu bar. When the window appears, place your mouse pointer there and move it around.

If we move the mouse quickly from left to right or up and down inside the display window, the ellipse width and height increase, depending on where we are heading. Drawing in such a small sketch window restricts our mouse movement, so let's use the size() method to increase the window size to [400,

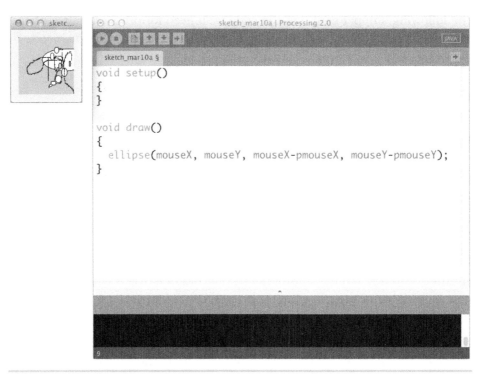

```
void setup()
{
}

void draw()
{
    ellipse(mouseX, mouseY, mouseX-pmouseX, mouseY-pmouseY);
}
```

Figure 4—Writing code in the Processing IDE. A sketch typically includes at least two methods: setup() and draw(). When we run the sketch, the separate window, shown in the upper left, displays the results.

400], as shown in Figure 3, *A simple sketch*, on page 10. We add the size() method to setup(), because we need to define the window size only once when we start up the sketch. In a typical Processing sketch, the idea is to keep everything strictly away from draw() so the application doesn't get bogged down executing extra statements at the rate of sixty times per second.

Go ahead and add the following statements to setup() in your Processing text editor:

```
size(400, 400);
```

Now rerun the sketch. With a bit more pixel real estate (400 x 400px), we now have the space to build up some speed.

Save the Sketch

Let's finish by saving the sketch as basicDrawing.pde into the Processing sketchbook, located in Documents on the hard drive. When the sketch is saved, the tab is renamed to the current sketch name. Press Open in the toolbar and see your sketch listed at the top in the sketchbook.

You've just completed your first Processing sketch in Java mode. Time now to make an Android app from the sketch and run it in the Android emulator.

1.3 Run a Sketch in the Android Emulator

Let's now switch our basic drawing sketch code, on page 11, to Android mode. Click Java in the upper right corner of the Processing IDE and use the drop-down menu to switch to Android mode. The structure and statements of a Processing sketch are identical across modes. So there is nothing we need to change in our sketch to run it on an Android.

When you switch modes, the Processing IDE turns from gray (Java mode) to green (Android mode), signaling the change. In the final 2.0 Processing release, the IDE will not turn green. Instead, the IDE will indicate the mode change through a different image at the top of the window. The code remains unchanged in the IDE. We are now ready to run the sketch in the Android emulator.

Run the App

To run the sketch in the emulator, select Sketch → "Run in Emulator" from the Processing menu.

The following lines should appear in the console area at the bottom of the IDE when the Android emulator launches for the first time:

```
Building Android project...
Waiting for device to become available...
Installing sketch on emulator.
Stating Sketch on emulator.
Sketch launched on the emulator.
```

The emulator starts up the Android OS exactly as a device would, just a bit more slowly. Once Android is running, Processing then installs the Android package (.apk) and launches the sketch. It looks identical to the Java mode sketch illustrated in Figure 5, *Running the drawing sketch in Android mode*, on page 14, and if you move the mouse in the emulator window, it responds the same way it did in Java mode. The frame rate is noticeably lower, and the screen has a different aspect ratio. In the emulator, the mouse methods are a stand-in for the touch screen interface.

Here's the first Android app for you. Congratulations! If you get an error, please jump to Section A1.4, *Troubleshooting*, on page 346.

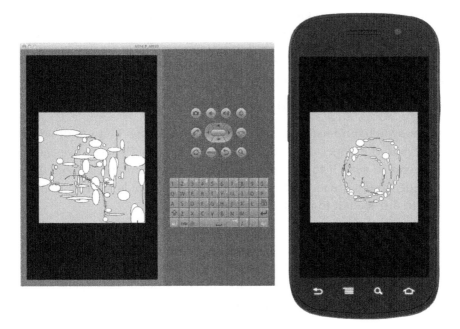

Figure 5—Running the drawing sketch in Android mode. We can run a sketch in either the Android emulator installed on our desktop computer (left) or directly on the Android device (right).

As you can see, the emulator is a good way to check whether your sketch is operational. When it comes to testing responsiveness or the touch screen user experience of your app, however, we need an actual device. So next up is testing the sketch on an actual Android device.

1.4 Run a Sketch on an Android Device

Let's run the sketch on a real Android device. First you'll need to check which version of Android it's running. Then you'll need to connect the device to your computer with a USB cable and enable USB debugging.

To determine which version of Android you're running, go to the home screen, tap Settings and then tap "About phone" (or "About phone/tablet") at the bottom of the menu that appears. Look for the version of Android that is installed on your device under "Android version" and make a note. The procedure for enabling USB debugging depends on that number. Now connect your device to your desktop.

- If you're running version 4.2 Jelly Bean or a more recent version of Android, activate the hidden "Developer options" menu by tapping "Build number" at the bottom of the "About phone/tablet" menu five times. Then navigate to the Settings → "Developer options" menu and check "USB Debugging." To respond to the warning that "USB debugging is intended for development purposes only," tap OK.

- If you're running version 4.1 Jelly Bean or an earlier version of Android, tap Settings and look for the "Developer options" menu under the System section at the bottom of the list. Click OK after the warning and check "USB Debugging" at the top of the list that appears.

If you are developing on Windows or Linux, you'll need a special USB device driver. You can find instructions on the Android website for downloading and installing it.[17]

With all the software tools in place and the Android device plugged into your desktop, let's run our basic drawing example on the device.

Run the App

Choose Run on Device from the Sketch menu, or use the shortcut ⌘R on a Mac or `Ctrl R` on Windows or Linux. The shortcut is a timesaver when we're testing and running a sketch frequently. Processing compiles the sketch and produces a basicDrawing.apk package, which it then moves onto the device and launches.

```
Building Android project...
Waiting for device to become available...
Installing sketch on DEVICE_ID.
Starting Sketch on DEVICE_ID.
Sketch launched on the device.
```

Your sketch is now up and running on your Android device. In contrast to running the sketch in the emulator, installing and launching it on an Android device goes fairly quickly. If you play with your sketch on the touch screen, you'll be able to tell how much more responsive the device is. This is because the device provides a higher frame rate. Being able to test the actual user experience more accurately while saving some time rerunning your sketch are the main reasons why testing on the Android device is preferable.

Let's also note what we are *not* doing! We are not signing up as a developer. We are not installing certificates, and we haven't used a credit card. Processing and Android are open platforms. The apps we create can be shared directly with other Android users. And if we intend to further develop our project in Eclipse or collaborate with Eclipse developers, Processing provides us with

---

17. http://developer.android.com/guide/developing/device.html

an Export Android Project option, which you can find on the Processing menu toolbar under File. This command will create a folder containing all the necessary Eclipse project files.

1.5 Wrapping Up

Let's summarize. You've seen how easy it is to use Processing to create graphics for the Android. You've downloaded the Processing IDE and the Android SDK, and you've installed the software tools to develop Android apps in Processing. You've written your first Processing sketch using the mouse as input, and you are now able to switch to Android mode and write basic Android apps in Processing. The Android emulator that comes with the Android SDK and the Android device you've used in this chapter will help you test the apps you'll write throughout the book.

In the next chapter, we'll work with the touch screen interface and device display. You'll learn how to work with color, use fingertip pressure on the screen surface, and work with multitouch gestures such as *tap* and *pinch* to manipulate the graphical elements on the device display.

CHAPTER 2

Working with the Touch Screen Display

Now that we've completed our first Android app, let's explore a device feature that has become particularly popular with mobile phones and tablets—multitouch. Virtually all Android devices ship today with a capacitive touch screen panel. It's a device we've gotten so accustomed to that we hardly "see" it as the hardware sensor that it is.

User interaction (UI) with Android touch screens differs somewhat from that of a mouse on a traditional computer display. First of all, we don't have one omnipresent mouse pointer for interacting with UI elements via rollovers, clicks, right-clicks, and double-clicks. In fact, we don't have a rollover or a physical "click" on the touch screen panel at all, hence UI interactions often require adjustments for the touch screen. Typically the Android device uses audiovisual cues such as click sounds or small device vibrations for user feedback.

There are a number of advantages to the multitouch screen interface to point out. First and foremost, the capacitive touch screen panel affords us more than one mouse pointer. We can work with two, five, even ten fingers on the Android, although more than three are rarely used. Multitouch allows us a variety of distinct finger gestures compared to the mouse,[1] which we can only use to interact with the UI elements and other components displayed on the screen. The two most common multitouch gestures are the pinch and rotate gestures, typically used for scaling and rotating objects on the screen.

In this chapter, we'll get started by learning to use the mouse callback methods available in Processing for Android. Then we'll dive into the different color modes Processing has to offer, an essential topic that we need to address to work with graphics and images throughout the book. Building on the basic

---

1.   http://en.wikipedia.org/wiki/Multi-touch

drawing sketch code, on page 11, we'll use the mouse speed to manipulate the hues of the ellipses we draw.

Finally, we'll dedicate the second part of the chapter to the multitouch features of the Android touch screen and create a sketch that showcases the most common gestures, including the tap, double-tap, long press, flick, pinch, and rotate gestures. In the sketch we'll develop, we'll manipulate the scale, position, rotation, and color of a rectangle using multitouch gestures.

To make working with multitouch gestures easy, we'll use the Ketai library for Processing,[2] which greatly simplifies the process. We'll work with Ketai throughout the book, as it also simplifies working with sensors, cameras, location, and networking—all the hardware features that are typically difficult to work with. We'll download and install the library step by step and take a quick look at the main Ketai classes.

Let's take a look at how the touch screen panel works.

2.1 Introducing the Android Touch Screen

The capacitive touch screen panel of an Android device consists of a glass insulator coated with a transparent conductor. When we interact with the touch screen surface, our fingertips act as electrical conductors—not very good ones, but good enough to be detected. A touch on the screen surface distorts the electrostatic field, causing a change in its electric capacitance, which can be located relative to the screen surface. The horizontal and vertical position of the fingertip relative to the screen is then made available to us through the Android OS; it is updated only when we touch or move a fingertip across the screen.

The apps we write in Processing have a flexible screen orientation by default, which means our app switches orientation automatically from portrait to landscape depending on how we are holding the phone or tablet—this is detected by the accelerometer sensor we'll get to know in Section 3.5, *Display Values from the Accelerometer*, on page 46. We can lock the orientation using Processing's *orientation()* method using either the PORTRAIT or the LANDSCAPE parameter.[3]

For compatibility, Processing uses the constants mouseX and mouseY when it's running in Android mode, corresponding in this case to the position of a user's fingertip relative to the upper left corner of the device touch screen

---

2.   http://ketai.googlecode.com

3.   http://wiki.processing.org/index.php?title=Android#Screen.2C_Orientation.2C_and_the_size.28.29_command

rather than the position of the mouse cursor on a desktop screen. This allows us to use the same code across modes. When using mouseX in Android mode, we refer to the horizontal position of the fingertip on the touch screen panel, and when we use mouseY, we refer the fingertip's vertical position. Both are measured relative to the coordinate system's origin in the upper left corner of the touch screen.[4] Moving the finger to the right on the screen will increase mouseX values; moving the finger down will increase mouseY.

In Android mode, we can also use the following mouse methods, which are available in all Processing modes. The Android touch screen gestures correspond to the following mouse events:

mousePressed()[5] This callback method is called every time a finger touches the screen panel. It corresponds to a mouse-pressed event on the desktop when the mouse button is pressed down.

mouseReleased()[6] This callback method is called every time a finger lifts off the touch screen surface, but only if its position has changed since first touching the panel. It corresponds to a mouse-up event on the desktop.

mouseDragged()[7] This callback method is called every time a new finger position is detected by the touch screen panel compared to the previously detected position. It corresponds to a mouse-dragged event on the desktop when the mouse moves while the button is pressed.

All three methods respond only to one finger's touch. When you use more than one finger on the multitouch surface, the finger that triggers callback events is the first one that touches the screen panel—the second, third, or more are ignored. If you hold down one finger on the screen surface, add another one on, and remove the first, then the second finger one will now be first in line and take over mouse events. We will work with multiple fingers and multitouch gestures in just a bit in Section 2.7, *Detect Multitouch Gestures*, on page 32.

Let's put the mouse callback methods to the test with a simple sketch that prints the mouse position and events into the Processing console. We'll need draw() to indicate that this sketch is running and listening to the mouse continuously. Then we add our callback methods and have each print a brief text string indicating which mouse method has been called at what finger position.

---

4.   http://processing.org/learning/drawing/
5.   http://processing.org/reference/mousePressed_.html
6.   http://processing.org/reference/mouseReleased_.html
7.   http://processing.org/reference/mouseDragged_.html

Create a new Android sketch by choosing File → New from the Processing menu. If your new sketch window is not yet in Android mode, switch it to Android using the drop-down menu in the upper right corner. Add a few lines of code to the sketch window:

```
void draw()
{
        // no display output, so nothing to do here
}

void mousePressed ()
{
        println("PRESSED x:" + mouseX + " y: " + mouseY);
}

void mouseReleased ()
{
        println("RELEASED x:" + mouseX + " y: " + mouseY);
}

void mouseDragged ()
{
        println("DRAGGED x:" + mouseX + " y: " + mouseY);
}
```

Let's go ahead and test the touch screen panel of an Android device.

Run the App

With your Android device connected to your desktop via a USB cable, run the sketch on the device by pressing the "Run on Device" button in the sketch window. When the sketch is installed and launched on the device, we don't need to pay attention to the screen output of the touch screen panel, but keep an eye on the Processing console at the bottom of the sketch window.

Hold your device in one hand and get ready to touch the screen surface with the other. Take a look at the console and tap the screen. In the console, you'll see output similar to this:

```
❰ PRESSED x:123 y:214
```

Lift your finger and see what happens. If you see no additional mouse event, don't be surprised. Although we might expect a RELEASED here, we shouldn't get this event if we just tap the screen and lift the finger. The mouseX and mouseY constants always store and maintain the last mouse position. To get a mouse-released event, touch the screen, move your finger a bit, and release. Now you should see something like this:

```
‹ PRESSED x:125 y:208
  DRAGGED x:128 y:210
  DRAGGED x:130 y:209
  RELEASED x:130 y:209
```

Because we touched the screen, we first trigger a mousePressed() event. By moving the finger slightly while touching the surface, we trigger mouseDragged() until we stop moving. Finally, we get a mouseReleased() event because we've updated our position since we pressed or touched the screen.

Now that we can now work with the mouse callback methods, we're ready to take a look at the color support that Processing provides, which is one of its strengths. Knowing how to control color values is a fundamental skill that we'll frequently return to as we work with graphics and images throughout the book. We'll come back to the Android touch screen and its multitouch features later in this chapter.

2.2   Using Colors

Any geometric primitive we draw on the screen uses a particular fill() and stroke() color. If we don't say otherwise, Processing will default to a black stroke and a white fill color. We can use the fill() and stroke() methods to change default values, and we can also use grayscale, RGB, HSB, or hexadecimal color in the Android apps we create. The background() method uses color in the same way, with the exception that it cannot set a value for opacity, formally known as the alpha value.

By default, Processing draws all graphic elements in the RGB (red, green, blue) color mode. An additional alpha value can be used as a fourth parameter to control the opacity of graphic elements drawn on the screen. An alpha value of 0 is fully transparent, and a value of 255 is fully opaque. Values of 0..255 control the level of opacity for an individual pixel.

The background() color of a Processing window cannot be transparent. If you provide an alpha parameter for background(), the method will just ignore its value. Within draw(), the background() method is used in most cases to clear the display window at the beginning of each frame. The method can also accept an image as a parameter, drawing a background image if the image has the same size as the Processing window.

Processing provides us with two different color modes that we can switch between using the colorMode() method.[8] The color mode can be set to RGB or HSB (hue, saturation, brightness), which we'll explore further in *Using HSB*

---

8.   http://processing.org/reference/colorMode_.html

Colors, on page 23. colorMode() changes the way Processing interprets color values. Both RGB and HSB can handle alpha values to make objects appear transparent.

We can adjust the value range of the parameters used in colorMode() as well. For example, white in the default RGB color mode is defined as color(255). If we change the range to colorMode(RGB, 1.0), white is defined as color(1.0).

Here are the parameters colorMode() can take. We can specify mode as either RGB or HSB and specify range in the value range we prefer.

- colorMode(mode)
- colorMode(mode, range)
- colorMode(mode, range1, range2, range3)
- colorMode(mode, range1, range2, range3, range4)

Let's now take a look at the three different color methods Processing has to offer. They are good examples of how Processing uses as few methods as possible to get the job done.

Using Grayscale and RGB colors

The fill() and stroke() methods can take either one, two, three, or four parameters. Since the background() method doesn't accept alpha values, it takes either one or three parameters:

- fill(gray)
  stroke(gray)
  background(gray)
- fill(gray, alpha)
  stroke(gray, alpha)
- fill(red, green, blue)
  stroke(red, green, blue)
  background(red, green, blue)
- fill(red, green, blue, alpha)
  stroke(red, green, blue, alpha)

As you can see, your results will differ depending on how many parameters you use. One parameter results in a grayscale value. Two parameters define a grayscale and its opacity (as set by an alpha value). If alpha is set to 0, the color is fully transparent. An alpha value of 255 results in a fully opaque color. Three parameters correspond by default to red, green, and blue values. Four parameters contain the red, green, and blue values and an alpha value for transparency. Through this approach, Processing reduces the number of core methods by allowing for a different number of parameters and by interpreting them differently depending on the color mode.

To recall the syntax of any particular method, highlight the method you want to look up in the sketch window and choose the Find in Reference option from Help. It's the quickest way to look up the syntax and usage of Processing methods while you are working with your code.

Using Hex Colors

Processing's color method can also handle hexadecimal values, which are often less intuitive to work with but are still fairly common as a way to define color. We'll take a closer look at hexadecimal color values in Section 9.5, *Read Comma-Separated Web Color Data*, on page 223. Hex color method parameters, such as the hex code #ff8800 for orange, are applied like this:

- fill(hex)
  stroke(hex)
  background(hex)
- fill(hex, alpha)
  stroke(hex, alpha)

Now let's take a look at the HSB color mode, which, as we learned earlier, can define a color using hue, brightness, and saturation.

Using HSB Colors

Why should we care about HSB? Because it's a rather excellent color mode for working algorithmically with color, such as when we want to change only the saturation of a UI element. When we switch the default RGB color mode to HSB, the values of the color parameters passed to fill() and stroke() are not interpreted any more as red, green, blue, and alpha values, but instead as hue, saturation, brightness, and alpha color values. We can achieve seamless transitions between more- and less-saturated color values for UI highlights, for instance, which is very difficult to do properly in RGB. So for the objective of algorithmic color combinations, transitions, and animations that need to be seamless, HSB is great.

When we switch to HSB using the colorMode(HSB), the fill(), stroke(), and background() methods will be interpreted like this:

- fill(hue, saturation, brightness)
  stroke(hue, saturation, brightness)
  background(hue, saturation, brightness)
- fill(hue, saturation, brightness, alpha)
  stroke(hue, saturation, brightness, alpha)

When we work algorithmically in HSB, we can access the hue directly using Processing's hue() method.[9] It takes a color as a parameter and extracts only the hue value of that color. Similarly, we can get the brightness by using the brightness() color method,[10] and we can access the saturation() separately as well.[11] The HSB color cylinder is a very useful illustration of this color space to further investigate and better understand the HSB color mode,[12] where all hues are represented within the 360-degree circumference of the color cylinder. Take a quick look at it; we'll come back to it in the next project, Section 2.3, *Use Mouse Speed to Control Hues*, on page 25.

Now that we've learned about the different ways to assign color values, let's also take a look at the Processing color type, which Processing provides for the specific purpose of *storing* colors.

Using the Color Type

The Processing color type can store RGBA or HSBA values in one variable, depending on the colorMode() you choose.[13] It's a great type for any app that we build using a color scheme of multiple colors. Using the color type, we simply call the color variable and apply it to the objects we draw. We can create a color palette in our app without requiring a bunch of individual variables for each value of an RGBA or HSBA color. We would apply the color type like this:

- fill(color)
- fill(color, alpha)

If color included an alpha value of, let's say, 127.5, a primitive drawn with fill(color) would be drawn with 50% opacity (given a possible max alpha value of 255). In the unlikely scenario that the same color that already contains an alpha value is used in conjunction with an additional alpha parameter, such as fill(color, 128), the resulting color would be drawn half as transparent as before, or at 25% opacity.

Processing color methods are overloaded, so they can handle a range of situations—you can use one method for many applications. In other languages, remembering which syntax to use for a particular color effect can be a challenge, but with Processing you need to remember only a small number of methods. When a color value exceeds the default maximum value of 255,

---

9.   http://processing.org/reference/hue_.html
10. http://processing.org/reference/brightness_.html
11. http://processing.org/reference/saturation_.html
12. http://upload.wikimedia.org/wikipedia/commons/1/16/Hsl-hsv_models_b.svg
13. http://processing.org/reference/color_datatype.html

Processing caps it for us. So fill(300) has the same result as fill(255) does. The same is true for values lower than the default minimum, 0.

Now that we've learned about the different color modes, methods, and types available to define colors in an Android app, let's refine our previous drawing sketch.

2.3 Use Mouse Speed to Control Hues

Now let's explore the HSB mode on the device touch screen display. By adding colorMode() to our sketch, we switch the color mode, and by modifying our fill() method to work with HSB values, we change our app from grayscale to shades of color. Here's the result:

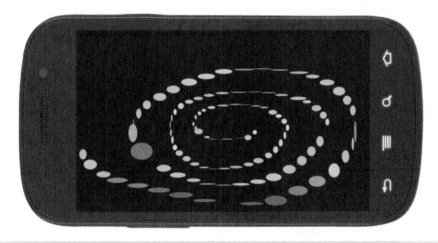

Figure 6—Using mouse speed to control color. The hue of the ellipses changes depending on how fast you move your finger across the touch screen surface. Slow movements result in greenish, medium in blueish, and fast movements in reddish values.

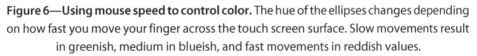

In this project, we'll keep the screen orientation() flexible, which is the default setting for our Processing apps, and we don't have to set anything to make the app change orientation when we hold the device upright or sideways. This means it will change orientation when the built-in device accelerometer sensor decides that the app should adapt to the particular orientation at that moment. When such an orientation change occurs, our setup() method will be called again, reinitializing the sketch and executing all the statements we've included in setup(). Because we set the screen to black, erasing its contents using the background(0) method, a change in the app's orientation will reset the background() to black, erasing all the ellipses we've drawn prior to changing the orientation.

We have only two modifications to make using the code, on page 11. First we switch the color mode to HSB, which also customizes its value range. Then we calculate the speed of our movement by measuring the distance between the previous and the current mouse position using Processing's dist()[14] method. The method takes two points as parameters and returns the distance between them. Finally, we apply the distance we've calculated to the hue in the fill() method for the ellipses we draw. The default value range for the HSB color modes is 0..255 by default. We'll override the default hue value to use floating point ranges of 0..100 instead, allowing us to use the calculated mouse speed directly to the hue parameter. For the saturation and brightness values, we'll override the default values to use floating point ranges of 0..1.0.

Let's take a look at the project code.

Display/MouseSpeedHue/MouseSpeedHue.pde

```
void setup()
{
  noStroke();
  background(0);
  colorMode(HSB, 100, 1, 1);
}

void draw()
{
  fill(dist(pmouseX, pmouseY, mouseX, mouseY), 1, 1);
  ellipse(mouseX, mouseY, mouseX-pmouseX, mouseY-pmouseY);
}
```

Here are the modifications we've made.

❶ Switch the default RGB color mode to HSB using the colorMode(HSB, 100, 1, 1) method. Set the second parameter for hue to 100, allowing for floating point hue values of 0..100. Set the third parameter to 1, defining the color saturation values for the range 0..1.0. Also set the brightness range as 0..1.0 in the fourth parameter.

❷ Now set the color fill() of the ellipse in our defined HSB mode. Use dist() to calculate the distance between the previous mouse position (pmouseX, pmouseY) and the current one (mouseX, mouseY), and apply the result to the hue parameter. Use 1 for saturation and brightness. We've defined 1 as the maximum saturation and brightness, so both are set to 100 percent.

Let's test the app.

---

14. http://processing.org/reference/dist_.html

Run the App

Rerun the sketch on the device now switched to HSB color, and see how the hue of the ellipses that are drawn changes depending on how fast you move your finger across the screen surface. The changes in the hues occur independently of their saturation and brightness, so all the colors are drawn with maximum saturation and brightness.

If you go back to the HSB color wheel we looked at earlier, you will see how the 360 degrees of the HSB or the wheel correspond to the different colored ellipses you draw on the screen. Slow movement results in yellow color values, and then, with increasing speed, you'll see green, cyan, blue, and magenta as the maximum speed values.

Now that we've mastered the use of color in Processing, let's continue our investigation into the multitouch screen panel. We'll go ahead and install a Processing library that will help us work with multitouch gestures and extend the core features Processing provides us. Besides multitouch, the Ketai library makes it easy for us to work with other hardware devices and sensors built into Android phones and tablets. Let's take a look at the Ketai classes and the features it provides. We'll be using these throughout the rest of the book.

2.4 Introducing the Ketai Library

The Ketai library for Processing focuses particularly on making it easy to work with the mobile hardware features built into Android phones and tablets.[15] The term "Ketai" is used in Japan to describe its cell phone culture, enabled by mobile handheld devices.[16] The mobile device translates as Keitai Denwa and literally means "something carried in the hand," or handheld.

The Ketai library is free software published under the GNU General Public License Version 3 (GPL v3),[17] and it is compatible with Android versions 2.3 Gingerbread, 3.0/3.1 Honeycomb, 4.0 Ice Cream Sandwich, and 4.1/4.2 Jelly Bean. NFC, Wi-Fi Direct, and updated camera features introduced in 4.0 Ice Cream Sandwich are not available in Gingerbread or Honeycomb. Therefore the Ketai library is available as separate downloads for Gingerbread/Honeycomb and for Ice Cream Sandwich/Jelly Bean.[18] Please refer to Section 1.4, *Run a Sketch on an Android Device*, on page 14, to find out which version of Android you are running on your device.

---

15. http://ketai.googlecode.com
16. http://iipc.utu.fi/imaginaryjapan/Kusahara.pdf
17. http://www.gnu.org/licenses/gpl.html
18. http://code.google.com/p/ketai/downloads/list

Compared to the desktop, the defining feature of a mobile handheld device is that we use it on the go, where we expect cameras, location, and orientation sensors to help us navigate traffic, find relevant locations near by, and snap pictures while we are on the move. We also might be networking with Bluetooth accessories, interacting with products through embedded NFC tags, or paying for merchandise with our mobile devices. The Ketai library helps us develop apps for all of these scenarios.

Libraries are arguably one of the most successful aspects of the open source Processing project. There are more than 130 libraries available for Processing; however, on the Android device we can only use those Java libraries that do not make use of desktop hardware. Libraries extend the easy-to-learn Processing core with classes written for particular contexts, including 3D, animation, compilations, computer vision, data and protocols, geometry, graphic interface, hardware interface, import and export, math, simulation, sound, tools, typography, and video—to name the main categories listed on the Processing website, where the libraries are organized.[19]

Many interface, sound, computer vision, and import/export libraries use code that is specific to the desktop context and are not designed for use on Android devices. Many libraries that could be compatible with Processing for Android are currently updated by library authors to eventually be available for us to use in Android mode. The Library Manager added to Processing 2.0 makes it easy to install libraries from within Processing. We'll use it to install the Ketai library in Section 2.5, *Install the Ketai Library*, on page 30.

There is hardly any computational topic that is not addressed in the Processing libraries. Because all libraries are open source and come with examples and tutorials, Processing is a favorite of students and creative coders alike. Most of the supplemental libraries have been developed for artists and designers for a particular project, so their use is often illustrated with the actual project that inspired it. Some of those projects can also be found in the online Processing exhibition.[20] This site makes browsing in and "shopping" for free libraries a fun activity and inspiring in its own right. As you download libraries and install them in your Processing sketchbook's libraries directory, they remain at this location and available even after you upgrade to a new version of the Processing IDE. The idea of this structure is to separate the Processing developer environment from the sketches that you write and the libraries you collect, keeping them independent of updates to Processing itself.

---

19. http://processing.org/reference/libraries/
20. http://processing.org/exhibition/

While there are scores of Processing libraries, only a small number of them work on Android phones and tablets. The Ketai library is designed particularly to provide programmer access to Android sensors, cameras, and networking; it is the only library that has been developed to run solely in Android mode.

I've been working on the Ketai library with Jesus Duran since 2010, with the objective to make it really easy to write apps that can effectively use the mobile hardware features built into Android phones and tablets. Convinced by the idea that phones and tablets evolve rapidly alongside the open source Android OS, the Ketai library makes it possible to consider such devices as a great complement to microcontrollers such as the Arduino—an open hardware sister project to Processing that is built on the same IDE.

Besides their compact form factor, multicore Android phones and tablets are computationally quite powerful, are equipped with a wide range of sensors, and run an operating system that is open source, free, and doesn't require subscriptions—characteristics that are advantageous to innovation, academic use, and DIY culture.[21] What's more, once a mobile phone or tablet is outdated, it remains an inexpensive device, available in abundance and way too functional for a landfill.[22]

The Ketai library values conciseness and legibility in its syntax and makes hardware features available using just a few lines of code. For example, the simple code we use for our accelerometer project (code, on page 46) uses less than thirty lines of code altogether, while the Java sample included in the Android SDK completes the task with more than one hundred lines of code.[23] This ratio increases significantly with more complex subjects such as Chapter 7, *Peer-to-Peer Networking Using Bluetooth and Wi-Fi Direct*, on page 151, and Chapter 8, *Using Near Field Communication (NFC)*, on page 189, where Ketai is significantly more concise and easier to understand than the SDK.

Ketai includes a number of classes that make Android hardware sensors and devices available within Processing. The following classes are included in the library, described in more detail in Section A1.2, *The Ketai Library Classes*, on page 341, and explained within the relevant chapters:

- KetaiSensor
- KetaiLocation
- KetaiCamera
- KetaiFaceDetector

---

21. http://en.wikipedia.org/wiki/DIY_culture
22. http://en.wikipedia.org/wiki/Mobile_phone_recycling
23. http://developer.android.com/tools/samples

- KetaiBluetooth
- KetaiWiFiDirect
- KetaiNFC
- KetaiData
- KetaiList
- KetaiKeyboard
- KetaiGesture

Let's go ahead and install the Ketai library now.

2.5 Install the Ketai Library

Follow these steps to activate the Processing library. It's a one-time process; you won't need to repeat it.

You can install the Ketai library from within the Processing IDE using the "Add Library..." menu item.

1. Choose "Add Library...," which you can find under Sketch → "Import Library..."

2. At the bottom of the window that opens, enter "Ketai."

3. Select the Ketai library that appears in the list and press the Install button on the right.

4. The download starts immediately, and a bar shows the download's progress. When the library is installed, the button on the right changes to Remove.

Alternatively, you can download and install the library manually from the dedicated website that comes with every Processing library. This process has the advantage that you can read about the library and preview its features alongside a reference and example code for the library.

1. Go to the Ketai library website, http://ketaiLibrary.org, and download the latest .zip file.

2. Extract the file to the Documents/Processing/libraries folder. If the libraries subfolder doesn't exist in your sketchbook, create it now and put the Ketai folder inside it.

3. Restart Processing so it can load the newly added library.

4. Check whether the installation was successful by opening Sketch→ "Import Library..." Under Contributed libraries you should now see the name

"Ketai." If it doesn't show up in the list, please refer to Section A1.4, *Troubleshooting*, on page 346.

The process for downloading and installing the Ketai library is identical for any other Processing library.

Let's now move on to our first project—putting the Ketai library to work.

2.6 Working with the KetaiGesture Class

KetaiGesture gives us access to the most common multitouch gestures used on mobile devices. It provides us with the callback methods that we need to highlight, scale, drag, and rotate objects and UI elements. To select, zoom, focus, and organize the elements we display on the touch screen, we can use a number of gestures that have become user interaction standards on mobile devices. Working off established UI standards, we can build apps that are more intuitive to use and that enable the user to get the job done quickly while on the move.

Using the KetaiGesture class,[24] we can work with the following callback methods, which report back to us when a certain event has occurred on the touch screen surface, which was triggered by a particular user interaction or multi-touch gesture.[25]

Let's take a look at the main methods included in KetaiGesture:

onTap(float x, float y) *Single Tap*—triggered by one short tap on the device screen. Returns the horizontal and vertical position of the single-tap gesture.

onDoubleTap(float x, float y) *Double Tap*—triggered by two successive short taps on the device screen. Returns the horizontal and vertical position of the double-tap gesture.

onLongPress(float x, float y) *Long Press*—triggered by tapping and holding a finger at one position on the touch screen for about one second. Returns the horizontal and vertical position of the long press gesture.

onFlick(float x, float y, float px, float py, float v) *Flick*—triggered by moving a finger in any direction, where the beginning and the end of the gesture occur at two different screen positions while the finger doesn't come to a full stop before lifting it from the screen surface. Returns the horizontal and vertical position where the flick is released, the horizontal and vertical position where the flick started, and the velocity of the flick.

---

24. http://ketai.googlecode.com/svn/trunk/ketai/reference/ketai/ui/KetaiGesture.html

25. http://en.wikipedia.org/wiki/Multitouch

onPinch(float x, float y, float d) *Pinch*—triggered by a two-finger gesture either away from each other (pinch open) or toward each other (pinch close). The pinch is typically used for zooming in and out of windows or for scaling objects. Returns the horizontal and vertical position of the pinch's centroid and the relative change in distance of the two fingers to each other.

onRotate(float x, float y, float angle) *Rotate*—triggered by the relative change of the axis rotation defined by two fingers on the touch screen surface. Returns the centroid of the rotation gesture and the relative change of the axis angle.

Let's build an app that puts KetaiGesture's multitouch methods to use.

2.7 Detect Multitouch Gestures

For this project, we'll implement the most common user interactions using just one simple geometric primitive—a rectangle—drawn on the screen using Processing's rect(x, y, width, height) method.[26] To begin, we'll place a rectangle in a specified size of 100 pixels in the center of the screen. Then we use a series of KetaiGesture callback events to trigger changes to the rectangle, including a change of scale, rotation, color, and position, as illustrated in Figure 7, *Using multitouch gestures*, on page 33.

We have a number of callback events for the touch surface to try out, so we'll assign each of them with a particular purpose. We'll zoom to fit the rectangle onto the screen using onDoubleTap(), randomly change its fill color onLongPress() using Processing's random() method,[27] scale it onPinch(), rotate it onRotate(), drag it using mouseDragged(), and change the background color onFlick(). Besides manipulating color properties and the rectangle, we'll keep track of the multitouch events as they occur by printing a text string to the Processing Console. The code we use to manipulate the properties and the callback methods themselves are not complicated in any way, but we're now dealing with a bit more code than we have before because we're using a series of callback methods in one sketch.

Introducing 2D Transformations

For this project, we'll lock our app into LANDSCAPE orientation() so we can maintain a clear reference point as we discuss 2D transformations in reference to the coordinate system. To center our rectangle on the screen when we start up, to scale from its center point using the pinch gesture, and to rotate it around

---

26. http://processing.org/reference/rect_.html
27. http://processing.org/reference/random_.html

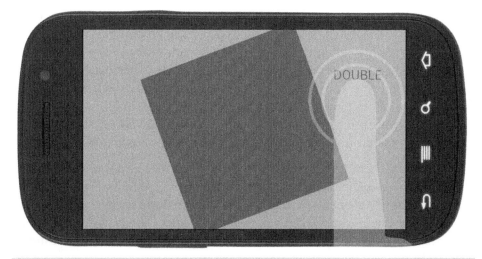

Figure 7—Using multitouch gestures. The illustration shows a rectangle scaled with a two-finger pinch gesture, turned by a two-finger rotation gesture, placed on a magenta background color, and triggered by a flick, as well as a gray fill color caused by a long press. The text "DOUBLE" appears due to a double-tap gesture at the position indicated by the hand silhouette.

its center point using the rotate gesture, we need to work with two-dimensional (2D) transformations.[28]

We'll use the Processing's rectMode(CENTER) method to overwrite the default way a rectangle is drawn in Processing,[29] which is from the upper left corner of the rectangle located at position [x, y] with a specified width and height. Instead we draw it from its center point using rectMode(CENTER), which allows us to rotate and scale it around its center point.

A common metaphor to explain 2D transformations is a grid or graph paper. Using this analogy, each grid cell stands for one pixel of our app's display window. The default origin in Processing's coordinate system is always the upper left corner of the window. Each graphic element is drawn relative to this origin onto the screen. To move and rotate our rectangle, we'll use Processing's transformation methods: translate() and rotate().[30] We also have a scale() method,[31] which we won't use in this sketch.

---

28. http://processing.org/learning/transform2d/

29. http://processing.org/reference/rectMode_.html

30. http://processing.org/reference/translate_.html and http://processing.org/reference/rotate_.html

31. http://processing.org/reference/scale_.html

When we draw graphic objects in Processing on our grid paper, we are used to specifying the rectangle's horizontal and vertical coordinates using x and y values. We can use an alternative method, which is necessary here, where we move our grid (paper) to specified horizontal and vertical coordinates, rotate, and then draw the rotated rectangle at position x and y [0, 0]. This way the rectangle doesn't move to our intended position, but our grid paper (coordinate system) did. The advantage is that we can now rotate() our rect() right on the spot around its center point, something we can't do otherwise.

What's more, we can introduce a whole stack of grid paper if we'd like to by using the Processing methods pushMatrix() and popMatrix(). When we move, rotate, and scale multiple elements and would like to transform them separately, we need to draw them on separate pieces of grid paper. The pushMatrix() method saves the current position of our coordinate system, and popMatrix() restores the coordinate system to the way it was before pushing it.

Like our first project in this chapter, in which we used Processing's mousePressed(), mouseReleased(), and mouseDragged() callback methods to identify touches to the screen, some of the multitouch gestures introduced here fulfill the same purpose. If we'd like to use Processing's mouse methods alongside multitouch methods provided by KetaiGesture, we'll need to notify the superclass method surfaceTouchEvent() to notify the Processing app that a surface touch event has occurred.[32]

Now let's take a look at our multitouch code.

```
Display/Gestures/Gestures.pde
① import ketai.ui.*;
② import android.view.MotionEvent;

③ KetaiGesture gesture;
④ float rectSize = 100;
  float rectAngle = 0;
  int x, y;
⑤ color c = color(255);
⑥ color bg = color(78, 93, 75);

  void setup()
  {
    orientation(LANDSCAPE);
⑦   gesture = new KetaiGesture(this);

    textSize(32);
    textAlign(CENTER, BOTTOM);
```

---

32. http://processing.org/reference/super.html

```
      rectMode(CENTER);
      noStroke();

⑧    x = width/2;
⑨    y = height/2;
    }

    void draw()
    {
      background(bg);
⑩    pushMatrix();
⑪    translate(x, y);
      rotate(rectAngle);
      fill(c);
      rect(0, 0, rectSize, rectSize);
⑫    popMatrix();
    }

⑬ void onTap(float x, float y)
    {
      text("SINGLE", x, y-10);
      println("SINGLE:" + x + "," + y);
    }

⑭ void onDoubleTap(float x, float y)
    {
      text("DOUBLE", x, y-10);
      println("DOUBLE:" + x + "," + y);

      if (rectSize > 100)
        rectSize = 100;
      else
        rectSize = height - 100;
    }

⑮ void onLongPress(float x, float y)
    {
      text("LONG", x, y-10);
      println("LONG:" + x + "," + y);

      c = color(random(255), random(255), random(255));
    }

⑯ void onFlick( float x, float y, float px, float py, float v)
    {
      text("FLICK", x, y-10);
      println("FLICK:" + x + "," + y + "," + v);

      bg = color(random(255), random(255), random(255));
    }
```

```
⑰ void onPinch(float x, float y, float d)
  {
    rectSize = constrain(rectSize+d, 10, 500);
    println("PINCH:" + x + "," + y + "," + d);
  }

⑱ void onRotate(float x, float y, float angle)
  {
    rectAngle += angle;
    println("ROTATE:" + angle);
  }

⑲ void mouseDragged()
  {
    if (abs(mouseX - x) < rectSize/2 && abs(mouseY - y) < rectSize/2)
    {
      if (abs(mouseX - pmouseX) < rectSize/2)
        x += mouseX - pmouseX;
      if (abs(mouseY - pmouseY) < rectSize/2)
        y += mouseY - pmouseY;
    }
  }

⑳ public boolean surfaceTouchEvent(MotionEvent event) {
    //call to keep mouseX and mouseY constants updated
    super.surfaceTouchEvent(event);
    //forward events
    return gesture.surfaceTouchEvent(event);
  }
```

Let's take a look at the steps we need to take to capture and use multitouch gestures on the Android touch screen.

❶ Import Ketai's ui package to give us access to the KetaiGesture class.

❷ Import Android's MotionEvent package.

❸ Define a variable called gesture of type KetaiGesture.

❹ Set a variable we call rectSize to 100 pixels to start off.

❺ Define the initial color c (white), which we'll use as a fill color for the rectangle and text.

❻ Define the initial color bg (dark green), which we'll use as a background color.

❼ Instantiate our KetaiGesture object gesture.

❽ Set the initial value for our variable x as the horizontal position of the rectangle.

⑨ Set the initial value for y as the vertical position of the rectangle.

⑩ Push the current matrix on the matrix stack so that we can draw and rotate the rectangle independent of other UI elements, such as the text.

⑪ Move to the position [x, y] using translate().

⑫ Pop the current matrix to restore the previous matrix on the stack.

⑬ Use the callback method onTap() to display the text string SINGLE at the location (x, y) returned by KetaiGesture.

⑭ Use the callback method onDoubleTap() to display the text string DOUBLE at the location returned by KetaiGesture, indicating that the user triggered a double-tap event. Use this event to decrease the rectangle size to the original 100 pixels if it's currently enlarged, and increase the rectangle scale to the display height minus 100 pixels if it's currently minimized to its original scale.

⑮ Use the callback method onLongPress() to display the text string "LONG" at the location (x, y) returned by KetaiGesture. Use this event to randomly select a new color c using random(), which we'll use as a fill color for the rectangle.

⑯ Use the callback method onFlick() to display the text string FLICK at the location x and y returned by KetaiGesture. Also, receive the previous location where the flick has been initiated as px and py, as well as the velocity v.

⑰ Use the callback method onPinch() to calculate the scaled rectSize using the pinch distance d at the location x and y returned by KetaiGesture.

⑱ Use the callback method onPinch() to calculate the scaled rectSize using the pinch distance d at the location x and y returned by KetaiGesture.

⑲ Use Processing's mouseDragged() callback to update the rectangle position (x and y) by the amount of pixels moved. Determine this amount by subtracting the previous pmouseX from the current mouseX, and pmouseY from mouseY. Move the rectangle only if absolute distance between the rectangle and the mouse position is less than half the rectangle's size, or when we touch the rectangle.

⑳ Use the Processing method surfaceTouchEvent() to notify Processing about mouse/finger-related updates.

Let's test the app.

Run the App

Run the app on your device. You'll see a square show up in the center of the screen. Drag it to a new location, flick to change the background color, and give it a long tap to change the foreground fill color.

To test the multitouch gestures, put two fingers down on the screen and pinch, and you'll see how the rectangle starts scaling. Now rotate the same two fingers to see the rectangle rotate. If you use more than two fingers, the first two fingers you put down on the screen are in charge.

Finally, double-tap the screen to zoom the square to full screen, and double-tap again to scale it to its initial size of 100 pixels.

This completes our investigation into the multitouch features of the touch screen panel.

2.8 Wrapping Up

You've used the touch screen panel as the first hardware device we've worked with. You've learned about mouse speed and all the different color features in Processing and worked with the HSB color mode to manipulate the hue values of the geometric primitive we've drawn. And finally, you are now able to use mouse events and multitouch gestures for your app's user interfaces to control the object you display on the device screen.

You are now well positioned to move on to the next chapter, where we'll focus on the hardware sensors built into Android devices. After all, the "native" user experience of mobile apps relies heavily on hardware devices and sensors, and we are now ready to incorporate them into our apps.

CHAPTER 3

Using Motion and Position Sensors

This chapter is about how to interact with sensors on an Android device using the Ketai library. Android devices come packed with sensors that allow us to write mobile apps that react to how we position and move the Android device to make them more engaging, useful, and interactive. Android sensors provide us with information about device motion, position, and environment. We'll focus on motion sensors in this chapter and take a look at some position sensors.

Motion sensors allow us to measure how the device is oriented in space and how it accelerates when we move it. The typical accelerometer sensor found on Android devices triggers screen rotations and is used for a wide range of apps to detect shakes, fist bumps, hand gestures, bumpy roads, and other features. Using Ketai, we'll list all the available sensors built into the Android and work with multiple sensors combined in an app that displays values for the magnetic field, light, proximity, and accelerometer sensors.

We'll work with the orientation of an Android device to create an interactive color mixer app. Step by step, we'll start by learning to display raw data from the accelerometer sensor, and then we'll use those values to generate the entire spectrum of color that the Android can generate. Next we'll learn how to store data in an array and how to use the array to display a palette of eight colors that we've created. Finally, we'll use the accelerometer to clear the color palette by shaking the device, and we'll detect that motion in our program. In the process, we'll acquire a sense for the accelerometer sensor, its value range, and its accuracy, and we'll learn to integrate it into the app's user interface. By the end of the chapter, you will know this sensor well enough to transpose this knowledge to other applications.

3.1   Introducing the Device Hardware and Software Layers

Writing sensor-based Android apps in Processing involves a series of software layers that build on each other. The list below describes the software stack running on the device hardware, all of which we put to use when we run our sketches—starting with the bottommost hardware layer.

Hardware   Besides the central (CPU) and graphics (GPU) processing unit, hardware devices built in the Android include: GSM/3G/4G antennas, digital cameras, an accelerometer sensor, a light sensor, a gyroscope, a geomagnetic field sensor, a capacitive touch screen panel, an audio interface, a speaker, a vibration motor, a battery, a Flash memory interface, and perhaps a hardware keyboard and a temperature sensor.

Linux kernel   The bottommost software layer running on the hardware is the Linux kernel,[1] a Unix-like operating system initially developed by Linus Torvalds in 1991. We access all the hardware resources of the device through this layer, which contains drivers for the display, cameras, Bluetooth, Flash memory, Binder (PC), USB, keypad, Wi-Fi, audio, and power.

Android and Java Core Libraries Above the Linux kernel sit the Android native libraries written in C/C++, including Surface Manager, Media Framework, SQLite , OpenGL/ES , FreeType, WebKit, SGL, SSL, and libc. This layer also includes Android Runtime, which contains the core Java libraries and the Dalvik virtual machine.[2] The Dalvik virtual machine creates compact executable files that are optimized for memory and processor speed. The virtual machine allows a high level of control over the actions an app is permitted to take within the operating system. Android applications are typically written in Java using the Java core libraries and compiled to bytecode, which is the format executed by a Java virtual machine. In the Android OS, bytecode is converted into a Dalvik executable (.dex) before an app is installed on the Android device.

Processing The language itself is the next layer in our software stack that builds on the Java core libraries. The Android mode in Processing works with the Android libraries in the Android layer. Processing's software architecture allows us to use Java and Android classes directly within the Processing code.

---

1.   http://en.wikipedia.org/wiki/Linux_kernel
2.   http://en.wikipedia.org/wiki/Dalvik_%28software%29

Ketai The library builds on the Processing for Android layer, taking advantage of the Processing, Java, and Android libraries. It's the highest layer in the software stack we'll be working with in projects, besides using a few other libraries that sit on the same level in the hierarchy. Ketai focuses specifically on the hardware features built into Android devices, including the multitouch screen panel, sensors, cameras, and networking devices.

Now that we are aware of the different hardware components and the software layers stacked on top of the hardware layer, let's start with the bottommost hardware layer and take a look at the most common sensors built into our Android device.

3.2 Introducing Common Android Sensors

In this chapter, we will work mostly with the accelerometer sensor and use the KetaiSensor class to access it. KetaiSensor is capable of working with all sensors. Some sensors found on the Android device are based on hardware; others are software-based and provided by the Android SDK. For the projects in this chapter, we'll focus on actual electronic hardware sensors built into the Android phone or tablet. Android distinguishes three different sensor-type categories: motion sensors,[3] position sensors,[4] and environment sensors.[5] Most environment sensors have been added to the Android SDK recently (Android 4.0 Ice Cream Sandwich), so they are not typically found in devices yet. Let's take a look at the different sensors Android supports.

Motion Sensors

The following sensors let you monitor the motion of the device:

Accelerometer (hardware) Determines the orientation of the device as well as its acceleration in three-dimensional space, which we'll use to detect shakes

Gravity (software-based) Calculates the orientation of the device, returning a three-dimensional vector indicating the direction and magnitude of gravity

Gyroscope (hardware) Measures the movement of the device, returning the rate of rotation around each device axis—if available, this sensor is often used for games that rely on immediate and precise responses to device movement.

---

3.   http://developer.android.com/guide/topics/sensors/sensors_motion.html

4.   http://developer.android.com/guide/topics/sensors/sensors_position.html

5.   http://developer.android.com/guide/topics/sensors/sensors_environment.html

Linear Acceleration (software-based) Calculates the movement of the device, returning a three-dimensional vector that indicates the acceleration of each device axis, excluding gravity

Rotation Vector (software-based) Calculates the orientation of the device, returning an angle and an axis—it can simplify calculations for 3D apps, providing a rotation angle combined with a rotation axis around which the device rotated.

Now let's take a look at the sensors that deal with the device's position.

Position Sensors

The following sensors let you to determine the location or position of the device:

Magnetic Field A three-axis digital compass that senses the bearing of the device relative to magnetic north

Proximity Senses the distance to an object measured from the sensor that is mounted in close proximity to the device speaker—this is commonly used to determine if the device is held toward, or removed from, the ear.

Now let's take a look at the sensors that measure the device's environment.

Environment Sensors

The following sensors let you monitor environmental properties or measure the device context:

Light Senses the ambient light level

Pressure Senses the air pressure (the atmospheric pressure)

Relative Humidity Senses the humidity of the air (in percent)

Temperature Senses the ambient air temperature

Since this list will grow and remain a moving target as new generations of devices and APIs are released, the Android Sensor website is the best source for keeping an eye on changes and additions.[6]

Let's start by looking at the KetaiSensor class, which we'll use when we work with sensors throughout the book.

---

6.   http://developer.android.com/reference/android/hardware/Sensor.html

3.3 Working with the KetaiSensor Class

For the sketches we'll write in this chapter, the following KetaiSensor methods are the most relevant:

list() Returns a list of available sensors on the device

onAccelerometerEvent() Returns x-, y-, and z-axis acceleration minus g-force in meters per second squared (m/s^2)

onMagneticFieldEvent() Returns the x, y, and z values for the ambient magnetic field in units of microtesla

onLightEvent() Returns the light level in SI units of lux

onProximityEvent() Returns the distance to an object measured from the device surface in centimeters—depending on the device, a typical output is 0/1 or 0/5—the sensor is typically located next to the speaker on the device.

onGyroscopeEvent() Returns the x, y, and z rates of rotation around the x-, y-, and z-axes in degrees

Because a multitude of devices on the market exist, it's important that we start by checking the sensors that are built into our Android device. Let's use the KetaiSensor class to see what sensors are built into our Android device.

3.4 List the Built-In Sensors on an Android Device

Let's find out what sensors are built into our device and available for us to work with. The KetaiSensor class offers a list() method that enumerates all Android sensors available in the device and lists them for us in the Processing console.

Open a new sketch window in Android mode and type or copy the following four lines of code; click on the green bar to download the SensorList.pde source file if you are reading the ebook.

Sensors/SensorList/SensorList.pde
```
import ketai.sensors.*;
KetaiSensor sensor;
sensor = new KetaiSensor(this);
println(sensor.list());
```

Take a look at the code. First we import the Ketai sensor package, then we create a sensor variable of the type KetaiSensor, and finally we create a sensor object containing all the KetaiSensor methods we need. As the last step, we print the sensor list() to the console.

Run the App

Run this code on your Android device and take a look at the Processing console. For example, the Google Nexus S reports the following list of sensors:

```
KetaiSensor sensor: KR3DM 3-axis Accelerometer:1
KetaiSensor sensor: AK8973 3-axis Magnetic field sensor:2
KetaiSensor sensor: GP2A Light sensor:5
KetaiSensor sensor: GP2A Proximity sensor:8
KetaiSensor sensor: K3G Gyroscope sensor:4
KetaiSensor sensor: Rotation Vector Sensor:11
KetaiSensor sensor: Gravity Sensor:9
KetaiSensor sensor: Linear Acceleration Sensor:10
KetaiSensor sensor: Orientation Sensor:3
KetaiSensor sensor: Corrected Gyroscope Sensor:4
```

The Asus Transformer Prime tablet reports the following sensors:

```
KetaiSensor sensor: MPL rotation vector:11
KetaiSensor sensor: MPL linear accel:10
KetaiSensor sensor: MPL gravity:9
KetaiSensor sensor: MPL Gyro:4
KetaiSensor sensor: MPL accel:1
KetaiSensor sensor: MPL magnetic field:2
KetaiSensor sensor: MPL Orientation:3
KetaiSensor sensor: Lite-On al3010 Ambient Light Sensor:5
KetaiSensor sensor: Intersilisl29018 Proximity sensor:8
```

The list includes some hardware info for each sensor, its type, and an ID. Your results, no doubt, will differ; there are a lot of Android makes and models out there today.

The list includes more than hardware sensors. The Android SDK also includes software-based sensors, known as *fused sensors*. Fused sensors use multiple hardware sensors and an Android software layer to improve the readings from one individual sensor. They make it easier for us as developers to work with the resulting data. The Gravity, Linear Acceleration, and Rotation Vector sensors are examples of such hybrid sensors, combining gyroscope, accelerometer, and compass data to improve the results. In the list of available sensors, however, no distinction is made between hardware sensors and fused sensors.

This also means that even if you don't update your device hardware, new versions of the Android API might include fused software-based sensor types that might be easier to use or might produce better results. For example, if you browse Android's sensor hardware overview and switch the "Filter by API Level" to 8 (http://developer.android.com/reference/android/hardware/Sensor.html), you will see a list of the sensor types and methods that have been added to the API since the release of API 8.

As you start adding methods from the Ketai library to the sketch, note that contributed libraries are not highlighted by the Processing IDE because they are not part of the core. This is not a big deal, but it's something you should be aware of.

Here's the code we'll typically use to interact with a device using the classes and methods that the Ketai library provides:

```
❶ import ketai.sensors.*;
❷ KetaiSensor sensor;

   void setup()
   {
❸    sensor = new KetaiSensor(this);
❹    sensor.start();
   }
   void draw()
   {
   }
❺ void onAccelerometerEvent(float x, float y, float z)
   {
   }
```

Let's take a look at the code that is specific to KetaiSensor.

❶ Import the Ketai sensor library package from Sketchbook/libraries.

❷ Declare a sensor variable of type KetaiSensor, and register it for any available Android sensors.

❸ Instantiate the KetaiSensor class to create a sensor object, which makes KetaiSensor methods available.

❹ Start listening for accelerometer sensor events.

❺ Each time the accelerometer changes value, receive a callback for the x, y, and z sensor axes.

Sensor values change at a different rate than the draw() method does. By default, draw() runs 60 times per second. The sensor can report much faster than that rate, which is why we work with an onAccelerometerEvent() callback method. It is called every time we receive a new value from the accelerometer.

Different devices use different accelerometers. Some contain hardware filters that stop reporting values altogether when the device is absolutely still. Others might be more accurate—or noisy—and keep reporting even when the device is seemingly still. Accelerometers are sensitive to the smallest motion. Let's take a look at the raw values such a device will display.

3.5 Display Values from the Accelerometer

Using the Ketai library, let's see what the accelerometer has to report. The accelerometer is the most common sensor found in mobile devices and is designed to detect device acceleration and its orientation toward g-force. It returns the *x-*, *y-*, and *z*-axes of the device, measured in meters per second squared. These axes are *not* swapped when the app's screen orientation changes.

The accelerometer sensor's shortcomings are related to the fact that it cannot distinguish between rotation and movement. For instance, moving the device back and forth on a flat table and rotating it about its axes can produce identical accelerometer values. To differentiate between movement and rotation, we require an additional sensor, the gyroscope, which we'll also use in Chapter 11, *Introducing 3D Graphics with OpenGL*, on page 265. When we want to find out how the device is oriented with respect to gravity, however, the accelerometer is the only sensor that can help us.

Let's add some code to output raw accelerometer values onto the screen. We're aiming for the result shown in Figure 8, *Accelerometer output*, on page 47. We use the text() method and some formatting to display accelerometer values. As we move the device, it will also come in handy to lock the screen orientation so we can keep an eye on the quickly changing values. Because we only need to set the screen orientation(PORTRAIT) once at startup, the method goes into setup().

Now let's dive into the code.

```
Sensors/Accelerometer/Accelerometer.pde
import ketai.sensors.*;

KetaiSensor sensor;
float accelerometerX, accelerometerY, accelerometerZ;

void setup()
{
  sensor = new KetaiSensor(this);
  sensor.start();
  orientation(PORTRAIT);
❶ textAlign(CENTER, CENTER);
❷ textSize(36);
}

void draw()
{
  background(78, 93, 75);
❸ text("Accelerometer: \n" +
```

Figure 8—Accelerometer output. The picture shows the acceleration of the *x-, y-,* and *z*-axes of the device in relation to g-force.

```
    "x: " + nfp(accelerometerX, 2, 3) + "\n" +
    "y: " + nfp(accelerometerY, 2, 3) + "\n" +
    "z: " + nfp(accelerometerZ, 2, 3), width/2, height/2);
}

void onAccelerometerEvent(float x, float y, float z)
{
  accelerometerX = x;
  accelerometerY = y;
  accelerometerZ = z;
}
```

Let's take a closer look at the Processing methods we've used for the first time.

❶ Align the text to the CENTER of the screen using textAlign().[7]

❷ Set the text size to 36 using textSize().[8] The default text size is tiny and hard to decipher in motion.

❸ Display the data using text().[9] We output a series of strings tied together via the plus sign (+), known as the concatenation operator. This way we can use only one text method to display all the labels and reformatted values we need.

Acceleration values are measured in m/s^2. If the device is sitting *flat* and *still* on the table, the accelerometer reads a magnitude of +9.81 m/s^2. This number represents the acceleration needed to hold the device up against g-force and the result of the following calculation: acceleration of the device (0 m/s^2) minus the acceleration due to gravity (-9.81 m/s^2).[10] If we move and rotate the device, we can observe values in the range of roughly -10 to 10 m/s^2. Shake the device and the values will surge momentarily to maybe +-20 m/s^2. Values beyond that become tricky to observe; feel free to try.

We format the numbers via nfp(), a method that helps us to maintain two digits to the left and three digits to the right of the decimal point. This way, values we observe don't jump around as much. The "p" in nfp() puts a "+" in front of positive accelerometer values and a "-" in front of negative values, helping us to understand the device orientation better with regard to the accelerometer's nomenclature.

Run the App

In case you didn't already run the sketch in anticipation, now is the time. Remember that the shortcut for Run on Device is ⌘R. Try placing your device in different positions and observe the acceleration due to gravity reported for each axis. If you lay your Android device flat on a table, for example, the z-axis will report an acceleration of approximately +9.81 m/s^2. When you hold it vertically in a reading position, notice how the acceleration due to gravity shifts to the *y*-axis. The screen output is similar to Figure 8, *Accelerometer output*, on page 47. Tiny movements of the device trigger very observable changes in value, which are reported back to us via onAccelerometerEvent().

Let's now see how a sketch would look using multiple sensors.

---

7.   http://processing.org/reference/textAlign_.html

8.   http://processing.org/reference/textSize_.html

9.   http://processing.org/reference/text_.html

10. http://en.wikipedia.org/wiki/G-force

3.6 Display Values from Multiple Sensors

So far we've worked with the accelerometer, which is a hardware motion sensor built into the Android device. In future chapters we'll want to work with multiple sensors, so let's fire up a few simultaneously and display their values on the Android screen. For this sketch, we'll activate the accelerometer again and add two position sensors and an environment sensor. The magnetic field sensor and the proximity sensors are considered position sensors; the light sensor is an environment sensor.

We could store the three axes returned by the accelerometer and magnetometer sensors in individual floating point variables. A better solution, however, is to work with Processing's PVector class.[11] It can store either a two- or a three-dimensional vector, which is perfect for us, since we can put any two or three values into this package, including sensor values. Instead of three variables for the *x*-, *y*-, and *z*-axes returned by the accelerometer and magnetometer, we can just use one PVector, called accelerometer. We refer later to an individual value or axis using the accelerometer.x, accelerometer.y, and accelerometer.z components of this PVector. The class is equipped with a number of useful methods to simplify the vector math for us, which we'll use later in this chapter to detect a device shake.

For this sketch, let's lock the screen orientation() into LANDSCAPE mode so we can display enough digits behind the comma for the floating point values returned by the sensors.

To create a sketch using multiple sensors, we follow these steps:

Sensors/MultipleSensors/MultipleSensors.pde
```
import ketai.sensors.*;
KetaiSensor sensor;
PVector magneticField, accelerometer;
float light, proximity;

void setup()  {
  sensor = new KetaiSensor(this);
  sensor.start();
  sensor.list();
  accelerometer = new PVector();
  magneticField = new PVector();
❶ orientation(LANDSCAPE);
  textAlign(CENTER, CENTER);
  textSize(28);
}
```

---

11. http://processing.org/reference/PVector.html

```
void draw()
{
  background(78, 93, 75);
  text("Accelerometer :" + "\n"
    + "x: " + nfp(accelerometer.x, 1, 2) + "\n"
    + "y: " + nfp(accelerometer.y, 1, 2) + "\n"
    + "z: " + nfp(accelerometer.z, 1, 2) + "\n"
    + "MagneticField :" + "\n"
    + "x: " + nfp(magneticField.x, 1, 2) + "\n"
    + "y: " + nfp(magneticField.y, 1, 2) + "\n"
    + "z: " + nfp(magneticField.z, 1, 2) + "\n"
    + "Light Sensor : " + light + "\n"
    + "Proximity Sensor : " + proximity + "\n"
    , 20, 0, width, height);
}

  void onAccelerometerEvent(float x, float y, float z, long time, int accuracy)
  {
    accelerometer.set(x, y, z);
  }
❷ void onMagneticFieldEvent(float x, float y, float z, long time, int accuracy)
  {
    magneticField.set(x, y, z);
  }

❸ void onLightEvent(float v)
  {
    light = v;
  }

❹ void onProximityEvent(float v)
  {
    proximity = v;
  }
❺ public void mousePressed() {
    if (sensor.isStarted())
      sensor.stop();
    else
      sensor.start();
    println("KetaiSensor isStarted: " + sensor.isStarted());
  }
```

Let's take a closer look at the different event methods.

❶ Rotate the screen orientation().[12]

❷ Measure the strength of the ambient magnetic field in microteslas along the *x*-, *y*-, and *z*-axes.

_____

12. http://wiki.processing.org/w/Android#Screen.2C_Orientation.2C_and_the_size.28.29_command

❸ Capture the light intensity, measured in lux ambient illumination.

❹ Measure the distance between the device display and an object (ear, hand, and so on). Some proximity sensors support only near (1) or far (0) measurements.

❺ Tap on the touch screen to invoke the start() and stop() methods for the sensors on the device. This will start and stop all sensors here, as all of them are registered with the same sensor object.

Let's take a look to see if all the sensors return values.

Run the App

Run the sketch on the device, and you should see output similar to this:

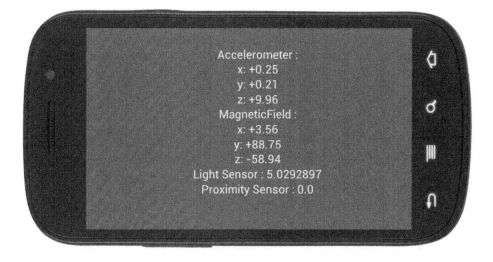

Figure 9—Using multiple Android sensors. The image shows the accelerometer, magnetic field, light, and proximity sensor output.

Move and rotate the device to see how sensor values change. The proximity sensor is located on the Android next to the speaker and is typically used to detect whether the device is held against or away from the ear. It returns values in centimeters, and you can use your hand to play with the returned proximity values. Depending on your Android make and model, you get a 0 if you are close to the device and either a 1 or a 5 if you are more than 1 or 5 centimeters away. Current proximity sensors are not accurate enough to use as a measuring tool just yet.

Tapping the screen calls the stop() method and stops all the sensors. If the app doesn't require sensor updates all the time, stopping sensors is a good way to save some battery power.

Your sensor list on page 43 might have already shown that your Android has a gyroscope built in. If not, Ketai will report, "Disabling onGyroscopeSensorEvent() because of an error" in the console.

To work with the gyro as well, add the following code snippet to the sketch code, on page 49, and rerun the app on the device:

```
void onGyroscopeEvent(float x, float y, float z) {
    rotationX = x;
    rotationY = y;
    rotationZ = z;
}
```

If you have a gyro, you are all set for Chapter 11, *Introducing 3D Graphics with OpenGL*, on page 265, where we use it to navigate a 3D environment. No worries though if your device doesn't support it. There are plenty of motion-based apps we'll develop based on the accelerometer, and there are numerous other projects to discover in this book that don't require the gyro.

Let's now move on to the main chapter project and use what we've learned so far to build an app that combines what we know about the accelerometer with the support the Processing language provides for working with colors.

3.7 Build a Motion-Based Color Mixer and Palette

We're going to build a color mixer that generates hues by mapping the orientation of an Android device relative to its x-, y-, and z-axes to the *R*, *G*, and *B* values of a color variable. We've already discussed the Processing color type in *Using the Color Type*, on page 24. When the sketch is complete, as shown in Figure 12, *Color mixer app*, on page 59, you'll be able to create every hue available to your device by rotating it in three-dimensional space.

In Section 3.10, *Erase a Palette with a Shake*, on page 62, we'll add a feature that lets you erase the stored colors by shaking the device. The color mixer will help us to get a better sense of the Processing color type and the value ranges of the accelerometer motion sensor, and it will provide us with a good foundation for working within the device coordinate system.

Mix a Color

Now let's move ahead and connect the accelerometer to change color hues. Since we successfully registered the accelerometer earlier, we can now take the code, on page 46, to the next level for our color mixer project. The global variables

Simulating Sensors in the Emulator

Please keep in mind that features that rely on built-in sensor hardware cannot be emulated on the desktop computer. Because the emulator doesn't have a built-in accelerometer, for example, it can only give you a default value. The emulator does a good job of showing us whether the Processing sketch is compiling happily, but we can't get to an actual user experience. If you'd like to explore further how the emulator can be fed with "simulated" sensor values, you need to download additional software.[a]

a.   OpenIntents SensorSimulator lets you simulate sensor data from accelerometer, compass, and orientation sensors, available at http://code.google.com/p/openintents/downloads/list.

accelerometerX, accelerometerY, and accelerometerZ keep track of raw values already, and it's a small step now to tie color values to device orientation. Earlier we observed magnitude values roughly in the range of -10 and 10 for each axis. We can now map these raw values to the RGB color spectrum in the default target range of 0..255. For that, we use the handy map() method, which takes one number range (in this case, incoming values of -10..10), and maps it onto another (our target of 0..255):

Here's a description of map() parameters. Once we've learned how to use it, we'll find ourselves using it all the time:

map(value, low1, high1, low2, high2)

value Incoming value to be converted

low1 Lower bound of the value's current range

high1 Upper bound of the value's current range

low2 Lower bound of the value's target range

high2 Upper bound of the value's target range

Now let's use map() to assign accelerometer values to the three values of an RGB color, and let's use background() to display the result, as shown in Figure 10, *Mapping accelerometer values to RGB color*, on page 54.

We need to add the accelerometer bounds for each axis and map() the values to three variables, called r, g, and b. Add the code snippet below to the code, on page 46, at the beginning of draw() and adjust the background() method:

```
float r = map(accelerometerX, -10, 10, 0, 255);
float g = map(accelerometerY, -10, 10, 0, 255);
float b = map(accelerometerZ, -10, 10, 0, 255);
background(r, g, b);
```

Figure 10—Mapping accelerometer values to RGB color. Accelerometer values for each axis in the range of -10..10 are mapped to about 50 percent red, 50 percent green, and 100 percent blue values, resulting in a purple background.

The three color variables (r, g, and b) now translate sensor values in the range of -10..10 to color values of 0..255. The sketch then looks something like Figure 10, *Mapping accelerometer values to RGB color*, on page 54.

Sensors/AccelerometerColor/AccelerometerColor.pde

```
import ketai.sensors.*;

KetaiSensor sensor;
float accelerometerX, accelerometerY, accelerometerZ;
float r, g, b;

void setup()
{
  sensor = new KetaiSensor(this);
  sensor.start();
  orientation(PORTRAIT);
  textAlign(CENTER, CENTER);
  textSize(36);
}
```

```
void draw() {
  float r = map(accelerometerX, -10, 10, 0, 255);
  float g = map(accelerometerY, -10, 10, 0, 255);
  float b = map(accelerometerZ, -10, 10, 0, 255);
  background(r, g, b);
  text("Accelerometer: \n" +
    "x: " + nfp(accelerometerX, 2, 3) + "\n" +
    "y: " + nfp(accelerometerY, 2, 3) + "\n" +
    "z: " + nfp(accelerometerZ, 2, 3), width/2, height/2);
}

void onAccelerometerEvent(float x, float y, float z) {
  accelerometerX = x;
  accelerometerY = y;
  accelerometerZ = z;
}
```

With this small addition, let's run the sketch on the device.

Run the App

When you run the sketch on the device, notice how the background() changes when you tilt or shake it. You are starting to use sketches and ideas from previous sections and reuse them in new contexts. The translation from raw sensor values into a color mixer project is not a big step. To understand how the accelerometer responds to your movement, it is a bit more intuitive to observe color changes displayed on the Android screen rather than fast-changing floating point values.

Now look more closely at the display as you rotate the device. Notice how the red value is linked to rotation around the *x*-axis, green to the *y*-axis, and blue to the *z*-axis. This helps us figure out how the Android coordinate system is aligned with the actual device. The coordinate system does *not* reconfigure when the screen orientation switches from PORTRAIT to LANDSCAPE. This is why we locked the app into orientation(PORTRAIT). We don't have to maintain the one-to-one relationship between the device coordinate system and the Processing coordinate system, but we'd sure have a harder time learning about it.

Let's now figure out how to save the colors we generate.

3.8 Save a Color

To save any color that we create by rotating our device about its three axes, we need a container that is good for storing color values. Processing provides us with the color type, which we looked at briefly in the previous chapter, *Using the Color Type*, on page 24.

To implement the color picker, let's rework our code, on page 46, and add a variable named swatch to store whatever color we pick when we tap the screen. We can then display the color pick value in an area at the bottom half of the screen, as shown here:

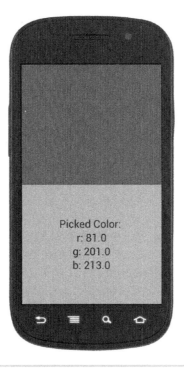

Figure 11—Saving a color swatch. The image shows a color picked from all the possible hues Android can generate, stored in a color swatch.

Let's also display the individual values that correspond to the red, green, and blue variables as text using the red(), green(), and blue() methods to extract color values from the swatch color variable.

Sensors/AccelerometerColorPicker/AccelerometerColorPicker.pde

```
import ketai.sensors.*;

KetaiSensor sensor;
float accelerometerX, accelerometerY, accelerometerZ;
color swatch;
float r, g, b;

void setup()
{
  sensor = new KetaiSensor(this);
```

```
    sensor.start();
    orientation(PORTRAIT);
    textAlign(CENTER, CENTER);
    textSize(36);
  }

  void draw()
  {
    // remap sensor values to color range
    r = map(accelerometerX, -10, 10, 0, 255);
    g = map(accelerometerY, -10, 10, 0, 255);
    b = map(accelerometerZ, -10, 10, 0, 255);
    // assign color to background
    background(r, g, b);
    // color picker
    fill(swatch);
    rect(0, height/2, width, height/2);
    fill(0);
    text("Picked Color: \n" +
      "r: " + red(swatch) + "\n" +
      "g: " + green(swatch) + "\n" +
      "b: " + blue(swatch), width*0.5, height*0.75);
  }

  void onAccelerometerEvent(float x, float y, float z)
  {
    accelerometerX = x;
    accelerometerY = y;
    accelerometerZ = z;
  }

  void mousePressed()
  {
    // updating color value, tapping top half of the screen
    if (mouseY < height/2)
      swatch = color(r, g, b);
  }
```

Let's take a second look at the methods we've added.

❶ Declare the variable swatch to be of type color.

❷ Apply the swatch color to the fill() before drawing the color picker rectangle.

❸ Draw the color picker rectangle.

❹ Extract the red, green, and blue values individually from the swatch color.

❺ Update the swatch color.

Let's test the app.

Run the App

Tapping the top half of the screen stores the current swatch color, which appears as a strip of color on the bottom half of the screen. The numeric color values displayed as text on the bottom of the screen are taken directly from the swatch variable.

The sequence of events can be summarized as follows: We receive the accelerometer values from the hardware sensor and remap them into color values that we then display via the background() method in real time. When we tap the screen and pick a color, all three color values are stored in swatch. The numeric color value displayed as text is derived directly from the swatch color by using Processing's red(), green(), and blue() extraction methods, grabbing each value from swatch individually.[13]

Clearly, though, storing one color is not enough. We've organized the screen and code so we can handle multiple colors, so let's take it a step further. We want to store multiple colors in such a way that we can recall them later individually. To implement this effectively, we need a color array.

3.9 Build a Palette of Colors

In this section, we'll build a palette of colors using a list of colors, or a color array,[14] as illustrated in Figure 12, *Color mixer app*, on page 59. When you see a color you like, you'll be able to store it as one of eight swatches on the screen. In our example, we are dealing with a color array and we want to store a list of colors in a palette[] array. Each data/color entry in the list is identified by an index number that represents the position in the array. The first element is identified by the index number, [0]; the second element, [1]; and the last element, palette.length. We need to define the array length when we create the array. ArrayList is an alternative here because it is able to store a varying number of objects. It's great, but it has a steeper learning curve. More info is available at http://processing.org/reference/ArrayList.html.

We can create arrays of any data type, for example int[], String[], float[], and boolean[]. For a color array that stores up to, let's say, eight colors, we need to change the swatch variable from the previous code, on page 56, into this:

```
color[] palette = new color[8];
```

As a result, we can then store eight colors sequentially within the palette array. This touches on a prime programming principle: build the code to be as

---

13. http://processing.org/reference/red_.html

14. http://processing.org/reference/Array.html

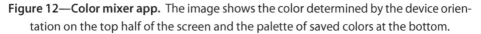

Figure 12—Color mixer app. The image shows the color determined by the device orientation on the top half of the screen and the palette of saved colors at the bottom.

adaptable and versatile as possible. In our case, we want the app to work with any number of colors, not just eight. So we need to aim at more (n) colors and introduce a num variable that can be set to the amount we want to work with (8). Sure, the UI might not adapt as neatly if we set num to 100, for example. But the code should be able to handle it without breaking. With adaptability in mind, we also program the GUI independent of the screen's size and resolution. In a diverse and rapidly changing device market, this approach prepares the app for a future filled with Android devices of every conceivable size.

Now that we have an array in which to store our colors, let's talk about its sidekick: the for loop.[15] Because arrays are equivalent to multiples, the for loop is typically used to parse the array. It's designed to iterate a defined number of times, here num times, until it reaches the end of our palette. The init, test, and update conditions in a for loop are separated by semicolons, here with i serving as the counter variable.

---

15. http://processing.org/reference/for.html

When Processing encounters the for loop, the counter variable is set to the init condition (i=0) and then tested (i<num); if the test passes, all statements in the loop are executed. At the end of the loop, the counter variable is updated (i++), which here means incremented by one and then tested again, and if the test passes, all statements in the loop are executed. This continues until the test condition is false, and Processing continues to interpret the statements following the for loop.

Let's now put this into the context of our color mixer sketch.

Sensors/AccelerometerColorPickerArray/AccelerometerColorPickerArray.pde

```
import ketai.sensors.*;
KetaiSensor sensor;
float accelerometerX, accelerometerY, accelerometerZ;
float r, g, b;
❶ int num = 8;
❷ color[] palette = new color[num];
❸ int paletteIndex = 0;

void setup() {
  sensor = new KetaiSensor(this);
  sensor.start();
  orientation(PORTRAIT);
  textAlign(CENTER, CENTER);
  textSize(36);
}

void draw() {
  // remap sensor values to color range
  r = map(accelerometerX, -10, 10, 0, 255);
  g = map(accelerometerY, -10, 10, 0, 255);
  b = map(accelerometerZ, -10, 10, 0, 255);
  // assign color to background
  background(r, g, b);
  fill(0);
  text("Current Color: \n" +
❹     "(" + round(r) + ", " + round(g) + ", " + round(b) + ")",
    width*0.5, height*0.25);
  // color picker
❺   for (int i=0; i<num; i++) {
❻     fill(palette[i]);
❼     rect(i*width/num, height/2, width/num, height/2);
  }
}
void onAccelerometerEvent(float x, float y, float z) {
  accelerometerX = x;
  accelerometerY = y;
  accelerometerZ = z;
}
```

```
void mousePressed() {
  // updating color value, tapping top half of the screen
  if (mouseY < height/2) {
    palette[paletteIndex] = color(r, g, b);
    if (paletteIndex < num-1) {
      paletteIndex++;
    }

    else {
      paletteIndex = 0;
    }
  }
}
```

Let's take a look at the main additions to the sketch.

❶ Set the quantity of colors to be stored to 8.

❷ Set up the color array to hold the previously defined number of colors.[16]

❸ Set an index variable that indicates the current color we are working with in the palette, represented by the index number in the color array.

❹ Round the floating point value of the color value to an integer so we can read it better.[17]

❺ Iterate through the color array using a for loop.[18]

❻ Step through all the colors in the list using the for loop, and set the fill color for the rectangle to be drawn.

❼ Display each color in the array with a rectangle set to the individual fill color in the list. Rectangles are displayed in sequence on the bottom of the screen; their width and position is defined by the number of colors in the list. The rectangle size is determined by the screen width and then divided by the total number of swatches, num.

❽ Assign the three color values to the palette, cast as color type.

❾ Increment the index number, moving on to the next position in the list.

❿ Reset the index when the palette is full.

Let's run the sketch now.

_____

16. http://processing.org/reference/Array.html
17. http://processing.org/reference/round_.html
18. http://processing.org/reference/for.html

Run the App

On the device, we can tap the screen and the color swatches on the bottom of the screen update to the current color we've mixed by moving the device. If we fill all the swatches, it continues again at the beginning of the buffer. This is because we are setting paletteIndex back to 0 when the array reaches its end.

Building on the code we've previously developed, we've compiled a number of features into a color mixer prototype. This iterative process is typical when building software. We take small and manageable steps, test/run frequently, and make sure we have always saved a stable version of the code we are working with. This is good practice so that we can always have a fallback version if we get stuck or called away.

Now that we've used the accelerometer to mix and save colors, we've also established that device motion is a UI feature that allows us to interact with the app. We can now continue to build on device motion and add a shake to clear all swatches in the palette. How can we detect a shake?

3.10 Erase a Palette with a Shake

Shaking a device can be used as a deliberate gesture for controlling UI elements. On smart phones, it is typically assigned to the Undo command so that a shake can reverse or clear a prior action. Let's take a look at how this gesture can be detected and used by our color mixer.

What is a shake? When we move the device abruptly side to side, forward or backward, up or down, the idea is that our sketch triggers a "shake" event. For the color mixer, we want to use the shake for clearing out all color swatches. The shake needs to be detected no matter how we hold the device and independent of what's up or down. You might already anticipate the issue: we know well that the accelerometer is the ideal sensor for us to detect a shake, but we can't just use its *x*, *y*, or *z* values to trigger the shake when a certain threshold is reached because we can't assume our swaying gesture is aligned any of these axes. So this approach won't work and we need something else.

Any movement in space can be described with a three-dimensional vector that describes both the magnitude and the direction of the movement. You might (or might not) envision such a vector as an arrow in three-dimensional space—a visual representation of the mathematical construct from the field of trigonometry. A vector is ideal to handle all three axes from our accelerometer.

We are using the PVector class again to store three variables in one package,[19] which we are going to use to detect the shake. If we imagine how the vector would react to a shake, it would change erratically in direction and magnitude. In comparison, movement at a constant velocity causes no significant changes to the vector. Hence, if we continuously compare the movement vector of our device to the previous vector, frame by frame, we can detect changes when they reach a certain threshold.

Processing provides a few very useful vector math methods, including angleIn-Between(vector1, vector2), to calculate the angle between two given vectors.[20] So if we compare the current accelerometer vector with the vector of the previous frame, we can now determine their difference in angle, summarized into a single numeric value. Because this value describes angular change, we use a threshold to trigger the shake. For now, let's say this threshold angle should be 45 degrees. Alternatively, we could use the mag() method to detect a sudden change to the vector's magnitude.[21] We'll work with the change to the vector angle in this example. OK, let's put it together.

Sensors/ColorPickerComplete/ColorPickerComplete.pde

```
import ketai.sensors.*;

KetaiSensor sensor;
PVector accelerometer = new PVector();
PVector pAccelerometer = new PVector();
float ch1, ch2, ch3;
int num = 8;
color[] palette = new color[num];
int paletteIndex = 0;
void setup()
{
  sensor = new KetaiSensor(this);
  sensor.start();
  orientation(PORTRAIT);
  textAlign(CENTER, CENTER);
  textSize(36);
}

void draw()
{
  // remap sensor values to color range
  ch1 = map(accelerometer.x, -10, 10, 0, 255);
  ch2 = map(accelerometer.y, -10, 10, 0, 255);
  ch3 = map(accelerometer.z, -10, 10, 0, 255);
```

---

19. http://processing.org/reference/PVector.html
20. http://processing.org/reference/PVector_angleBetween_.html
21. http://processing.org/reference/PVector_mag_.html

```
     // calculating angle between current and previous accelerometer vector in radians
④    float delta = PVector.angleBetween(accelerometer, pAccelerometer);
⑤    if (degrees(delta) > 45) {
       shake();
     }
     // assign color to background
     background(ch1, ch2, ch3);
     fill(0);
     text("Current Color: \n" +
       "(" + round(ch1) + ", " + round(ch2) + ", " + round(ch3) + ")",
     width*0.5, height*0.25);
     // color picker
     for (int i=0; i<num; i++) {
       fill(palette[i]);
       rect(i*width/num, height/2, width/num, height/2);
     }
     // storing a reference vector
⑥   pAccelerometer.set(accelerometer);
   }

   void onAccelerometerEvent(float x, float y, float z)
   {
⑦   accelerometer.x = x;
     accelerometer.y = y;
     accelerometer.z = z;
   }

   void mousePressed()
   {
     // updating color value, tapping top half of the screen
     if (mouseY < height/2) {
       palette[paletteIndex] = color(ch1, ch2, ch3);
       if (paletteIndex < num-1) {
         paletteIndex++;
       }
       else {
         paletteIndex = 0;
       }
     }
   }

   void shake()
   {
     // resetting all swatches to black
     for (int i=0; i<num; i++) {
⑧     palette[i] = color(0);
     }
     paletteIndex = 0;
   }
```

Here's how we proceed to implement the shake detection using PVector.

❶ Create a processing vector of type PVector.

❷ Create a second vector as a reference to compare change.

❸ Use the first .x component of the accelerometer vector. The second component can be accessed via .y, and the third component via .z.

❹ Calculate the delta between the current and the previous vector.

❺ Check the delta in radians against a threshold of 45 degrees.

❻ Set the reference vector to the current one as the last step in draw().

❼ Assign raw accelerometers to the accelerometer PVector.

❽ Set all palette colors in the array to the color black.

Let's run the code first and test the shake detection on the device. It helps us better understand some of the shake detection we talked about.

Run the App

If we play with the app, we can mix and pick colors as we did previously, as shown in Figure 12, *Color mixer app*, on page 59. Small wiggles go undetected. As soon as we move the device quickly and a shake is triggered, all color swatches are erased from the palette.

Let's compare some of the small adjustments we made to the code, on page 63, to the previous code, on page 60, and check what we've added. First of all, we eliminated the three floating point variables we had used globally for incoming accelerometer values. Instead, we are using the PVector variable accelerometer to do the same job. This means we need to update our map() method so it uses the vector components .x, .y, and .z of the accelerometer vector.

We use the same approach for the onAccelerometerEvent() method, where incoming values are now assigned to individual vector components. To assign all three components at once to a vector, we can also use the set() method, as illustrated with pAccelerometer at the very end of draw().

In terms of additions, we've added the pAccelerometer variable so we have something to compare against. We use angleBetween() to calculate the angle difference between the current and previous frame and assign it to delta. If the difference is larger than 45 degrees, we trigger the shake() method, resetting all palette colors to black and paletteIndex to 0.

The degrees() method used here converts radian values provided by the angleBetween() method into degrees. Degrees (ranging 0..360) are far more intuitive to work with than trigonometric measurements in radians,[22] whose range is 0..TWO_PI.

When you take a second look at the app, you can also confirm that shake() is triggered consistently independent of device rotation. The shake detection feature completes our color mixer project.

3.11 Wrapping Up

You've completed a series of sensor-based apps in this chapter, and you've worked with motion, position, and environment sensors using the KetaiSensor class of the Ketai library. You've learned the difference between software- and hardware-based sensors and determined which sensors your device supports. You've used multiple sensors in one app, and you could go on to imagine other uses for motion-based features for your apps, such as speedometers for cars, shake detectors for putting your phone in silent mode, "breathome-ters" for biofeedback and analysis of breathing patterns...and the list goes on. You've also mastered working with color and learned how to mix and map it. You've learned how to work with Processing vectors to store multiple sensor values and to detect shakes.

Now that you know how the accelerometer can be used to determine the movement of an Android device, you are now ready to explore a more complex set of devices, such as GPS. Our next topic explores how to determine the device's geographic location using Android's geolocation features, which are typically used for navigation and location-based services.

---

22. http://processing.org/reference/degrees_.html and http://processing.org/reference/radians_.html.

Part II

Working with Camera and Location Devices

CHAPTER 4

Using Geolocation and Compass

Location-based services have changed the way we navigate, share, and shop. Since the FCC ruling in 1996 requiring all US mobile operators to be able to locate emergency callers, location has become embedded in the images we take, the articles we blog, the commercials we watch, and the places we check into. These services rely on location information using latitude and longitude—and sometimes altitude—to describe a north-south and east-west position on the Earth's surface.

When we search for local information, get directions to public transportation, or find the nearest bar or bargain, the Android enables us to zero in on the information that is relevant to us at a particular geographic location. Because the device is aware of its own geolocation, we can navigate, detect where we are heading, and know how we are holding the device in relation to magnetic north. A built-in Global Positioning System (GPS) receiver, accelerometer, and digital compass allow the Android to have a full picture about its location and orientation, which plays an important role for navigation apps and location-based services.[1]

Android apps make use of the Android's Location Manager to calculate a location estimate for the device.[2] Its purpose is to negotiate the best location source for us and to keep the location up-to-date while we are on the move. Updates typically occur when the device detects that we've changed location or when a more accurate location becomes available. An Android device uses two different location providers to estimate its current geographic coordinates:[3] GPS on the one hand and network on the other, the latter based either on

---

1. http://en.wikipedia.org/wiki/Location-based_service
2. http://developer.android.com/reference/android/location/LocationManager.html
3. http://en.wikipedia.org/wiki/GSM_localization

the calculated distance to multiple cell towers or on the known location of the Wi-Fi network provider to which we are connected.[4]

Compared with the Global System for Mobile Communications (GSM) and Wi-Fi network localization, GPS is the most well-known and accurate method for determining the location of a device. With thirty-one GPS satellites orbiting about 20,000 kilometers above any spot on the Earth's surface twice a day (every 11 hours, 58 minutes), it's just fantastic how the fingertip-sized GPS receivers built into our smart phones are able to determine the device's latitude, longitude, and altitude at a theoretical accuracy of about three meters.

In this chapter, we'll build a series of navigation apps. We'll start by working with the Android's current geolocation. We'll continue by measuring how far we are located from a predefined destination. Finally, we'll build an app that helps us navigate toward another mobile device.

Let's first take a look at how the Android device estimates its location.

4.1 Introducing the Location Manager

Given its ubiquitous use, working with geolocation data should be simple. In the end, it's just the latitude, longitude, and maybe altitude we are looking to incorporate into our apps. Because there are various location techniques, however, we are interacting with a fairly complicated system and continuously negotiating the best and most accurate method to localize the device. The Location Manager that does that work for us is a software class that obtains periodic updates of the device's geographic location from three sensors available on an Android phone or tablet, including a built-in GPS receiver, a cellular radio, and a Wi-Fi radio. Both the KetaiLocation and Android Location classes draw their data from the Location Manager, which in turn gets its information from the onboard devices.

The Global Positioning System, which you'll learn about in detail on page 72, can provide a fairly precise location estimate. However, it is not available indoors or if a building obstructs a direct "view" for GPS satellites overhead. In addition, the GPS receiver also uses a significant amount of battery power.

Another localization method uses cellular tower signals to determine the location of a device by measuring the distances to multiple towers within reach. This triangulation method is less precise because it depends on weather conditions and relies on a fairly high density of cell towers.[5]

---

4. http://developer.android.com/guide/topics/location/obtaining-user-location.html
5. http://en.wikipedia.org/wiki/Triangulation

The third method doesn't require GPS or cell towers at all but the presence of a Wi-Fi network. This technique uses the known locations of nearby Wi-Fi access points to figure out the approximate location of the mobile device. Wi-Fi access points themselves lack GPS receivers and therefore lack knowledge of their own geographic locations, but such information can be associated with their physical MAC (media access control) addresses by third parties.[6] The most notorious case was Google's now abandoned effort to associate GPS coordinates with the MAC address of every wireless access point it encountered as it photographed the streets of US cities and towns with GPS-enabled vehicles for its Google Maps Street View project.[7]

Nowadays, we're the ones who do this work for Google whenever we take an Android device for a stroll. If we have activated Google's location service by selecting Settings → "Location services" on the main menu of our device, then by default we have agreed to "collect anonymous location data" and that "collection may occur even when no apps are running." The MAC addresses of available Wi-Fi networks are sent to Google during this collection process, along with their geographic coordinates. The next user who walks through the same geographic area can then geolocate solely via the Wi-Fi network information, even if GPS is turned off.

It takes a few seconds for the Android to narrow the location estimate and improve its accuracy, so we typically need to start KetaiLocation as soon as the app launches. With fewer than ten lines of code, KetaiLocation can provide us with our geographic coordinates and notify us of changes in our location via the onLocationEvent() callback method. For the location-based apps we'll develop in this chapter, we'll use the following Ketai library and Android classes:

KetaiLocation A class that simplifies working with Android's Location Manager—it instantiates the Location Manager, registers for location updates, and returns geolocation data.[8]

Location[9] A wrapper for Android's Location Manager that provides us with many useful methods for determining our position, bearing, and speed—if we're only interested in our location, we won't need this class, but we will use some of its features for later projects in this chapter.

Now let's take a look at the KetaiLocation methods we'll be using in this chapter.

---

6. http://en.wikipedia.org/wiki/MAC_address
7. http://www.nytimes.com/2012/05/23/technology/google-privacy-inquiries-get-little-cooperation.html
8. http://ketai.googlecode.com/svn/trunk/ketai/src/ketai/sensors/KetaiLocation.java
9. http://developer.android.com/reference/android/location/Location.html

Introducing GPS

The transmitters built into GPS satellites broadcast with about 50 watts, similar to the light bulb in a desk lamp, and yet the GPS module in the phone is able receive a sequence of numbers sent by all the satellites simultaneously, every microsecond. The atomic clock in each satellite takes care of that. The satellite doesn't know anything about us; it's only transmitting. The receiver in our mobile device makes sense of the transmission by deciphering the sequence of numbers the satellite sends. The GPS receiver then determines from the number sequence (which includes the time it was sent by the satellite) how far each individual radio signal has travelled, using the speed of light as its velocity. If a satellite is close by (about 20,000 kilometers), the signal would take about 67 microseconds to travel. The distance is measured by multiplying the time it has taken the radio signal to reach your phone by the speed of light.

We need to "see" at least four satellites to determine latitude, longitude, and altitude (or three if we assume an incorrect altitude of zero). It's clear that a 50-watt signal from 20,000 kilometers away cannot penetrate buildings. We can only "see" satellites if there are no obstructions. If the signal bounces off a building surface, the estimate is less accurate as a consequence. Because the satellite orbits are arranged so that there are at always six within the line of sight, it's fine if one or two are not "seen" or are inaccurate. Accuracy is higher for military receivers getting a signal every tenth of a microsecond, bringing it theoretically down to 0.3 meters (or about 1 ft). High-end receivers used for survey and measurement can increase accuracy even more—to within about 2 mm.

4.2 Working with the KetaiLocation Class

The KetaiLocation class is designed to provide us with the longitude, latitude, and altitude of the device, as well as the accuracy of that estimate. Besides the typical start() and stop() methods, KetaiLocation also provides a method to identify the location provider that has been used to calculate the estimate. Let's take a look.

onLocationEvent() Returns the device location, including latitude, longitude, altitude, and location accuracy

latitude Describes the angular distance of a place north or south of the Earth's equator in decimal degrees—positive lat values describe points north of the equator; negative values describe points south of the equator (for example, Chicago is located at 41.87338 degrees latitude in the northern hemisphere; Wellington, New Zealand, is located at -41.29019 degrees latitude in the southern hemisphere).

longitude Describes the angular distance of a place east or west of the meridian at Greenwich, England, in decimal degrees (for example, Chicago, which is west of the Greenwich meridian, is located at -87.648798 degrees longitude; Yanqi in the Xinjiang Province, China, is located at 87.648798 degrees longitude.)

altitude Returns the height of the device in relation to sea level measured in meters

accuracy Returns the accuracy of the location estimate in meters

getProvider() Returns the identity of the location provider being used to estimate the location: gps or network—it does not distinguish between cellular or Wi-Fi networks.

Let's go ahead and write our first location-based app.

4.3 Determine Your Location

As our first step, let's write some code to retrieve and display your device's location, as shown in Figure 13, *Displaying location data*, on page 73.

Figure 13—Displaying location data. The screen output shows geolocation (latitude, longitude, and altitude), estimation accuracy (in meters), and the current location provider.

This exercise will familiarize us with the kinds of values we'll use to determine our current location on the Earth's surface. Let's display the current latitude, longitude, and altitude on the screen as determined by the Location Manager, as well as display the accuracy of the values and the provider that is used for the calculation. The following example uses KetaiLocation to gather this info.

Geolocation/Geolocation/Geolocation.pde

```
import ketai.sensors.*;
❶ KetaiLocation location;
   double longitude, latitude, altitude;
   float accuracy;

   void setup() {
     orientation(LANDSCAPE);
     textAlign(CENTER, CENTER);
     textSize(36);
❷    location = new KetaiLocation(this);
   }

   void draw() {
     background(78, 93, 75);
❸    if (location.getProvider() == "none")
       text("Location data is unavailable. \n" +
         "Please check your location settings.", width/2, height/2);
     else
❹      text("Latitude: " + latitude + "\n" +
         "Longitude: " + longitude + "\n" +
         "Altitude: " + altitude + "\n" +
         "Accuracy: " + accuracy + "\n" +
         "Provider: " + location.getProvider(), width/2, height/2);
   }

   void onLocationEvent(double _latitude, double _longitude,
❺    double _altitude, float _accuracy) {  //  longitude = _longitude;
     latitude = _latitude;
     altitude = _altitude;
     accuracy = _accuracy;
     println("lat/lon/alt/acc: " + latitude + "/" + longitude + "/"
       + altitude + "/" + accuracy);
   }
```

Let's take a look at how the newly introduced class and methods are used in this example.

❶ Declare the variable location to be of type KetaiLocation. We'll use this variable to store location updates.

❷ Create the KetaiLocation object we've called location.

❸ Check whether we currently have a location provider via the getProvider() method.[10] If none is available, display a warning.

---

10. http://developer.android.com/reference/android/location/LocationManager.html#get-Provider%28java.lang.String%29

❹ Display location values latitude, longitude, altitude, accuracy, and the location provider using getProvider().

❺ Whenever a location update occurs, use the onLocationEvent() method to retrieve location data and print them to the screen.

Ketai defaults the Location Manager to provide location updates every ten seconds or whenever the device moves more than one meter. This preset number is geared toward applications that strive for a certain level of accuracy. You can change this update rate by calling the KetaiLocation method setUpdateRate(int millis, int meters). The app will try to retrieve a gps location first via the Location Manager, and if that fails it will fall back to network localization.

Before we run the app, we need to take a look at the permissions the sketch needs to access this data.

4.4 Setting Sketch Permissions

By default, Android denies permissions to any app that requests access to private data or wants to perform privileged tasks, such as writing files, connecting to the Internet, or placing a phone call.[11] Working with privileged information such as geolocation is no exception.[12]

If we'd like to use the device's location data, we need to ask for permission. Android prompts the user to grant permission if an app requests permission that has not been given to the app before. The Processing IDE (PDE) helps us administer permission requests through the Android Permission Selector, which is available from the menu by selecting Android → Sketch Permissions. There we'll find a list of all the permissions that can be requested by an app on the Android.

As illustrated in Figure 14, *Sketch permissions*, on page 76, the location permissions need to be set for this app. When we run the sketch on the device and Processing compiles the Android package, it generates a so-called AndroidManifest.xml file that corresponds to our permission settings. We don't need to worry much about the details of AndroidManifest.xml;[13] however, we can see below how Processing's Permissions Selector translates our selection into a user-permissions list.

Geolocation/Geolocation/AndroidManifest.xml
```
<?xml version="1.0" encoding="UTF-8"?>
<manifest xmlns:android="http://schemas.android.com/apk/res/android"
```

---

11. http://developer.android.com/guide/topics/security/security.html#permissions
12. http://www.nytimes.com/2012/04/01/us/police-tracking-of-cellphones-raises-privacy-fears.html
13. http://developer.android.com/guide/topics/manifest/manifest-intro.html

```
        android:versionCode="1" android:versionName="1.0" package="">
  <uses-sdk android:minSdkVersion="8"/>
  <application android:debuggable="true"
        android:icon="@drawable/icon" android:label="">
    <activity android:name="">
      <intent-filter>
        <action android:name="android.intent.action.MAIN"/>
        <category android:name="android.intent.category.LAUNCHER"/>
      </intent-filter>
    </activity>
  </application>
<uses-permission android:name="android.permission.ACCESS_COARSE_LOCATION"/>
  <uses-permission android:name="android.permission.ACCESS_FINE_LOCATION"/>
  <uses-permission
        android:name="android.permission.ACCESS_LOCATION_EXTRA_COMMANDS"/>
</manifest>
```

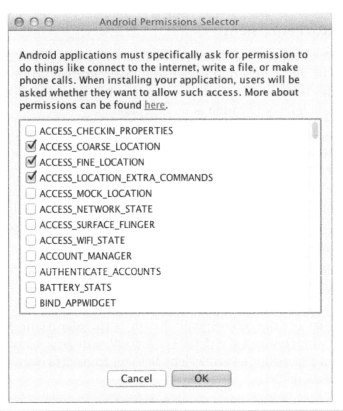

Figure 14—Sketch permissions. The Android Permissions Selector lists all permissions that can be requested by the Android app. The location permissions required by the first geolocation app are checked.

To make sure our location app is able to work with location data, we need to check Google's location service on the device under Settings → "Location services" and agree to the prompt, shown below:

❰ Allow Google's location service to collect anonymous location data.
Some data may be stored on your device.
Collection may occur even when no apps are running.

Otherwise our app will will display the following warning:

❰ Location data is unavailable. Please check your location settings.

We've programmed this warning into our sketch, assuming that getProvider() returns none, which is also the case if Google's location service is switched off.

Run the App

With the location service turned on, let's run the sketch on our device. Type or copy the code on page 74 into your Processing environment and run it on your Android phone or tablet. You should now see your current geographic location. If you are inside a building, chances are that the location estimate is based on the network provider, as shown in Figure 13, *Displaying location data*, on page 73. In this example, the Location Manager calculated the estimate with an accuracy of 46 meters, which means that the estimate can range from 46 meters, worst case, to "right on" in the best case.

Next, let's disconnect the phone and take it for a little walk. Step outside your building. Watch for a location update and a change in provider.

Great—now head back inside. Take a peek again at your latitude and longitude coordinates, and double-check the location accuracy in Google Maps, as described. How far off are you? If you walk a block, you will be able to observe a change to the third digit after the decimal in either the latitude or longitude, depending on where you are headed. The seemingly small change in this digit represents about 200 feet, which brings us to our next application.

4.5 Working with the Location Class

The event method onLocationEvent() we worked with earlier returns the latitude, longitude, altitude, and accuracy of the device location—or alternatively, an Android Location object. If we look at the onLocationEvent() method in more detail, we can use it with the following sets of parameters:

onLocationEvent(double latitude, double longitude, double altitude, float accuracy) Four parameters return the latitude, longitude, altitude, and accuracy of the location estimate.

onLocationEvent(Location location) One parameter returns an Android location object, where Android location methods can be applied directly.[14]

Depending on what location data we need for our location-based app, we can choose our preferred set of parameters from either latitude, longitude, altitude, accuracy, or the Location type. We can also select a few parameters if we don't require them all. The Location object returned in the second iteration of the onLocationEvent() implementation listed here allows us to access any Android Location method.[15]

The Location class is loaded with useful methods for dealing with the data they contain, and it is a great way to package returned location data for use in an app. Ketai gives us complete access to the Location class; let's take a look at some of the Location methods we'll be working with.

getBearing()[16]   Returns the direction of travel in degrees, measured clockwise in relation to magnetic north

getSpeed()[17]   Returns the speed of the device over ground in meters per second (One meter per second is equivalent to 2.236 miles per hour.)

distanceTo()[18]   Returns the distance to a given location in meters (The method takes a Location object as parameter.)

setLatitude()[19]   Sets the latitude of a Location.

setLongitude()[20]   Sets the longitude of a Location.

Now let's work on the next project, where we'll put Location methods to work and write an app that determines the distance between two locations.

4.6   Determine the Distance Between Two Locations

In this project, we'll calculate the distance between our current device location and another fixed location that we predetermine.[21] We provide the fixed location coordinate through latitude and longitude decimal degree values. To get

---

14. http://developer.android.com/reference/android/location/LocationProvider.html

15. http://developer.android.com/reference/android/location/Location.html

16. http://developer.android.com/reference/android/location/Location.html#getBearing%28%29

17. http://developer.android.com/reference/android/location/Location.html#getSpeed%28%29

18. http://developer.android.com/reference/android/location/Location.html#distanceTo%28android.location.Location%29

19. http://developer.android.com/reference/android/location/Location.html#setLatitude%28double%29

20. http://developer.android.com/reference/android/location/Location.html#setLongitude%28double%29

21. http://en.wikipedia.org/wiki/Wikipedia:Obtaining_geographic_coordinates

a better idea about what those values represent, let's first obtain the latitude and longitude values of our current geographic location via Google Maps.[22]

Browse Google Maps on your desktop, and find a location close to a landmark you recognize and know your approximate distance to. Now right-click anywhere close to that landmark on the map. From the menu, choose "Directions to here." You need to be zoomed in all the way so Maps doesn't grab the close-by landmark and display only the landmark's name instead of the latitude and longitude. If you hit a non-landmark spot, Maps will display the lat and lon values of the location inside the site's destination field. My current location at the University of Illinois at Chicago, for instance, looks like this:

❰ 41.87338,-87.648798

Write down your location—we'll use it in the next project. If you use the format shown above, lat,lon (latitude comma longitude), Google Maps will understand and take you to this location. This approach is a quick and easy way to double-check a location when you want to test a location app.

Now let's create a sketch to determine the distance between a fixed point and the device, as shown in Figure 15, *Calculating distance*, on page 79.

Figure 15—Calculating distance. The screen output shows the device's current location, the calculated distance to the predefined uic destination, and the current location provider.

We'll use both the KetaiLocation and Android's Location classes. KetaiLocation provides us with the current device latitude and longitude, Location lets us define a destination location object that we can use to calculate the distance between both points. We then convert the resulting distance from the default measurement unit returned by the Android, meters, into miles by multiplying distance

---

22. http://maps.google.com

by 0.000621371192. Finally, we'll use the round() method to calculate the closest integer and display full meters.

Let's take a look at the code.

Geolocation/LocationDistance/LocationDistance.pde

```
import ketai.sensors.*;
double longitude, latitude, altitude, accuracy;
KetaiLocation location;
Location uic;

void setup() {
  location = new KetaiLocation(this);
  // Example location: the University of Illinois at Chicago Art Building
  uic = new Location("uic");
  uic.setLatitude(41.874698);
  uic.setLongitude(-87.658777);
  orientation(LANDSCAPE);
  textAlign(CENTER, CENTER);
  textSize(36);
}

void draw() {
  background(78, 93, 75);
  if (location.getProvider() == "none") {
    text("Location data is unavailable. \n" +
      "Please check your location settings.", 0, 0, width, height);
  } else {
    float distance = round(location.getLocation().distanceTo(uic));
    text("Location data:\n" +
      "Latitude: " + latitude + "\n" +
      "Longitude: " + longitude + "\n" +
      "Altitude: " + altitude + "\n" +
      "Accuracy: " + accuracy + "\n" +
      "Distance to Destination: "+ distance + " m\n" +
      "Provider: " + location.getProvider(), 20, 0, width, height);
  }
}

void onLocationEvent(Location _location)
{
  //print out the location object
  println("onLocation event: " + _location.toString());
  longitude = _location.getLongitude();
  latitude = _location.getLatitude();
  altitude = _location.getAltitude();
  accuracy = _location.getAccuracy();
}
```

Here's what's new in this sketch compared to our previous project.

❶ Create an Android Location object to store a fixed location against which to compare your current device location. I named mine "uic" (for University of Illinois at Chicago). We'll use the setLatitude() and setLongitude() Android methods to set its values.[23]

❷ Use the distanceTo() method to compare the device's location via location.get-Location() with the fixed uic location. The round() method calculates the closest integer number to the floating point value returned by distanceTo().[24]

❸ Receive a location update using onLocationEvent(), which now returns a Location object instead of individual values for latitude, longitude, altitude, and accuracy. The different parameter options for onLocationEvent() are described next.

❹ Use the Android toString() method to print a concise, human-readable description of the location object to the console.[25]

Let's try this sketch.

Run the App

Run the sketch on the device and take a look at the location info, including the distance to your fixed location. In this example, the app calculates the distance to the uic Location in Chicago's South Loop. So the distance will vary significantly depending on the state or country you are currently located in.

Go back to the geolocation you've previously noted via Google Maps. Use this location now to adjust the uic location object in setup(), and adjust the setLatitude() and setLongitude() parameters to match your location. Feel free to also adjust the uic variable and the Location name called "uic" to reflect your location—it's not crucial for this sketch though.

Rerun the sketch on the device, and notice how the distance has changed. You should be able to confirm the distance to the landmark you've Googled using this app.

Now that you know how to calculate the distance between two points, you're ready to use some additional Android Location methods to determine the bearing and speed of an Android phone or tablet when it's in motion. We'll take a look at that topic in the next section.

---

23. http://developer.android.com/reference/android/location/Location.html#setLatitude%28double%29 and http://developer.android.com/reference/android/location/Location.html#setLongitude(double).

24. processing.org/reference/round_.html

25. http://developer.android.com/reference/android/location/Location.html#toString%28%29

4.7 Determine the Speed and Bearing of a Moving Device

To determine the speed and bearing of a device, three other useful Android Location methods can be applied in ways that are similar to what we did with distanceTo(). Let's create a new sketch and focus for a moment on travel speed and bearing.

We've mastered latitude, longitude, and altitude and calculated the distance between two points. The next step is to determine where we are heading and how fast we are going. Because these parameters are only fun to test while we are on the move, let's create a simple new sketch that focuses on speed and bearing. Then we'll bring it all together in the next section, Section 4.8, *Find Your Way to a Destination*, on page 83.

Let's take a look.

Geolocation/LocationSpeed/LocationSpeed.pde

```
import ketai.sensors.*;
KetaiLocation location;
float speed, bearing;

void setup() {
  orientation(LANDSCAPE);
  textAlign(CENTER, CENTER);
  textSize(36);
  location = new KetaiLocation(this);
}

void draw() {
  background(78, 93, 75);
  text("Travel speed: "+ speed + "\n"
    + "Bearing: "+ bearing, 0, 0, width, height);
}

void onLocationEvent(Location _location) {
  println("onLocation event: " + _location.toString());
❶  speed = _location.getSpeed();
❷  bearing = _location.getBearing();
}
```

Here are the two new Android Location methods we are using for this sketch.

❶ Get the current travel speed using the Android Location method getSpeed(), which returns the speed of the device over ground in meters per second.

❷ Get the current device bearing using the Android Location method getBearing(), which returns the direction of travel in degrees.

Let's run the sketch and get ready to go outside.

Run the App

Run the sketch on the device and take the Android for a little trip—again, the app can only give us reasonable feedback when we're on the move. The onLocationEvent() method returns a Location object containing speed and bearing info, which we extract using the getSpeed() method and the getBearing() method. The numeric feedback we receive on speed and bearing is useful for the navigation apps we write. If we want to calculate bearing toward a fixed destination instead of magnetic north, however, we should use the bearingTo() method instead of getBearing().[26]

We'll look at bearingTo() in the next section, where we'll build on a destination finder app.

4.8 Find Your Way to a Destination

If we are heading toward a destination and want to use our Android device like a compass to guide us there, we need to calculate the angle toward the destination relative to our location. And to make it at all useful, we also need to consider the direction the device is "looking" relative to geographic north. When used together, these two numbers can then successfully point us to where we want to go. We'll build on the code, on page 80, and add a simple triangle to our user interface that points toward our destination no matter which way the device itself is facing.

The core idea here is that we'll calculate the bearing and then use it to rotate a graphic object, a triangle, which will serve as our compass needle. The rotation of our graphic object and text will be performed by moving the triangle to the center of the screen using translate(). Then we'll rotate() the compass needle by the angle resulting from the difference of the device orientation toward north and the calculated bearing toward the destination. We'll calculate the bearing using the bearingTo() method, which returns values ranging -180..180 measured from true north—the shortest path between our device location and the destination.

Then we'll draw the triangle and the text. Because bearing is measured in degrees and so is the compass azimuth, we'll need to convert it into radians() first before performing the rotation. Degree values range 0..360 degrees and radians range 0..TWO_PI.[27] All trigonometric methods in Processing require parameters to be specified in radians.

---

26. http://developer.android.com/reference/android/location/Location.html#bearingTo%28android.location.Location%29

27. http://processing.org/reference/TWO_PI.html

We'll use the PVector class we've already used earlier so we can keep the code concise and don't use more variables than we need. For numeric feedback, we use the mousePressed() method to display the location values and the bearing we'll calculate.

Let's build.

Geolocation/DestinationCompass/DestinationCompass.pde

```
import ketai.sensors.*;
import android.location.Location;

KetaiLocation location;
KetaiSensor sensor;
Location destination;
PVector locationVector = new PVector();
```
❶ `float compass;`

```
void setup() {
  destination = new Location("uic");
  destination.setLatitude(41.824698);
  destination.setLongitude(-87.658777);
  location = new KetaiLocation(this);
  sensor = new KetaiSensor(this);
  sensor.start();
  orientation(PORTRAIT);
  textAlign(CENTER, CENTER);
  textSize(28);
  smooth();
}

void draw() {
  background(78, 93, 75);
```
❷ `  float bearing = location.getLocation().bearingTo(destination);`
```
  float distance = location.getLocation().distanceTo(destination);
  if (mousePressed) {
    if (location.getProvider() == "none")
      text("Location data is unavailable. \n" +
        "Please check your location settings.", 0, 0, width, height);
    else
      text("Location:\n" +
        "Latitude: " + locationVector.x + "\n" +
        "Longitude: " + locationVector.y + "\n" +
        "Compass: "+ round(compass) + " deg.\n" +
        "Destination:\n" +
        "Bearing: " + bearing + "\n" +
        "Distance: "+ distance + " m\n" +
        "Provider: " + location.getProvider(), 20, 0, width, height);
  }
  else {
```
❸ `    translate(width/2, height/2);`

```
④    rotate(radians(bearing) - radians(compass));
     stroke(255);
⑤    triangle(-width/4, 0, width/4, 0, 0, -width/2);
     text((int)distance + " m", 0, 50);
⑥    text(nf(distance*0.000621, 0, 2) + " miles", 0, 100);
  }
}

void onLocationEvent(Location _location) {
  println("onLocation event: " + _location.toString());
⑦  locationVector.x = (float)_location.getLatitude();
  locationVector.y = (float)_location.getLongitude();
}
⑧ void onOrientationEvent(float x, float y, float z, long time, int accuracy) {
  compass = x;
  // Azimuth angle between magnetic north and device y-axis, around z-axis.
  // Range: 0 to 359 degrees
  // 0=North, 90=East, 180=South, 270=West
}
```

Let's take a look at the code additions.

❶ Introduce the compass variable to store the rotation around the z-axis.[28]

❷ Apply the bearingTo() method to determine the direction of the destination pointer.

❸ Move the triangle to the center of the screen using translate().[29] Translate horizontally by half of the width and vertically by half of the height.

❹ Rotate the triangle toward the destination. The angle is calculated by subtracting the device bearing toward the destination from the device orientation toward north stored in compass. Both angles are calculated in degrees and need to be converted into radians() for the trigonometric rotate() method.[30] rotate() adds a rotation matrix to the stack, which makes all objects drawn after the method call appear rotated in relation to the default screen orientation.

❺ Draw the destination pointer using triangle().[31] Draw the triangle pointing up using three points, starting with the left base, followed by the right base, and finally by the top point, which provides direction.

❻ Convert the distance to the destination from meters to miles.

---

28. http://developer.android.com/reference/android/hardware/SensorManager.html#getOrientation%28float[],%20float[]%29

29. http://processing.org/reference/translate_.html

30. http://processing.org/reference/radians_.html and http://processing.org/reference/rotate_.html.

31. http://processing.org/reference/triangle_.html

❼ Use the PVector variable locationVector to store the device latitude and longitude.

❽ Receive bearing values from the onOrientationEvent() method, returning azimuth (z-axis), pitch (x-axis), and roll (y-axis).

We are now using two methods, onLocationEvent() and onOrientationEvent(), that operate in concert with each other. One tracks the location of the device in latitude, longitude, and altitude values, and the other determines where the device is pointing.

Run the App

Let's run the app on the device and find out whether we are being pointed in the right direction. Make sure to set the correct permissions again, as we've discussed in Section 4.4, *Setting Sketch Permissions*, on page 75. For this test, it's quite helpful that we've looked up the destination earlier so we can better gage how well the app is doing.

If you tap the screen, you can observe raw device location values, the compass variable we've calculated, and the calculated bearing angle of the device. The distance toward the destination and the location provider are also displayed on the screen, as shown in Figure 16, *Compass app*, on page 87.

We've now used several pieces of location info in concert and created an app that guides us home (or to work, or wherever destination is pointing to). Before you rely on your app to find your way, please make sure destination is pointing to the right place.

Now that we've seen how to find our way to a fixed destination, the next task in line is to create an app that targets a moving destination. For our next project let's navigate toward another mobile device and address some of the challenges when it comes to sharing locations.

4.9 Find a Significant Other (Device)

At first sight, it seems there is not much of a difference between the compass app we've just made and one that guides us toward another mobile device. If we think about it, though, using a hard-coded latitude and longitude as we did in our previous sketch is quite different from retrieving another device's location data in real time. We'll explore networking techniques in detail in Chapter 6, *Networking Devices with Wi-Fi*, on page 127. The difficulty is that two mobile devices separated by some distance will not share a common IP address that we can use to exchange our location data. So for this task, we

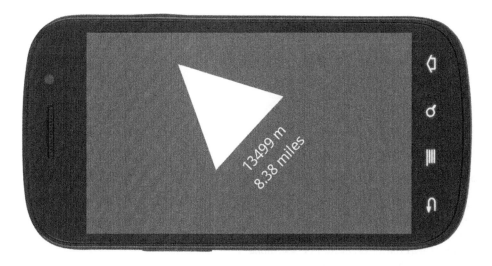

Figure 16—Compass app.   The triangle points to the second device, whose distance is displayed at its base in meters and miles.

need a shared place where each device can write its own latitude and longitude and where each can read the other device's location in return.

For this project, we'll use a web server to facilitate sharing, and we'll equip it with a simple PHP script that takes the location info from each device and writes it to a text file. If one device knows the (made-up) name of the other, it can look it up on that server and we'll have a significant-other location to navigate to. You can certainly download the script code, on page 344, and host it on your own web server as well.

Let's get started. This sketch works with the PHP script on the dedicated web server for this book project. If you point the serverURL variable to another destination, you'll store your locations there.

Geolocation/DeviceLocator/DeviceLocator.pde

```
import ketai.sensors.*;
double longitude, latitude, altitude, accuracy;
❶ KetaiLocation location;
❷ Location otherDevice;
KetaiSensor sensor;
String serverMessage="";
String myName, deviceTracked;
❸ String serverURL = "http://www.ketaiProject.com/rad/location.php";
float compass;
```

```
void setup() {
  otherDevice = new Location("yourNexus");
  sensor = new KetaiSensor(this);
  sensor.start();
  location = new KetaiLocation(this);
  orientation(PORTRAIT);
  textAlign(CENTER, CENTER);
  textSize(28);
  myName = "yourNexus";
  deviceTracked = "myNexus";
}

void draw() {
  background(78, 93, 75);
  float bearing = location.getLocation().bearingTo(otherDevice);
  float distance = location.getLocation().distanceTo(otherDevice);
  if (mousePressed) {
    if (location.getProvider() == "none")
      text("Location data is unavailable. \n" +
        "Please check your location settings.", 0, 0, width, height);
    else
      text("Location data:\n" +
        "Latitude: " + latitude + "\n" +
        "Longitude: " + longitude + "\n" +
        "Altitude: " + altitude + "\n" +
        "Accuracy: " + accuracy + "\n" +
        "Distance to Other Device: "+ nf(distance, 0, 2) + " m\n" +
        "Provider: " + location.getProvider()+ "\n" +
        "Last Server Message: " + serverMessage, 20, 0, width, height );
  }
  else {
    translate(width/2, height/2);
    rotate(radians(bearing) - radians(compass));
    stroke(255);
    triangle(-width/4, 0, width/4, 0, 0, -width/2);
    text((int)distance + " m", 0, 50);
    text(nf(distance*0.000621, 0, 2) + " miles", 0, 100);
  }
}
void onLocationEvent(Location _location)
{
  // Print out the location object
  println("onLocation event: " + _location.toString());
  longitude = _location.getLongitude();
  latitude = _location.getLatitude();
  altitude = _location.getAltitude();
  accuracy = _location.getAccuracy();
  updateMyLocation();
}
void updateMyLocation()
```

```
  {
    if (myName != "")
    {
      String url = serverURL+"?update="+myName+
        "&location="+latitude+","+longitude+","+altitude;
      String result[] = loadStrings(url);
      if (result.length > 0)
        serverMessage = result[0];
    }
  }

  void mousePressed()
  {
    if (deviceTracked != "")
    {
      String url = serverURL + "?get="+deviceTracked;
      String result[] = loadStrings(url);
      for (int i=0; i < result.length; i++)
        println(result[i]);
      serverMessage = result[0];
      // Let's update our target device location
      String[] parameters = split(result[0], ",");
      if (parameters.length == 3)
      {
        otherDevice = new Location(deviceTracked);
        otherDevice.setLatitude(Double.parseDouble(parameters[0]));
        otherDevice.setLongitude(Double.parseDouble(parameters[1]));
        otherDevice.setAltitude(Double.parseDouble(parameters[2]));
      }
    }
    updateMyLocation();
  }
  void onOrientationEvent(float x, float y, float z, long time, int accuracy)
  {
    compass = x;
    // Angle between magnetic north and device y-axis, around z-axis.
    // Range: 0 to 359 degrees
    // 0=North, 90=East, 180=South, 270=West
  }
```

There are a few new statements to look at.

❶ Create a KetaiLocation type variable to be updated when our device detects a location update.

❷ Create an Android Location object to store latitude and longitude data from the target device. The Location object also contains a number of useful methods for calculating bearing and distance.

❸ Set the PHP script URL responsible for writing location files.

❹ Provide a (unique) phrase or identifier to store the location info.

❺ Point to the identifier of the other device.

❻ Use Location object to retrieve location updates as opposed to individual variables.

❼ Assemble the string that calls the PHP script with attached device name and location data.

❽ Trigger the PHP script to write a string containing latitude, longitude, and altitude.

❾ Read the other device's location file via the PHP script.

❿ Check if we get a valid location containing latitude, longitude, and altitude, as well as parsing numbers contained in the string.

⓫ Write our location to the server via the PHP script.

For this device locater app, we maintain a location variable that stores our location. We also keep the otherDevice Location, which this time is responsible for keeping track of a moving target. If we explore the code snippets that we've added to the destination compass app on page 84, the serverURL variable stands out. It's the path to the web server as a shared place for both devices; the server hosts the PHP script that writes and reads the device locations, which is discussed in the next section. We also introduced two string variables that identify each device. Those are necessary and need to be known to both devices—a shared "phrase" or ID that allows us to look up the other device's location. For instance, our location is identified via myName, the other device refers to the location via otherDevice, and vice versa. This is how the exchange is enabled.

Every time we receive a location update from onLocationEvent(), updateMyLocation() is called to send the device name, latitude, longitude, and altitude to the server. When we tap the screen, we check if there is location info for the remote device called deviceTracked. We connect to the same PHP script that takes care of writing the file, this time with a get request instead of an update request. When the server returns a message, we check if we have a complete data package containing all three parameters: latitude, longitude, and altitude. If that's the case, we parse the info and assign it to the otherDevice location object.

This is how the processing sketch triggers location updates to flows from and to the server to exchange location info between two known devices. If you feel comfortable writing your location to the book's project server defined in serverURL, you can give it a shot now and run the sketch on two Android devices (otherwise, please jump to Section A1.3, *Writing to a Text File on a Web Server*, on page 343). For each, you will have to swap the identifier stored in myName and deviceTracked for obvious reasons. Now let's test the app.

Run the App

Tap the screen on each device to trigger a location update on the server and observe. You should get a distance between both devices somewhere between 0 and 15 meters. Because our GPS satellites move constantly and the location provider estimates the device location on a constant basis,[32] location, distance, and compass direction will change even when both devices are static. The closer the devices get to each other, the more erratic the compass changes. To test the compass needle, keep your devices are at least 30 feet apart from each other. You can then take the test to the next level by moving with both devices at increasing distances, which is significantly easier with another set of hands.

You can certainly host the PHP script that is responsible for writing the location data to the web server on your own server. Instructions on how the script (and how PHP) works are located in Section A1.3, *Writing to a Text File on a Web Server*, on page 343.

4.10 Wrapping Up

In this chapter, you've created a series of apps where you've learned how to work with location data provided by Android's Location Manager. You've learned that Android devices use the GPS and network methods to determine their geographic location. Given a choice, they will choose the most accurate method available. You can access this information using either the Ketai Library's KetaiLocation or the Android's Location class.

You are now able to determine the distance between two geolocations and calculate the bearing toward a fixed location. You've also learned how to write a way-finding app that points to another mobile device on the move. You are able to tackle a wide range of apps that build on geolocation. To complete our investigation into Android sensors, we'll look at another very sophisticated device and common sensor next—the Android camera.

---

32. http://developer.android.com/guide/topics/location/obtaining-user-location.html#BestPerformance

CHAPTER 5

Using Android Cameras

Now that we've learned to work with several of the most important Android sensors, let's take a look at another device that's found on every Android phone and tablet—the digital camera. Your device includes at least one and sometimes two cameras: the back-facing camera, which you commonly use to take high-resolution pictures and capture video, and the front-facing camera, designed for video calls and chat at a lower resolution. The digital camera can also be used as a sophisticated light-sensitive sensor to build a variety of interactive applications that go beyond pictures and video clips. We'll explore each of these uses and more in this chapter.

We'll start with the back-facing camera and learn how to display what it "sees" as an image on the Android screen. Next we'll learn how to switch between the front- and back-facing cameras found on most devices and add a feature that allows us to save their images to the Android's *external storage*,[1] which is a default public location on the device that can be read by other apps. Depending on the device settings, this can be located on an SD card, in internal storage, or on media mounted over the network. To make it easier to use these features, we'll add a few UI buttons to initiate each task.

Once we have stored an image from a camera, we may want to make further use of it. Additional APIs allow us to stack stored images to create a composite image that consists of a foreground and a background. We'll put this function-ality to work by building a photo booth app, where we will create a fake backdrop and superimpose a snapshot on it.

But there's more. The Processing language also provides us with APIs that we can use to analyze the content of the images that we capture at the pixel level. We'll use that capability to build a game that can detect the color of a

---

1.   http://developer.android.com/guide/topics/data/data-storage.html#filesExternal

moving object—red or blue—and display the pattern of its motion on the device screen. To make the activity into a game, two players will compete to fill the screen by waving colored objects above it. The first to fill more than 50 percent of the screen wins. In building the game, we'll get to know the Processing PImage class, which allows us to manipulate images and work directly with pixel values.

Finally, we'll end the chapter with a brief look at Android's built-in face recognizer. This lesser-known camera feature is made possible by computer vision algorithms and the increased processing power that's finding its way into Android devices. Android provides a face-finder API that uses pixel-level image analysis to make inferences about what's going in the device's field of view. We'll demonstrate its use with a brief example.

Before we get started on our first project, let's first take a look at some of the camera features and classes we'll be using throughout the chapter to build our camera apps.

5.1 Introducing the Android Camera and APIs

Android phones and tablets are typically equipped with two cameras. Camera hardware varies across phones and tablets, but typically the back-facing camera is used to capture images and HD video at a resolution of 5 megapixels. The lower-resolution, front-facing camera is designed for video calls. The Google Nexus S phone, for example, features a 5-megapixel rear-facing camera (2560 x 1920 pixels) with a built-in LED flash and a 3-megapixel front-facing VGA camera (640 x 480 pixels).

Mobile cameras don't rely on hardware alone. The Android SDK provides a variety of features through its Camera class that make the camera more than just a camera.[2] We can use code to work with camera metering, focus, exposure, white balance, zoom, image capture, and even face detection. Geolocation data can also be added to image metadata so that images can be organized by the location where they were taken. The Google Camera app that ships with Android devices allows users to manipulate those features in its UI. But we're going to learn how apps can use them as well.

To implement the camera features in this chapter, we'll work mainly with a single Ketai library class and a highly versatile Processing type:

---

2.   http://developer.android.com/guide/topics/media/camera.html and http://developer.android.com/reference/android/hardware/Camera.html.

KetaiCamera[3]   This Ketai library class provides simplified access to the cameras on a device by making Android's Camera class available to Processing. When we work with KetaiCamera, we define the width, height, and frame rate for the camera preview we'd like to work with. It provides the necessary methods to define basic camera settings (such as resolution) and camera controls. It also provides access to the camera flash and Android's built-in face recognizer.

PImage[4] This is a Processing datatype for storing images (.gif, .jpg, .png, .tif, and .tga). It provides a number of methods that help us load, save, and filter images, including access to the image pixels[] array that contains information on pixel color values. The methods we are using in this chapter are described further in *Working with the PImage Class*, on page 109.

Now let's take a closer look at the KetaiCamera methods we'll be using.

5.2   Working with the KetaiCamera Class

Besides providing the typical start() and stop() methods that we use to control the sensors on a device, we'll use the following more specialized KetaiCamera methods for the projects in this chapter:

onCameraPreviewEvent() Returns a preview image from the camera when a new frame is available—the image can then be read into the KetaiCamera object using the read() method.

addToMediaLibrary() Makes a picture publicly available in the default preferred media storage on the device—the method requires a picture filename or path to the picture. After using the method, pictures are also available as an album in the Gallery app.

manualSettings() and autoSettings() Toggles between manual and automatic camera settings—manualSettings() locks the current camera exposure, white balance, and focus. autoSettings() lets the device adjust exposure, white balance, and focus automatically.

enableFlash() and disableFlash() Switches the built-in rear-facing camera flash on and off—this can only be used if the rear camera is on.

savePhoto() Saves a picture in the current camera preview size to the preferred media storage

---

3.   http://ketai.googlecode.com/svn/trunk/ketai/reference/ketai/camera/KetaiCamera.html

4.   http://processing.org/reference/PImage.html

setPhotoSize(),   Sets the picture's size to be saved in a different, for example, higher, resolution

setSaveDirectory() Defines where to save the pictures to—by default, pictures are saved to the public media storage on the device. The path can also be set to another destination, including private folders. Requires testing whether the directory path is valid.

KetaiSimpleFace()[5] A Ketai wrapper for the Face class in Android's FaceDetector package,[6] which returns the midpoint location and distance between the eyes recognized by the device cameras

KetaiSimpleFace[] A PVector list containing the position data of detected faces within a camera image—the center point between the left and right eyes and the distance between the eyes are stored in this array.

With this brief summary of KetaiCameramethods for this chapter, let's get started with our first camera app.

5.3 Display a Back-Facing Camera Full-Screen Preview

For this initial camera app shown below, we'll display the view seen by the back-facing Android camera.

Figure 17—**Camera preview app.** The illustration shows a camera preview image at a resolution of 640 x 480 pixels, displayed on the touch screen of a Google Nexus S, whose resolution is 800 x 480 pixels.

---

5.   http://ketai.googlecode.com/svn/trunk/ketai/reference/ketai/cv/facedetector/KetaiSimpleFace.html
6.   http://developer.android.com/reference/android/media/FaceDetector.Face.html

We'll use the KetaiCamera class to connect to and start the camera. The KetaiCamera class streamlines this process significantly for us. For example, creating a simple camera preview app using KetaiCamera takes about ten lines of code, compared with about three hundred documented on the Android developer site.[7] KetaiCamera helps us set up and control the camera, and it also decodes the YUV color format provided by the Android camera into the RGB format used in Processing.[8]

KetaiCamera works similarly to other Ketai classes that we've explored in *Using Motion and Position Sensors*. First we create a KetaiCamera object and start() the camera. Then we update the screen as soon as we receive a new image from the camera via onCameraPreviewEvent(). And finally, we use Processing's own image() method to display the camera preview.

The code for a basic camera sketch looks like this:

Camera/CameraGettingStarted/CameraGettingStarted.pde

```
import ketai.camera.*;
KetaiCamera cam;

void setup() {
  orientation(LANDSCAPE);
① cam = new KetaiCamera(this, 640, 480, 30);
② imageMode(CENTER);
}

void draw() {
  if (cam.isStarted())
③   image(cam, width/2, height/2);
}

④ void onCameraPreviewEvent() {
⑤ cam.read();
}

void mousePressed() {
  if (cam.isStarted())
  {
⑥   cam.stop();
  }
  else
    cam.start();
}
```

---

7. http://developer.android.com/resources/samples/ApiDemos/src/com/example/android/apis/graphics/CameraPreview.html

8. http://en.wikipedia.org/wiki/YUV#Conversion_to.2Ffrom_RGB

Let's take a closer look at the steps you take and the methods you use to set up a camera sketch.

❶ Create an instance of the KetaiCamera class to generate a new camera object with a preview width and height of 640 x 480 pixels and an update rate of 30 frames per second.

❷ Call imageMode() to tell Android to center its camera images on its screen. All images are now drawn from their center point instead of from the default upper left corner.

❸ Display the camera preview using the image() method.[9] It requires an image source as well as the x and y coordinates of the image to display. Optionally, the image can be rescaled using an additional parameter for the image width and height.

❹ Use the onCameraPreviewEvent() callback method for notification that a new preview image is available. This is the best time to read the new image.

❺ Read the camera preview using the read() camera method.

❻ Toggle the camera preview on and off when you tap the screen.

Let's try the sketch on the Android phone or tablet.

Run the App

Before we run the sketch, we need to give the app permission to use the camera. Here's how: On the Processing menu bar, select Android → Sketch Permissions. In the Android Permissions Selector that appears, select Camera. As we've done already in *Using Geolocation and Compass* earlier in Section 4.4, *Setting Sketch Permissions*, on page 75, the Android must allow the app to use the camera through a certificate, or it must prompt the user to approve the request to use the camera. If the app has permission to use the camera, the device will remember and not prompt the user anymore. For this app, we only need to check the permission for CAMERA.

Now run the sketch on the device. The rear-facing camera preview starts up as illustrated in Figure 17, *Camera preview app*, on page 96, in a resolution of 640px width and 480px height, known as NTSC.[10] Android cameras are set to auto mode, so they adjust focus and exposure automatically. On a Google Nexus S developer phone with a native screen resolution of 800 x 480 pixels, the preview image covers the screen height but not all of the screen

---

9. http://processing.org/reference/image_.html
10. http://en.wikipedia.org/wiki/Display_resolution

width. You can certainly scale and stretch the preview image, which also changes the image aspect ratio and distorts the image. For instance, if you set the width and height parameters in the image() method to screenWidth and screenHeight as in the code below, the camera preview will always stretch full screen independent of the screen's size and resolution.

```
image(cam, width/2, height/2, width, height);
```

Go ahead and try the fullscreen mode on your device. For a preview image in a camera app, it doesn't seem like a good idea to stretch the image, though. When we write apps that scale seamlessly across devices, we typically lock and maintain aspect ratios for images and UIs.

As we can see in the code on page 97, the steps we take to get the camera started are like the steps we took working with other sensors (*Using Motion and Position Sensors*). First we instantiate a KetaiCamera object using a defined width, height, and frameRate. Then we start the camera. And finally, we read new images from the camera using onCameraPreviewEvent() and display them. The frame rate in this sketch is set to 30 frames per second, which is the typical playback speed for digital video, giving the appearance of seamless movement. Depending on your device and image conversion performance, the image preview might not be able to keep up with the designated thirty previews per second. In that case, the sketch will try to approach the set frame rate as best it can.

With less than ten lines of code added to the typical processing sketch methods, we've completed our first camera app. The onPause() and exit() methods are responsible for releasing the camera properly when we pause or exit the app. The methods make sure that other apps can use the cameras and that we don't keep them locked down for our app alone. You can only have one active connection to the cameras at a time.

Now let's add some code so we can toggle between the front and rear cameras as well as between some controls to give the user greater control over the app.

5.4 Toggle Between the Front- and Back-Facing Cameras

Most mobile Android devices come with both the front-facing and back-facing cameras. We need a UI button that toggles between the front and back camera. Let's also activate the flash that's built into most back-facing cameras and add an additional pair of button controls to start and stop the camera. The final app then looks like this:

Figure 18—Camera preview app with UI. The UI added to the Preview app allows users to start and stop the cameras, toggle between the front- and back-facing cameras, and activate the built-in flash.

Android lists all built-in device cameras and allows us to pick the one we'd like to work with. For instance, the Nexus S uses the camera index ID 0 for the rear camera and 1 for the front camera. Future Android devices might add more cameras to the device, potentially for 3D applications, so having an enumerated list enables Android OS to incorporate them.

Let's build on the previous sketch on page 97, adding some camera controls that will remain pretty much the same throughout the chapter. Because this sketch is longer than the previous one, we'll separate it into two tabs: a main tab containing the essential setup() and draw() methods, which we'll name CameraFrontBack (identical to the sketch folder), and a second tab, which we'll call CameraControls and will contain the methods we need to read() the camera preview, the methods to start() and stop() the camera, and the UI buttons we'll use to control the camera via the touch screen.

Separating the code this way helps us reduce complexity within the main tab and focus on relevant code for the projects we are working on. We'll store each tab in its own Processing source file, or .pde file, inside the sketch folder. You can always check what's inside your sketch folder using the menu Sketch → Show Sketch Folder, or the shortcut K.

Let's first take a look at the main tab:

Camera/CameraFrontBack/CameraFrontBack.pde
```
import ketai.camera.*;

KetaiCamera cam;

void setup() {
  orientation(LANDSCAPE);
  cam = new KetaiCamera(this, 640, 480, 30);
❶  println(cam.list());
  // 0: back camera; 1: front camera
❷  cam.setCameraID(0);
  imageMode(CENTER);
  stroke(255);
❸  textSize(24);
}

void draw() {
  image(cam, width/2, height/2);
❹  drawUI();
}
```

In the main CameraFrontBack tab, we've added new features.

❶ Print all available device cameras to the Processing console using the list() method included in KetaiCamera.

❷ Set the back-facing camera ID to 0 via setCameraID().

❸ Increase the textSize() for the UI buttons to 24 pixels.

❹ Call the custom drawUI() method, taking care of drawing UI buttons.

The draw() method contains only a call to the image() method, used for displaying the camera preview, and a call to the custom drawUI() method we defined for our UI elements.

Now let's explore the second sketch tab called CameraControls, where we'll keep all the code that controls the camera.

Camera/CameraFrontBack/CameraControls.pde
```
❶ void drawUI() {
  fill(0, 128);
  rect(0, 0, width/4, 40);
  rect(width/4, 0, width/4, 40);
  rect(2*(width/4), 0, width/4, 40);
  rect(3*(width/4), 0, width/4, 40);
  fill(255);
❷  if (cam.isStarted())
    text("stop", 10, 30);
  else
    text("start", 10, 30);
```

```
      text("camera", (width/4)+10, 30);
      text("flash", 2*(width/4)+ 10, 30);
    }
❸ void mousePressed() {
❹   if (mouseY <= 40) {
❺     if (mouseX > 0 && mouseX < width/4) {
        if (cam.isStarted())
        {
          cam.stop();
        }
        else
        {
          if (!cam.start())
            println("Failed to start camera.");
        }
      }
❻     else if (mouseX > width/4 && mouseX < 2*(width/4))
      {
        int cameraID = 0;
        if (cam.getCameraID() == 0)
          cameraID = 1;
        else
          cameraID = 0;
        cam.stop();
        cam.setCameraID(cameraID);
        cam.start();
      }
❼     else if (mouseX >2*(width/4) && mouseX < 3*(width/4))
      {
❽       if (cam.isFlashEnabled())
          cam.disableFlash();
        else
          cam.enableFlash();
      }
    }
  }
  void onCameraPreviewEvent() {
    cam.read();
  }
  void exit() {
    cam.stop();
  }
```

In this CameraControls tab, we use the following UI elements and camera methods
to complete these steps.

 Display the UI on the screen using a custom void function called drawUI().
Void functions execute but don't return a value. The UI in this example
consists of buttons that use half-transparent rectangles for their back-
grounds and text labels for their names.

❷ Check if the camera is running using the boolean method isStarted(). If the method returns TRUE, we display "stop"; otherwise show "start."

❸ Capture touch screen input for camera controls using mousePressed().

❹ Check if the user is interacting with the UI at the top of the screen using the mouseY constant. If we receive user input within the top 40 pixels of the screen, we continue checking the horizontal position via mouseX.

❺ Check if the user presses the leftmost button to start and stop the camera. Each button occupies one-fourth of the screen width, so we check if the horizontal tap position is within the range (0..width)/4. We take the same approach for the other buttons.

❻ Check if the user taps the second button, which is responsible for toggling between the rear and the front cameras. We acquire the current camera ID using getCameraID() and toggle using setCameraID().

❼ Check if the user taps the third button, which is responsible for toggling the camera flash on and off.

❽ Check the camera's flash status using the isFlashEnabled() method and toggle the flash by calling enableFlash() or disableFlash(), depending on the returned boolean value.

Let's go ahead and test the app now.

Run the App

Load or enter the two tabs of the sketch, run it on your device, and take a look at the Processing console. You should see a list of all the built-in cameras on your device with their respective IDs, as shown below.

```
[camera id [0] facing:backfacing, camera id [1] facing:frontfacing]
```

When the app launches, the rear-facing camera becomes the default camera, but it remains paused until we start it up. Press the Start button now. The camera preview should appear on the screen at the defined resolution of 640 x 480 pixels. Toggle the camera from the front to the back using the Camera button. Start and stop the flash. The camera flash belongs to the back-facing camera and works only when the rear camera is active.

Now that we know how to preview and control the camera, it's time to put it to work—let's snap some pictures. In our next project, we'll learn how to store images on the device.

5.5 Snap and Save Pictures

To snap pictures and save them to the external storage of our device, we'll first need to add a savePhoto() method to the previous sketch on page 99. The method takes care of capturing the image and writing it to the device's external storage in a folder that bears the app's name. When the photo is written to this public directory on the SD card, we receive a callback from onSavePhotoEvent() notifying us that the writing process is complete. This callback method is also useful if we'd like to notify the device's media library to make the photos available to other applications, which we accomplish with a call to the addToMediaLibrary() method. Once we've added photos to the media library, we can browse them in the Gallery—Android's preinstalled app for organizing pictures and video clips shown in Figure 19, *Android gallery*. The larger the captured photo size, the longer it takes to transfer the image buffer and store it on the disk.

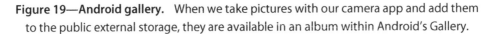

Figure 19—Android gallery. When we take pictures with our camera app and add them to the public external storage, they are available in an album within Android's Gallery.

To refine the camera app UI, let's also add a Save button that allows us to save the image by tapping the touch screen. Some status info on the current camera settings also seems useful.

For the Save feature, we need to modify the draw() method in the main CameraSavingImages tab and make some adjustments to CameraControls. The code snippets below show only the modifications to the previous code in CameraFrontBack.pde on page 101 and CameraControls.pde on page 101. You can also download the complete .pde source files from the book's website, and if you're reading the ebook, just click the green rectangle before the code listings.

Let's take a look.

Camera/CameraSavingImages/CameraSavingImages.pde

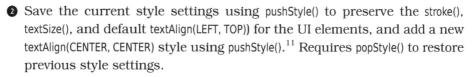

```
void draw() {
  background(128);
  if (!cam.isStarted())
  {
    pushStyle();
    textAlign(CENTER, CENTER);
    String info = "CameraInfo:\n";
    info += "current camera: "+ cam.getCameraID()+"\n";
    info += "image dimensions: "+ cam.width +
      "x"+cam.height+"\n";
    info += "photo dimensions: "+ cam.getPhotoWidth() +
      "x"+cam.getPhotoHeight()+"\n";
    info += "flash state: "+ cam.isFlashEnabled()+"\n";
    text(info, width/2, height/2);
    popStyle();
  }
  else
  {
    image(cam, width/2, height/2);
  }
  drawUI();
}
```

Now let's take a look at the new code we've added to draw() and what it does.

❶ Check the status through the boolean method isStarted(). Returns TRUE if the camera is on and FALSE if it's off.

❷ Save the current style settings using pushStyle() to preserve the stroke(), textSize(), and default textAlign(LEFT, TOP)) for the UI elements, and add a new textAlign(CENTER, CENTER) style using pushStyle().[11] Requires popStyle() to restore previous style settings.

❸ Get the index number of the currently chosen camera using getCameraID().

❹ Get the preview image width (in pixels) of the current camera using getImageWidth().

❺ Get the preview image height (in pixels) of the current camera using getImageHeight().

❻ Get the image width (pixels) of a photo taken by the current camera using getPhotoWidth(). The photo size is separate from the camera preview size.

---

11. http://processing.org/reference/pushStyle_.html

Get the image height (pixels) of a photo taken by the current camera using getPhotoHeight().

 Inquire about the status of the flash using the boolean method isFlashEnabled(). (The flash belongs to the rear camera and can only be used if the back-facing camera is on.)

 Restore the previous style settings using popStyle().

Changes to draw() mostly concern the text output that gives us some feedback on the camera settings. Next let's examine the modifications to the camera controls.

Camera/CameraSavingImages/CameraControls.pde

```
void drawUI() {
  fill(0, 128);
  rect(0, 0, width/4, 40);
  rect(width/4, 0, width/4, 40);
  rect(2*(width/4), 0, width/4, 40);
  rect(3*(width/4), 0, width/4-1, 40);

  fill(255);
  if (cam.isStarted())
    text("stop", 10, 30);
  else
    text("start", 10, 30);

  text("camera", (width/4)+10, 30);
  text("flash", 2*(width/4)+ 10, 30);
  text("save", 3*(width/4)+10, 30);
}

void mousePressed() {
  if (mouseY <= 40) {
    if (mouseX > 0 && mouseX < width/4)
    {
      if (cam.isStarted())
      {
        cam.stop();
      }
      else
      {
        if (!cam.start())
          println("Failed to start camera.");
      }
    }
    else if (mouseX > width/4 && mouseX < 2*(width/4))
    {
      int cameraID = 0;
      if (cam.getCameraID() == 0)
```

```
        cameraID = 1;
      else
        cameraID = 0;
      cam.stop();
      cam.setCameraID(cameraID);
      cam.start();
    }
    else if (mouseX >2*(width/4) && mouseX < 3*(width/4))
    {
      if (cam.isFlashEnabled())
        cam.disableFlash();
      else
        cam.enableFlash();
    }
❷   else if (mouseX > 3*(width/4) && mouseX < width)
    {
❸     if (cam.isStarted()) cam.savePhoto();
    }
  }
}

❹ void onSavePhotoEvent(String filename)
  {
❺   cam.addToMediaLibrary(filename);
  }
```

Take a look at how the code adds the following features.

❶ Add a UI button text() label for saving images.

❷ Add a condition to check if the user taps the added Save button.

❸ Save the photo to the device's external storage using savePhoto(). The method can also take a parameter for a custom file name.

❹ Receive notification from the onSavePhotoEvent() callback method when a picture is saved to external storage.

❺ Add the picture to the device's public preferred media directory on the external storage using addToMediaLibrary().

With the addition of the savePhoto() and addToMediaLibrary(), the app is now ready to store pictures in external storage, which makes the images public and available for other apps, such as the Android Gallery app. Once again, let's make sure we've set the permissions we need to write to external storage (see also *Setting Sketch Permissions*). In the Android Permissions Selector, check the boxes next to Write_External_Storage in addition to Camera. This time, we need both to run this sketch successfully.

Run the App

Run the modified sketch on an Android device and tap Save to save the picture.

Now let's take a look at the Gallery and see if the photos we took show up there properly. Press the Home button on the device and launch the Gallery app, which comes preinstalled with the Android OS. The images you took will appear in the CameraSavingImages album that bears the same name as the app. Making the images available publicly allows us to share them with other apps. The use of addToMediaLibrary() is certainly optional. If we use only the savePhoto() method, the images are still saved to the publicly available external storage, but they won't be visible to other apps using the external storage.

We've now learned how to save images to the external storage of an Android device. In the next project, we'll create a photo booth app that allows us to blend and superimpose the images we capture. To accomplish this task, we'll blend multiple image sources into one. Let's take a look.

5.6 Superimpose and Combine Images

In this project, we'll superimpose a snapshot on a background image, as we might do with a friend in a photo booth at a carnival. Using the Android's front-facing camera, we'll create an app that works like a photo booth, with the small twist that we use scenery loaded from a still resource image as the image's background instead of the physical backdrop we might find in an actual photo booth. We want to be able to use the app anywhere, independent of our current surroundings or lighting level. This is why we need to separate the foreground image from its background. Using color pixel calculations, we can erase a background image and superimpose a snapshot onto a scene loaded from an image in a resource file, as shown in Figure 20, *Photo booth app*, on page 109.

The photo booth app combines images from two sources: the preview image acquired by the front-facing camera and an image loaded from a file that will be included with the app.

First, take a snapshot with the device sitting still on the table. When you take the snapshot, be sure to stay out of the camera's field of view. We'll use this snapshot as a reference image, which we'll subtract from the camera's preview image. If we've held the camera steady, this subtraction will leave behind an empty, black image by eliminating all the pixels that have not changed. For example, if the live camera and the snapshot images are identical, any pixel[n] that we choose at random will have the identical value in both images. Let's

Figure 20—Photo booth app. The image shows the photo booth app using the rover background image we've chosen.

say, for the sake of argument, that the color of a particular pixel is color(135, 23, 245). If we subtract the color value of the pixel in one image from the corresponding pixel in the other—color(135, 23, 245) minus color(135, 23, 245)—the result is color(0, 0, 0).

When this subtraction of color values is performed for all of the pixels in an image pair, the resulting effect is that when someone enters the frame of the camera again, the image of the subject will appear to be "floating" in front of the background image of our choosing: the landscape of Mars or a view of Lake Michigan from the grounds of the World's Fair. The result: a portable photo booth that we can use to transport ourselves into any scene we'd like.

Let's start by looking in more detail at some of the PImage features we'll use.

Working with the PImage Class

PImage is a datatype for storing images that supports .tif, .tga, .gif, .png, and .jpg image formats. Listed below are some of the PImage methods that we'll be using for this project:[12]

loadImage()[13]   Loads the pixel data for the image into its pixels[] array

---

12. http://processing.org/reference/PImage.html
13. http://processing.org/reference/loadImage_.html

loadPixels()[14]	Loads the pixel data for the image into its pixels[] array—this function must always be called before reading from or writing to pixels[].
updatePixels()[15]	Updates the image with the data in the pixels[] array—the method is used in conjunction with loadPixels().
pixels[][16]	Array containing the color of every pixel in the image
get()[17]	Reads the color of any pixel or grabs a rectangle of pixels
set()[18]	Writes a color to any pixel or writes an image into another
copy()[19]	Copies the entire image
resize()[20]	Resizes an image to a new width and height—to resize proportionally, use 0 as the value for the width or height parameter.
save()[21]	Saves the image to a TIFF, TARGA, GIF, PNG, or JPEG file

Now let's write some code.

For this project, we'll create a new sketch, again with two tabs, and copy the code into each tab individually. We'll call the main tab CameraPhotoBooth and the second tab CameraControls, which we'll reuse from the previous sketch code, on page 106.

Let's first take a look at the main tab.

Camera/CameraPhotoBooth/CameraPhotoBooth.pde

```
import ketai.camera.*;

KetaiCamera cam;
PImage bg, snapshot, mux;

void setup() {
  orientation(LANDSCAPE);
  cam = new KetaiCamera(this, 720, 480, 30);
❶ cam.setCameraID(1);
  imageMode(CENTER);
  stroke(255);
  textSize(24);
  snapshot = createImage(720, 480, RGB);
❷ bg = loadImage("rover.jpg");
```

---

14. http://processing.org/reference/loadPixels_.html
15. http://processing.org/reference/PImage_updatePixels_.html
16. http://processing.org/reference/pixels.html
17. http://processing.org/reference/PImage_get_.html
18. http://processing.org/reference/set_.html
19. http://processing.org/reference/copy_.html
20. http://processing.org/reference/PImage_resize_.html
21. http://processing.org/reference/save_.html

```
    bg.loadPixels();
    mux = new PImage(640, 480);
  }

  void draw() {
    background(0);
    if (cam.isStarted()) {
      cam.loadPixels();
      snapshot.loadPixels();
      mux.loadPixels();
      for (int i= 0; i < cam.pixels.length; i++)
      {
        color currColor = cam.pixels[i];
        float currR = abs(red(cam.pixels[i]) - red(snapshot.pixels[i]) );
        float currG = abs(green(cam.pixels[i]) - green(snapshot.pixels[i]));
        float currB = abs(blue(cam.pixels[i]) - blue(snapshot.pixels[i]));
        float total = currR+currG+currB;
        if (total < 128)
          mux.pixels[i] = bg.pixels[i];
        else
          mux.pixels[i] = cam.pixels[i];
      }
      mux.updatePixels();
      image(mux, width/2, (height-40)/2);
    }
    drawUI();
  }
```

Here are the steps we need to take in the main tab.

 Set the camera ID to the front-facing camera using setCameraID(), which has the index number 1.

❷ Load the rover.jpg resource image from the data folder using loadImage(), which will serve as a replacement for the background.

❸ Load the camera pixel array using loadPixels().

❹ Load the snapshot picture pixel array using loadPixels().

❺ Load the mux pixel array using loadPixels() to store the composite photo booth image.

❻ Parse the pixels array and get the current screen pixel color at array position i.

❼ Calculate the red() difference between the individual camera and snapshot pixel values. Convert the result into an absolute, always positive number using abs().[22] Make the same calculation for the green and blue pixel values.

❽ Add the differences for the red, green, and blue values to calculate the total difference in color, which will be used as a threshold for the composite image. Values can range from 0 (no change) to 255 (maximum change) for total. Use 128 (50 percent change) as the threshold to choose between the live camera or the background image.

❾ Set the composite mux image to the background image bg pixel for small changes in the camera image.

❿ Set mux to the camera pixel if the camera preview changed a lot.

⓫ Update the composite mux pixels used to display the calculated result using updatePixels().

⓬ Display the composite image mux on the screen using the image() method, which now contains the combined pixel data from the live camera and the background image.

In this app, we've changed the draw() method from our previous camera app on page 105. We focus on combining images in draw(), where we use a background image—a snapshot taken from the camera preview—and the current camera preview taken in the same location. We calculate the difference between this current camera preview and the snapshot to determine which pixels changed. Then we display the stored background image in all the pixels that did not change and display the live camera pixels where the preview changed. When a person enters the scene after taking the snapshot, those changed pixels function as a mask for the background image. This is why it's also important that the camera doesn't move during the process.

Adding Media Assets to a Sketch

The setup() method contains a reference to a "canned" image called rover.jpg. The image is stored in the sketch's data folder. We load the image into the PImage variable bg at the beginning, when the app starts up. Here we use PImage only to store the image. We'll discuss this datatype further in the next project, *Working with the PImage Class*, on page 109, where we rely on some useful PImage methods to work with pixel values.

---

22. http://processing.org/reference/abs_.html

The sole purpose of the sketch's data folder is to host all necessary media assets and resource files for our sketch, such as images, movie clips, sounds, or data files. If a resource file is outside the sketch's data, we must provide an absolute path within the file system to the file. If the file is online, we need to provide a URL. There are three ways to add a media asset to a sketch:

- Drag and drop the file you want to add onto the sketch window from your file system (for example, from the desktop) onto the Processing sketch window you want to add the file to. Processing will create the data folder for you in that sketch and place the resource file inside it.

- Choose Sketch → Add File... from the Processing menu, and browse to the asset.

- Browse to the sketch folder (choose Sketch → Show Sketch Folder).

Now let's check what's changed in CameraControls.

Camera/CameraPhotoBooth/CameraControls.pde

```
❶      cam.manualSettings();
❷      snapshot.resize(cam.width, cam.height);
       snapshot.copy(cam, 0, 0, cam.width, cam.height,
❸        0, 0, snapshot.width, snapshot.height);
       mux.resize(cam.width, cam.height);
     }
   }
 }

void onCameraPreviewEvent()
{
  cam.read();
}

void exit()
{
  cam.stop();
}
```

In the Camera Controls tab, we reuse the UI button for the flash from the previous code on page 106 and label it "Snapshot." Because the flash belongs to the back-facing camera and it's much easier for us to use the front camera here, we don't need the flash any more for this project. The Snapshot button is now responsible for copying the pixels from cam to snapshot, as shown below.

❶ Set the camera to manual mode using the manualSettings() method, locking the current camera exposure, white balance, and focus.

❷ Match the resolution between the camera and the snapshot image using resize().

❸ Use the copy() method to take the snapshot. Use the snapshot image to subtract from the camera preview, erasing the background, and extracting the image foreground of the camera.

Run the App

Now lean the Android upright against something solid so it can remain static, and run the app. When it starts up, press the Snapshot button, capturing a snapshot image from the camera preview. Make sure you are out of the camera field of view; if not, you can always retake the snapshot. Now, reenter the scene and see yourself superimposed on the landscape of Mars. Adjust the threshold value of 128 to be higher or lower to best match your lighting situation. You can use any resource image stored in CameraPhotoBooth/data, so go ahead and swap it with another image resource of your choice.

This project showed us how to take control of two different image sources and combine them in creative ways. The project can easily be expanded to create a chroma-key TV studio, in which we could superimpose live video of a TV show host onto a studio green screen. But we'll leave that as an exercise for the reader.[23]

Now that we've gained some experience in manipulating images, let's use our ability to process information about pixels to create a two-person drawing game.

5.7 Detect and Trace the Motion of Colored Objects

In the drawing game that we'll build in this section, two players will compete to see who can fill the screen of an Android device with the color of a red or blue object first. Without touching the device screen, each player scribbles in the air above it with a blue or red object in an attempt to fill as much space as possible with the object's color. When more than 50 percent of the screen is filled, the player that filled in the most pixels wins. We'll use the front-facing camera as the interactive interface for this game. It's job is to detect the presence of the colors blue or red within its field of vision and capture them each time it records a frame. The game code will increase the score of each player who succeeds in leaving a mark on the screen.

---

23. http://en.wikipedia.org/wiki/Chroma_key

The camera remains static during the game. As Figure 21, *Magic marker drawing game*, illustrates, only the primary colors red and blue leave traces and count toward the score. If the red player succeeds in covering more pixel real estate than the blue, red wins. If blue dominates the screen, blue wins. If you are using an Android tablet you can step a little bit further away from the device than is the case for a phone, where the players are more likely to get in each other's way, making the game more competitive and intimate.

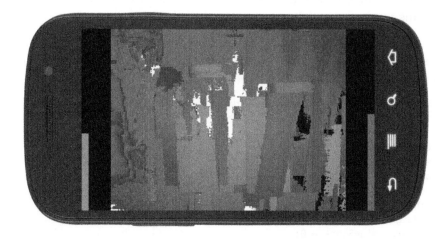

Figure 21—Magic marker drawing game. Red- and blue-colored objects leave color marks, gradually covering the camera preview. The color that dominates wins the game.

The magic marker drawing game uses color tracking as its main feature. As we implement this game, we put Processing's image class, called *PImage*, to use. The main purpose of this datatype is to store images, but it also contains a number of very useful methods that help us manipulate digital images. In the context of this game, we'll use PImage methods again to retrieve pixel color values and to set pixel values based on some conditions we implement in our sketch.

Manipulating Pixel Color Values

To create this magic marker drawing game, we need to extract individual pixel colors and decide whether a pixel matches the particular colors (blue and red) we are looking for. A color value is only considered blue if it is within a range of "blueish" colors we consider blue enough to pass the test, and the same is true for red. Once we detect a dominant color between the two, we need to call a winner.

For an RGB color to be considered blue, the blue() value of the pixel color needs to be relatively high,[24] while at the same time the red() and green() values must be relatively low.[25] Only then does the color appear blue. We are using the Processing color methods red(), green(), and blue() to extract *R*, *G*, and *B* values from each camera pixel. Then we determine whether we have a blue pixel, for instance, using a condition that checks if blue() is high (let's say 200) and at the same time red() and green() are low (let's say 30) on a scale of 0..255. To make these relative thresholds adjustable, let's introduce variables called high and low for this purpose.

Let's take a look. The sketch again contains CameraControls, which we don't discuss here because we already know the method to start() and stop() the camera.

Camera/CameraMagicMarker/CameraMagicMarker.pde

```
import ketai.camera.*;

KetaiCamera cam;
PImage container;
int low = 30;
int high = 100;
int camWidth = 320;
int camHeight = 240;
int redScore, blueScore = 0;
int win = 0;

void setup() {
  orientation(LANDSCAPE);
  imageMode(CENTER);
  cam = new KetaiCamera(this, camWidth, camHeight, 30);
  // 0: back camera; 1: front camera
  cam.setCameraID(1);
❶ container = createImage(camWidth, camHeight, RGB);
}

void draw() {
  if (win == 0) background(0);
  if (cam.isStarted()) {
    cam.loadPixels();
❷   float propWidth = height/camHeight*camWidth;
❸   if (win == 0) image(cam, width/2, height/2, propWidth, height);
    for (int y = 0; y < cam.height; y++) {
      for (int x = 0; x < cam.width; x++) {
❹       color pixelColor = cam.get(x, y);
        if (red(pixelColor) > high &&
```

---

24. http://processing.org/reference/blue_.html

25. http://processing.org/reference/red_.html and http://processing.org/reference/green_.html.

```
⑤      green(pixelColor) < low && blue(pixelColor) < low) {
⑥      if (brightness(container.get(x, y)) == 0) {
          container.set(x, y, pixelColor);
          redScore++;
        }
      }
      if (blue(pixelColor) > high &&
⑦        red(pixelColor) < low && green(pixelColor) < low) {
        if (brightness(container.get(x, y)) == 0) {
          container.set(x, y, pixelColor);
          blueScore++;
        }
      }
    }
  }
⑧  image(container, width/2, height/2, propWidth, height);
   fill(255, 0, 0);
   rect(0, height, 20, map(redScore, 0, camWidth*camHeight, 0, -height));
   fill(0, 0, 255);
   rect(width-20, height, 20, map(blueScore, 0, camWidth*camHeight, 0, -height));
⑨  if (redScore+blueScore >= camWidth*camHeight * 0.50) {
     win++;
⑩   if (redScore > blueScore) {
        fill(255, 0, 0, win);
      }
      else {
        fill(0, 0, 255, win);
      }
      rect(0, 0, width, height);
    }
    if (win >= 50) {
⑪     container.loadPixels();
      for (int i = 0; i < container.pixels.length; i++) {
⑫       container.pixels[i] = color(0, 0, 0, 0);
        redScore = blueScore = win = 0;
      }
    }
  }
 }
}

void mousePressed()
{
  if(cam.isStarted())
    cam.stop();
  else
    cam.start();
}
```

There are a couple of new methods for us to look at.

❶ Create an empty PImage called container using the createImage() method to hold red and blue color pixels that have been detected in the camera preview image. The empty RGB image container matches the size of the camera preview image.

❷ Calculate the fullscreen camera preview image width propWidth proportional to the camera preview aspect ratio. We get the ratio by dividing the screen height by the camera preview height camHeight and multiplying that with the camWidth.

❸ Draw the camera preview image in fullscreen size using image() if no player has won the game yet (win equals 0). Match the image height with the screen height and scale the image width proportionately.

❹ Get the color value at the image pixel location x and y using the PImage method get(). Store the value in the color variable pixelColor.

❺ Check for reddish pixel values within the camera preview using the red(), green(), and blue() PImage methods to extract individual color values from the color datatype. Consider only pixel values with a red content greater than the high threshold and low green and blue values. Use the globals high and low for the upper and lower limits of this condition.

❻ Check if the pixel is already taken by a color using brightness(). If the container is empty and not set yet, it has a brightness value of 0.

❼ Check for blueish pixel value in the camera image. It requires a color with a high blue content, while the red and green values are low.

❽ Draw the container using the image() method. This PImage contains all the red and blue pixels we grabbed from the camera's preview image.

❾ Check for the winner when at least 50 percent of the image is covered, comparing the combined redScore and blueScore values against 0.50 of all camera preview pixels.

❿ Fade to the winning color by changing the fill() opacity of a colored rectangle covering the screen. To achieve a continuous fade, use the win variable for the alpha parameter so that the following rectangle is drawn with decreasing opacity (0: fully opaque, 255 fully transparent).

⓫ Load the pixel data from the container PImage into the pixels[] array. The function must be called before writing to (or reading from) pixels[].

⓬ Empty all pixels[] in the container image pixel array. Set all pixels to the color(0, 0, 0, 0), which is a fully transparent black color. The Processing rule is that you must call loadPixels() before you read from or write to pixels[], even if some renderers seem not to require this call.

Now let's test the game using some blueish and reddish objects and test how well the camera picks up their colors. Any kind of object will do as long as its color is a vibrant red or blue—the more intense its hue and brightness the better.

Run the App

Grab a friend and a few blueish and reddish objects, and get ready to scribble madly mid-air and fight for pixel real estate on the Android device. Run the sketch on the device. When the game starts up, the camera preview will appear centered on the screen, stretched to fullscreen size. Reddish and blueish colors are instantly picked up and drawn on top of the preview image. This immediate feedback lets us play with different objects and quickly get an idea about which objects have the greatest color impact as we try to cover the screen.

Try it. The status bar on either side of the screen grows as colors are picked up, showing us how much pixel real estate each player owns. Individual scores are compared with the total number of available pixels. If 50 percent of all pixels are grabbed by the red player, for instance, the red progress bar covers half of the screen height. Once more than 50 percent of all available pixels are taken, the sketch calls a winner and fades to the winning color. It resets the game to start over.

This game has taken us deep into the world of pixels using all the prior color knowledge we've acquired in Section 3.7, *Build a Motion-Based Color Mixer and Palette*, on page 52. The PImage datatype is a convenient way to work with images, which are in principle "just" lists of colors containing red, green, blue, and alpha (transparency) values that we can use for our own purposes, such as our magic marker drawing game.

If your device is up to the challenge, feel free to double the camera resolution via camWidth and camHeight for better image quality, but consequently you'll have to lower the frame rate. We've discussed that pixel-level calculations are computationally expensive and hence require a speedy Android device to run smoothly. In Chapter 11, *Introducing 3D Graphics with OpenGL*, on page 265, we will learn a few tricks that help us put the graphics processing unit (GPU) to use, keeping the central processing unit (CPU) free for other tasks.

Since you've successfully interpreted images on a pixel level, let's take it a step further now and explore how pixel-level image algorithms are used for advanced image processing and computer vision purposes, specifically for Android's face detection API.

5.8 Detect Faces

One of the most amazing hidden features of the camera software is the ability to detect faces. We've seen that access to the pixel values enables us to interpret images and make inferences about their content. Such computer vision algorithms have many applications in robotics, automation, and security. The Android face detection API is designed to trigger an event when one or more faces are detected.[26]

Facial recognition is an Android feature that uses complex computer vision algorithms to detect typical facial features, which are recognized by their shape and the position of a person's eyes within the camera's field of view. The Android device uses so-called Haar cascades for face recognition.[27] The Camera app, for instance, uses this feature to set the focus of the camera on the eyes of a person when taking a photo. Face Unlock added to Ice Cream Sandwich uses face recognition to unlock your device. When you first activate Face Unlock (Security Settings → Face Unlock), you provide an image of your face and a PIN. The device remembers the shape and other characteristics of your face and uses those metrics to compare it to a live camera image when you unlock the screen. Depending on the amount of available light, this feature works uncannily well.

Face detection is part of Android's Camera class, exposed by KetaiCamera so we can use it within the camera apps we develop using the Ketai library. The information we receive about facial features includes the location of the leftEye(), the rightEye(), the mouth(), an individual id for each detected face, and a score of the confidence level for the detection of the face, with a range of 1..100. The ability to detect facial features might come as a surprise when we use and expose it. However, modern digital cameras use similar algorithms to auto-set the focus and auto-correct red-eye effects.

The face finder sketch we are writing is based on Android's Face detection API. For the sketch, we use the camera's preview image and send it to the face detector. It returns an array of faces to us that contains the metrics of individual facial features that we can use to draw a rectangle where a face is detected. We test the app on the device, point the Android camera to a web page that displays the results of a Google Image search on the term "faces."

---

26. http://developer.android.com/reference/android/hardware/Camera.Face.html
27. http://en.wikipedia.org/wiki/Haar-like_features

This way we can see how well the detection works when it has to respond to a variety of faces of different scales and quality. Let's take a look.

Figure 22—Face Finder app. The image illustrates Android's Face Detector API, which here displays fourteen faces found by an image search engine. The API does not recognize faces shown in side profiles or cropped portraits.

Camera/CameraFaceFinder/CameraFaceFinder.pde
```
import ketai.camera.*;
import ketai.cv.facedetector.*;
KetaiCamera cam;
❶ KetaiSimpleFace[] faces;
boolean findFaces = false;
void setup() {
  orientation(LANDSCAPE);
  cam = new KetaiCamera(this, 640, 480, 24);
❷ rectMode(CENTER);
  stroke(0, 255, 0);
❸ noFill();
}

void draw() {
  background(0);
  if (cam != null) {
    image(cam, 0, 0, 640, 480);
❹   if (findFaces)
    {
❺     faces = KetaiFaceDetector.findFaces(cam, 20);
❻     for (int i=0; i < faces.length; i++)
      {
```

```
⑦         rect(faces[i].location.x, faces[i].location.y,
⑧           faces[i].distance*2, faces[i].distance*2);
        }
⑨       text("Faces found: " + faces.length, 680, height/2);
      }
    }
  }

void mousePressed () {
  if(!cam.isStarted())
    cam.start();
  if (findFaces)
    findFaces = false;
  else
    findFaces = true;
}
void onCameraPreviewEvent() {
  cam.read();
}
```

Let's take a look at the face finder methods used by the sketch.

❶ Create an array to store the list of faces found. It contains the *x* and *y* location of each face and the distance between the eyes.

❷ Center the rectangles that mark found faces around their center points.

❸ Turn off the fill color for the green rectangle markers so we can see though them.

❹ Check the boolean that lets us turn the face finder on and off.

❺ Call the findFaces() method in the FaceFinder class with the two parameters for the image input (cam) and the maximum number of faces to be found (20).

❻ Parse the results returned from the faces array. The array length varies by the number of faces that are found, so we check how often to iterate through the array by testing faces.length with the for loop.

❼ Draw a rectangle based on the returned face location PVector. Use .x() and .y() to access the horizontal and vertical positions of the face location.

❽ Use twice the distance between the eyes to draw an approximate rectangle marking the detected face.

❾ Display the total number of faces found; a maximum of 20 can be found based on our findFaces() settings.

Let's give it a try.

Run the App

Run the app and set the device aside. Now go to your PC and do a Google image search on the word "face." Pick up the Android and aim the camera at the PC display. Google displays a grid of images showing a wide range of faces at different exposures and angles. Now tap the screen to start face detection. You immediately experience a performance hit caused by the face detection algorithm. We've instructed findFaces() to extract up to twenty faces from the camera's preview.

Once the camera has a clear and steady shot of the faces on the PC display, you can see on the Android screen where green rectangles are overlaid onto the detected areas, as illustrated in Figure 22, *Face Finder app*, on page 121. Overall it does a pretty good job. When portraits are cropped or only show faces in profile, the algorithm doesn't consider it a face. To confirm this rule, do a Google search on the term "face profile" and see what happens. Finally, see what "cartoon face" will produce. Using these different search strings helps us to understand what the algorithm requires to interpret a certain pixel area as a face.

Let's move on to the detection of moving human subjects. Use setCameraID(1) just before cam.start(); in setup() to switch to the front-facing camera. Run the app again, and test the face detection algorithm on your own face. You should observe that the face detection feature begins to work as soon as you face the camera. You need to keep enough distance so your face doesn't appear cropped in the camera preview. If you turn your head to present a profile to the camera, your face won't be detected anymore because the camera can't "see" both of your eyes.

We haven't looked deeply into what the Face API does exactly to extract faces from a list of pixel values, and in this case, we don't need to. Android provides us with a list of faces, the midpoint between the eyes, and their distance. Edge detection and decision trees are the concern of the API. Clearly, this feature, which ships with all current Android devices, can be used for different purposes.

Unlike social media sites that employ face detection algorithms to match a person or identity with an image, the Android is not concerned about that. If we start up face detection in our app, the Android OS will trigger a face event when it "sees" a face, whether or not it knows the identity of that person. For some of your apps, it can be relevant to know whether a person is looking at the screen or not.

Now that you are aware of this feature, it's up to you to use it or look at your device from now on with the level of scrutiny this feature calls for. The face detection project is a good example of why we need to ask for permission to use the CAMERA (Section 4.4, *Setting Sketch Permissions*, on page 75). If we do, the user is prompted to grant or deny this request. Once granted, the app will retain the permission certificate to use the camera, and we won't be prompted any more. In Section 12.7, *Control a Virtual Camera with Your Gaze*, on page 310, we'll use the face detection feature to rotate a 3D object based on how we look at the screen. It is one example of where the face detection API serves as an interactive user interface within a 3D environment.

5.9 Wrapping Up

In this chapter, you've learned how to work with the cameras on Android devices. You've also learned how to display the images the cameras acquire, how to save them, and how to work with them when they're stored in memory. You're now able to manipulate images down to the pixel level, use the camera to detect colored objects in motion, and display their paths on the screen. You've also learned how to activate and use Android's face recognition feature.

This completes our investigation of a diverse range of sensors found on Android devices. You know how to interact with their touch screens and how to determine their orientation and bearing as well as their motion and geographic location. You can also take pictures with the Android and start to make sense of what the device is seeing. You're ready now to move on to the second part of this book, where we'll learn how to network the Android with PCs and other mobile devices and work with large amounts of data.

Part III

Using Peer-to-Peer Networking

CHAPTER 6

Networking Devices with Wi-Fi

Social media, location-based services, and multiplayer games are just a few examples of mobile applications that rely on frequent updates delivered over the Internet via cellular, cable, or satellite networks. In this chapter we'll focus on wireless local area networks. The ability to exchange data between Android devices and PCs within a local area network allows us to write mobile apps that can connect multiple users without a mobile carrier data plan.

By the end of this chapter, you'll be able to send data between computers and Androids within a Wi-Fi network. You will be able to write real-time interactive apps running on multiple devices that take advantage of the high bandwidth offered by a Wi-Fi network. This can be useful, for example, to inventory stock in a retail store, monitor a patient, view data from a home security or automation system, or participate in a multiplayer game.

There are four ways to connect devices without sending data over the Internet: Wi-Fi, Wi-Fi Direct, Bluetooth, and near field communication (NFC), listed in decreasing order in terms of connection distance, power consumption, and speed. We will cover peer-to-peer networking, to which Wi-Fi Direct and Bluetooth belong, in the next chapter, called Chapter 7, *Peer-to-Peer Networking Using Bluetooth and Wi-Fi Direct*, on page 151, and cover NFC in the following one, called Chapter 8, *Using Near Field Communication (NFC)*, on page 189.

We'll start this chapter by creating an app that exchanges data between an Android device and a desktop PC using the Open Sound Control (OSC) networking format. Then we'll build a collaborative drawing app, where we use the Wi-Fi network to share a drawing canvas between two Android devices. As the final project for this chapter, we'll create a game for two players using the accelerometer on each device to control the tilt of a shared playing surface with two balls in play. Local Wi-Fi networks offer us the bandwidth and response time we need for multiplayer games while freeing us from worry about data plans and transmission quotas.

6.1 Working with Wi-Fi on Android Devices

Wi-Fi is so ubiquitous in cities that you can find a Wi-Fi network virtually anywhere you go. It's true that most Wi-Fi networks that you encounter while you're on the move are protected and won't allow devices to connect. But most domestic and workplace destinations that we visit regularly—including many coffee shops, libraries, and airports—do offer the opportunity to subscribe or connect for free. Once connected, the phones, tablets, and laptop devices that you carry will remember a particular Wi-Fi network, making it easy to connect again when you return.

Most Wi-Fi networks are set up to connect to the Internet. But you can also use a wireless network access point to set up a local Wi-Fi network for the sole purpose of connecting multiple Wi-Fi–enabled devices between one another. Many Android devices will even let you create a Wi-Fi hotspot using the device itself (Settings → Wireless & networks → More... → Tethering & portable hotspots).

When a Wi-Fi–enabled device connects to a Wi-Fi access point, it is assigned an IP address. An IP address is a unique identifier (see also *Peer-to-Peer Networking (P2P)*, on page 130) that is used to identify the device within a network. It functions as a numeric label that other devices can use to access it. Likewise, to connect our Android to other devices within the network, we need to know their IP addresses as well.

When two devices wish to communicate, they must also share a common port number in addition to knowing each other's IP addresses.[1] A port is an agreed-upon number that establishes communication in conjunction with the IP address. Certain ports are reserved for services such as FTP (Port 21) or HTTP (Port 80) and should not be used.[2] Port numbers greater than 1000 usually work just fine.

If we're on the move and a known Wi-Fi network is not available to us, the Android device requests an IP address from the cell phone carrier's 3G or 4G network. Although it is possible to network two devices over the carrier network, we cannot sustain a peer-to-peer network as the device connects from cell tower to cell tower. Connecting two (or more) devices inside a Wi-Fi network is significantly different from connecting them outside the network, which is

---

1. http://en.wikipedia.org/wiki/Port_%28computer_networking%29
2. http://en.wikipedia.org/wiki/Well-known_ports#Well-known_ports

described in further detail in *Peer-to-Peer Networking (P2P)*, on page 130. In this chapter, we'll stay focused on Wi-Fi communications.

Let's first take a look at the networking classes we'll be using in this chapter.

6.2 Working with Networking Classes

For the networking projects in this chapter, we'll be working with the following classes provided by Processing, Ketai, and oscP5 libraries.

netP5[3] Processing's core library for reading and writing data across networks—it allows the creation of clients and servers over a specified port. A server connects to a list of clients for reading and writing data. A client is able to read and write data to that server.

KetaiNet[4] A library containing Android-device–specific methods to complement netP5, including a method to look up the Android device IP address, as it frequently changes when we are on the move

oscP5[5] An Open Sound Control library for Processing developed by Andreas Schlegel—OSC is a networking protocol for communication among computers, sound synthesizers, and other multimedia devices in many application areas.

When two or more devices communicate in a distributed application through a network, they typically interact through a server-client computing model. The server provides resources, and a client requests them. There can be more than one client connected to the central server, and multiple clients can communicate with each other through that server. The server is responsible for establishing a connection between itself and one or more clients.

To transfer data between devices, we need a protocol to package, send, and receive different data types in an efficient manner. We'll use the Open Sound Control protocol for that. Let's take a look at what OSC has to offer.

6.3 Using the Open Sound Control Networking Format

Open Sound Control (OSC) is a very flexible and popular data protocol. We can wrap pretty much any data format into an OSC message and send it over the network. We can also package several messages at a time in an OSC bundle before sending it on its way, giving us a lot of control over how much we send at once. So instead of taking our data, chopping it into individual

---

3. http://processing.org/reference/libraries/net/
4. http://ketai.googlecode.com/svn/trunk/ketai/reference/ketai/net/KetaiNet.html
5. http://www.sojamo.de/libraries/oscP5/

Peer-to-Peer Networking (P2P)

When it comes to peer-to-peer networking, the difference between an IP address provided by a local area network and an IP address from a 4G or 3G cellular network is that we can send data to a local area network address directly. If we go outside the local area network, our IP address undergoes network address translation, or NAT.[a] There is no way to connect directly to a device without knowing exactly how to translate that new number in reverse. "Getting through" the NAT router is often referred to as "traversing" the NAT, or NAT-busting. Applications such as Skype (voice-over-IP), Hamachi, or LogMeIn (remote desktop) are very good at traversing. IP addresses are managed centrally, and the techniques that companies use to traverse the NAT are proprietary. It is clear, though, that NAT-busting is a messy and complicated process, one that exploits NAT router and firewall loopholes. Why the trouble? Because of the great benefit that we can have very efficient peer-to-peer connections that provide high update rates at no cost while "off-the-grid".[b]

If we are on the move, we will lose the IP address provided by a cellular network and will get a new one as we hop from tower to tower. A cellular provider might also have services in place that try to maintain a particular address using an address translation that takes place on the carrier's side. Being handed over from cell tower to cell tower or from Wi-Fi network to Wi-Fi network, however, is the nature of being on the move.

In short, for true P2P, we need a public IP address.[c] In the prevalent IPv4 addressing system, there are virtually too few IP addresses available for the number of devices on the planet. An enormous global transition to the new IPv6 addressing system is currently underway, rendering NAT practically obsolete. You can keep an eye on the IPv6 deployment as it unfolds.[d] For now we need to sit tight; all our toasters, clothes, and children have a dedicated IP address.

---

a. http://en.wikipedia.org/wiki/Network_address_translation
b. http://en.wikipedia.org/wiki/Peer-to-peer
c. http://en.wikipedia.org/wiki/Public_IP_address#Public_address
d. http://en.wikipedia.org/wiki/IPv6_deployment

pieces (bytes), and precariously assembling it on the other side of a network, we can send different data types within one OSC message. OSC allows us to change how many pieces of data we put into a message as well, and we don't have to change the way we package it. This is particularly useful when we build networking apps, where we start with a simple message and add data to the payload as we get more complex.

For the projects in this chapter, we'll use the netP5 library to read and write data over the network. It's already available because it's part of Processing's core library. The KetaiNet class is also available because it's part of the Ketai library, which we've already installed.

Let's go download the oscP5 library now. You can find it at http://www.sojamo.de/libraries/oscP5/ and also among other Processing libraries in the Data/Protocols section of the Processing libraries website.[6]

Let's follow the same process we already used to install the Ketai library, which is the same process we use for installing any Processing library:

1. Choose "Add Library...," which you can find under Sketch → "Import Library..."

2. On the bottom of the window that opens, enter oscP5.

3. Select the Ketai library that appears in the list, and press the Install button on the right.

4. The download starts immediately, and a bar shows the download's progress. When the library is installed, the button on the right changes to Remove.

Alternatively, you can use your web browser to download the library and install it manually within Processing's library folder:

1. Download and unzip the oscP5 library folder.

2. Check what's inside the folder. Locate the library subfolder that contains the actual Processing library .jar. The OSC library and most other Processing libraries also include reference, examples, and src subfolders.

3. Move the complete oscP5 directory, including library, reference, examples, and src into the Processing sketchbook, located at Documents/Processing/libraries.

The sketchbook libraries folder now looks something like Figure 23, *Placing oscP5 in the Libraries folder*, on page 132. Now let's put OSC to work and network the Android with the PC.

6.4 Network an Android with a Desktop PC

For our first project, we're going to network a desktop PC and an Android device and then use the Wi-Fi network to exchange data between them. Wireless local area networks provide us with a high-bandwidth connection, which allows us to write applications that let us interact with peers within the network in real time. We can send fairly large data payloads without noticeable delays, making it a good choice for a diverse range of multiuser applications.

---

6. http://processing.org/reference/libraries/#data_protocols

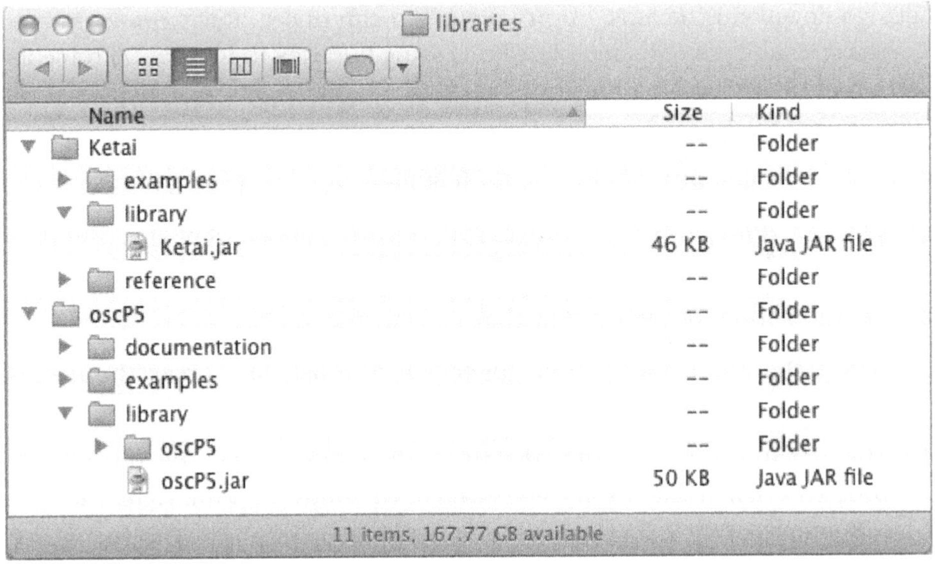

Figure 23—Placing oscP5 in the Libraries folder. After installing the library, it is located inside the libraries folder of the sketchbook, where all of the other Processing libraries are stored.

We'll need to import the networking classes described in Section 6.2, *Working with Networking Classes*, on page 129, so we can exchange data over a common port, as illustrated in Figure 24, *Connecting an Android to a PC*, on page 133. We'll use oscP5, which builds on and requires Processing's core netP5 library for the exchange of data. We also use the KetaiNet class to look up the Android's IP address, and we'll use the familiar KetaiSensor class to receive accelerometer data.

Before we get started, let's make sure that both devices are connected to the same Wi-Fi network. Go ahead and check the Android (Settings → Wireless & networks) to activate Wi-Fi. If your device is not already connected to a Wi-Fi network, choose the same network that the PC is connected to. Once connected, write down the IP address that has been assigned to the Android device. On your desktop machine, check your network settings so your desktop computer is connected to the same network as the Android. You can use an Ethernet connection for the PC as well, as long as you are connected to the same network as the Android.

We'll build this application in two steps: first we'll write a sketch for the Android device and then for the PC.

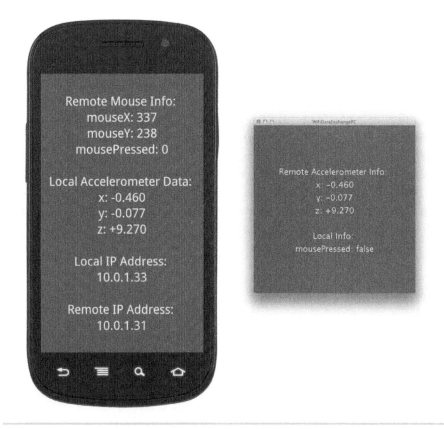

Figure 24—Connecting an Android to a PC. The screen output shows remote mouse data from the PC on the Android screen (left) and accelerometer data from the Android in the PC display window (right). The local Android IP address and the remote PC address are shown at the bottom of the Android screen.

Program the Android Device

Before you can connect your Android to the PC, you first need to figure out the IP address of the desktop computer on the local network. Make sure your PC is on the same network as the Android via Wi-Fi.

- On a Mac, you'll find your IP address under System Preferences → Network.
- On a PC, try Control Panel → Network and Internet.
- On Linux you can go to Administration → Network Tools.

My IP address looks like this:

❰ 10.0.1.31

Your address most likely looks different. Write yours down, as it is not very intuitive, and this needs to be correct to connect successfully.

We'll first code the Android sketch using the oscP5 NetAddress class to specify the destination of the OSC message.[7] We'll create a NetAddress object called remoteLocation and consisting of the IP address of the remote device—in this case our PC—and the port number (12000) that both devices will use to communicate. For this first sketch, the OSC message we send will consist of three floating point numbers, the values of the x-, y-, and z-axes of the accelerometer that we'll add() to the message before it's sent. In turn, we'll receive three integer values from the desktop PC, consisting of the x and y positions of the mouse cursor, followed by a 0 or a 1, depending on whether the mouse button is pressed (1) or not (0).

Now let's take a look at the code for the sketch:

Networking/WiFiDataExchangeAndroid/WiFiDataExchangeAndroid.pde

```
❶ import netP5.*;
   import oscP5.*;
   import ketai.net.*;
   import ketai.sensors.*;

   OscP5 oscP5;
   KetaiSensor sensor;

   NetAddress remoteLocation;
   float myAccelerometerX, myAccelerometerY, myAccelerometerZ;
   int x, y, p;
   String myIPAddress;
❷ String remoteAddress = "10.0.0.103";  // Customize!

   void setup() {
     sensor = new KetaiSensor(this);
     orientation(PORTRAIT);
     textAlign(CENTER, CENTER);
     textSize(36);
     initNetworkConnection();
     sensor.start();
   }

   void draw() {
     background(78, 93, 75);

❸   text("Remote Mouse Info: \n" +
       "mouseX: " + x + "\n" +
       "mouseY: " + y + "\n" +
```

---

7. http://www.sojamo.de/libraries/oscP5/reference/netP5/NetAddress.html

```
        "mousePressed: " + p + "\n\n" +
        "Local Accelerometer Data: \n" +
        "x: " + nfp(myAccelerometerX, 1, 3) + "\n" +
        "y: " + nfp(myAccelerometerY, 1, 3) + "\n" +
        "z: " + nfp(myAccelerometerZ, 1, 3) + "\n\n" +
        "Local IP Address: \n" + myIPAddress + "\n\n" +
        "Remote IP Address: \n" + remoteAddress , width/2, height/2);
    }

    void oscEvent(OscMessage theOscMessage) {
④   if (theOscMessage.checkTypetag("iii"))
      {
⑤      x =  theOscMessage.get(0).intValue();
        y =  theOscMessage.get(1).intValue();
        p =  theOscMessage.get(2).intValue();
      }
    }

    void onAccelerometerEvent(float x, float y, float z)
    {
      myAccelerometerX = x;
      myAccelerometerY = y;
      myAccelerometerZ = z;

⑥    OscMessage myMessage = new OscMessage("accelerometerData");
⑦    myMessage.add(myAccelerometerX);
      myMessage.add(myAccelerometerY);
      myMessage.add(myAccelerometerZ);
⑧    oscP5.send(myMessage, remoteLocation);
    }

    void initNetworkConnection()
    {
⑨    oscP5 = new OscP5(this, 12000);
⑩    remoteLocation = new NetAddress(remoteAddress, 12000);
⑪    myIPAddress = KetaiNet.getIP();
    }
```

Here are the steps outlining what the sketch does.

❶ Import the Processing networking library netP5 to read and write data over the network. Import the oscP5 library to send data using the OSC protocol. Import the Ketai networking class to look up the device's current IP address and the KetaiSensor class to work with the accelerometer sensor.

❷ Set the remote IP address variable (remoteAddress) of the desktop to exchange data with.

❸ Print all info about remote mouse position, state, and local accelerometer data. Android accelerometer data myAccelerometerX, myAccelerometerY, and myAccelerometerZ are presented with one digit to the left and two digits to the right of the decimal point and a plus or minus number prefix using the nfp() method. At the bottom of the screen we display our local Android IP address followed by the remote desktop IP.

❹ Check the incoming OSC message for the iii value pattern, which specifies a packet of three integer values.

❺ Once a complete OSC data package containing three integers is detected, we set x, y, and p to the incoming values.

❻ Create a new outgoing OSC message (myMessage) with an assigned label (accelerometerData) that contains our local accelerometer info. OSC labels can also be used on the receiving side to distinguish between multiple incoming messages.

❼ Add the x, y, and z accelerometer axes to the outgoing OSC message.

❽ Send the OSC message myMessage to remoteLocation.

❾ Instantiate an OSC object from the oscP5 library and start an OSC connection on port 12000.[8]

❿ Set the destination IP and port number to the remoteAddress at port number 12000; the port number must be identical to successfully exchange data.

⓫ Look up the Android IP address assigned by the Wi-Fi network using getIP().

The oscP5 library relies on some methods from the core network library in Processing called netP5,[9] which is why we import both at the beginning of the code. To work with the accelerometer, we use the KetaiSensor class again, which is why we import the ketai.sensors package. To look up the Android's assigned Wi-Fi IP address we use the getIP() method contained in the ketai.net package.[10] Make sure to customize remoteAddress to match your desktop IP address.

Now we are ready on the Android side to start talking.

Run the App

Before we run the sketch, let's check the INTERNET permissions in the Android Permissions Selector that we'll need in order to send data through the network. We've already worked with different types of permissions for geolocation and

---

8. sojamo.de/oscP5
9. http://processing.org/reference/libraries/net/index.html
10. http://ketai.googlecode.com/svn/trunk/ketai/reference/index.html

Open Sound Control

Developed by Matt Wright and Adrian Freed at the Center for New Music and Audio Technologies in 1997,[a] the OSC protocol has been used for a variety of applications, including sensor-based electronic music instruments, mapping data to sound, multiuser controls, and web interfaces, to name a few. OSC messages consist of numeric and symbolic arguments, 32-bit integers and floats, time tags, strings, and blobs.[b] Messages can be bundled so they can act simultaneously when received. Pattern matching allows OSC to specify multiple targets for a single message as well. This allows us to broadcast values to a number of devices. Optional time tags (64 bit) allow highly accurate synchronization of timed events. Many data exchange applications don't require the optional time tags, as they utilize only the OSC data structure, triggering events upon delivery.

Although less convenient and more fundamental in nature, other widespread communication protocols include TCP (Transmission Control protocol),[c] UDP (User Datagram protocol),[d] and asynchronous serial communication. They use different ports to exchange data,[e] and they "shake hands" slightly differently. Handshaking is the process of negotiating communication parameters on both sides before the actual communication begins.

---

a. http://archive.cnmat.berkeley.edu/ICMC97/OpenSoundControl.html
b. opensoundcontrol.org/
c. http://en.wikipedia.org/wiki/Transmission_Control_Protocol
d. http://en.wikipedia.org/wiki/User_Datagram_Protocol
e. http://en.wikipedia.org/wiki/List_of_TCP_and_UDP_port_numbers

cameras, and we follow the same procedure (Section 4.4, *Setting Sketch Permissions*, on page 75) in the Permissions Selector, choosing INTERNET from the Android → Sketch Permissions dialog.

We'll take the following steps to network the Android and the PC. First, we'll run the Android sketch we've just created on the Android device. Then we'll check the Processing console to see if OSC is up and running. Since the Android device is connected to the PC via USB, it gives us some feedback with regard to the OSC status when the app starts up. Finally, when the app is running on the device and the OSC server is running, we move on to run the PC sketch and start the connection.

Now run the sketch on the Android device. It should start up fine, even if we don't have a partner to talk to yet. When the app is starting up, the device reports to the console that OSC is initialized and that the OSC server is running on port 12000.

Here's the output you can expect to see in the PDE (Processing IDE) console.

❰ PROCESS @ UdpClient.openSocket udp socket initialized.
  PROCESS @ UdpServer.start() new Unicast DatagramSocket created @ port 12000
  INFO @ OscP5 is running. you (127.0.0.1) are listening @ port 12000
  PROCESS @ UdpServer.run() UdpServer is running @ 12000

With the app launched on the Android, let's shift our focus to the desktop to complete the OSC server-client network.

Program the PC

The sketch for the PC is nearly identical to the one for the Android sketch. It's a bit more concise because there's no accelerometer data to capture on the desktop, and we don't have to look up the device IP address because we've already written it down. The desktop sketch receives accelerometer values from the Android and sends its mouseX, mouseY, and mousePressed values in return. Let's take a look:

Networking/WiFiDataExchangePC/WiFiDataExchangePC.pde

```
import oscP5.*;
import netP5.*;

OscP5 oscP5;
NetAddress remoteLocation;
float accelerometerX, accelerometerY, accelerometerZ;

void setup() {
  size(480, 480);
  oscP5 = new OscP5(this, 12000);
❶ remoteLocation = new NetAddress("10.0.1.41", 12000); // Customize!
  textAlign(CENTER, CENTER);
  textSize(24);
}

void draw() {
  background(78, 93, 75);
  text("Remote Accelerometer Info: " + "\n" +
    "x: "+ nfp(accelerometerX, 1, 3) + "\n" +
    "y: "+ nfp(accelerometerY, 1, 3) + "\n" +
    "z: "+ nfp(accelerometerZ, 1, 3) + "\n\n" +
    "Local Info: \n" +
    "mousePressed: " + mousePressed, width/2, height/2);

  OscMessage myMessage = new OscMessage("mouseStatus");
❷ myMessage.add(mouseX);
❸ myMessage.add(mouseY);
❹ myMessage.add(int(mousePressed));
❺ oscP5.send(myMessage, remoteLocation);
}

void oscEvent(OscMessage theOscMessage) {
```

```
⑥  if (theOscMessage.checkTypetag("fff"))
   {
⑦    accelerometerX = theOscMessage.get(0).floatValue();
      accelerometerY = theOscMessage.get(1).floatValue();
      accelerometerZ = theOscMessage.get(2).floatValue();
   }
}
```

On the desktop, we make the following adjustments.

❶ Point OSC to the remote Android IP address remoteLocation, displayed on the Android as "Local IP Address." Go ahead and customize this address using your Android's IP address now.

❷ Add the horizontal mouse position mouseX to the OSC message.

❸ Add the vertical mouse position mouseY to the OSC message.

❹ Add the mousePressed boolean, cast as an integer number to send either 0 or 1 via OSC.

❺ Send the OSC message myMessage on its way to the Android via port 12000.

❻ Check the OSC message for packages containing three incoming floating point values patterned "fff."

❼ Assign incoming floating point values to accelerometerX, accelerometerY, and accelerometerZ, shown on the desktop screen.

We are sending three global integers x, y, and p from the desktop to the Android (the horizontal and vertical mouse position and mousePressed) and will receive accelerometerX, accelerometerY, and accelerometerZ in return. For the data exchange, we are using port 12000 in both sketches. This port number (12000) could change, but it must be identical on both sides to work properly and shouldn't conflict with the lower numbers for ports already in use.[11]

Run the App

Let's run the sketch on the PC in Java mode. The display window starts up on the desktop, and we can now move the mouse in the window to send OSC messages containing mouse info to the Android. On the Android screen we see the horizontal and vertical position of the mouse update and the mouse button state change. Changing the orientation of the Android device gives us a range of accelerometer values, which we can observe on the desktop screen. Value updates seem to occur instantaneously. There is no perceivable lag

---

11. http://en.wikipedia.org/wiki/List_of_TCP_and_UDP_port_numbers

time, and while we are certainly only sending a few values, it gives us an idea about the bandwidth Wi-Fi has to offer—a highly interactive setup.

If communication fails, make sure you've adjusted remoteAddress in the Android sketch to match the IP address of your desktop PC. It's close to impossible that your Wi-Fi router assigned the same IPs used in the example sketches here. And while you are at it, go ahead and also check that the port number matches on both sides. The IP address must be correct, and port numbers must match to exchange data successfully.

Let's note that when we use OSC networking, it won't complain if there is no other device to talk to. The connection sits and waits until another device enters the conversation on port 12000. Likewise, OSC doesn't throw a networking error when a device leaves the conversation; it can also reconnect at any time. This is another great feature of the OSC communication protocol, whether we use it on the Android or the desktop—a robust connection process combined with a straightforward method to send messages containing different data types.

In terms of networking across devices, this is a major milestone we can continue to build on. It's a small step for us to change the values we've sent via OSC to take on different new tasks. So for the next project, we'll use the code on page 134 to create a drawing canvas that the Android and the PC can share.

6.5 Share Real-Time Data

For our next project, we're going to create a program for the Android and the PC that allows users of the two devices to draw on a shared surface, or virtual whiteboard, as shown in Figure 25, *Networked drawing app*, on page 141. We'll refine the previous sketches on page 134 and on page 138 that we've written to connect the Android and the desktop PC. The Wi-Fi network has the necessary bandwidth and update rates that we need to draw collaboratively. Whatever one of the users draws will appear instantaneously on the other's device, and vice versa.

Let's start by programming the Android; then we'll program the PC.

Program the Android

Compared to the previous sketch, where we sent accelerometer data from the Android to the desktop and mouse info from the desktop to the Android, we'll focus now on the mouseX and mouseY integer values we'll need to draw, sending only those two constants back and forth using OSC. The sketches for the Android and the PC are identical, with the exception of the single line of code that specifies the remote IP address. Since we now know the IP addresses of

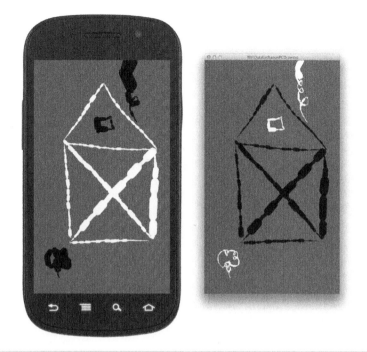

Figure 25—Networked drawing app. The image illustrates the app running on the Android (left) and the sketch running on the desktop PC (right).

both the Android and the PC, we can complete this project using only the oscP5 and netP5 libraries.

Let's take a look:

Networking/WiFiDataExchangeAndroidDrawing/WiFiDataExchangeAndroidDrawing.pde

```
import oscP5.*;
import netP5.*;

OscP5 oscP5;
NetAddress remoteLocation;
int x, y, px, py;

void setup() {
  orientation(PORTRAIT);
  oscP5 = new OscP5(this, 12001);
❶ remoteLocation = new NetAddress("10.0.1.66", 12001);
  background(78, 93, 75);
}

void draw() {
  stroke(0);
```

```
❷    float remoteSpeed = dist(px, py, x, y);
❸    strokeWeight(remoteSpeed);
❹    if (remoteSpeed < 50) line(px, py, x, y);
❺    px = x;
❻    py = y;
     if (mousePressed) {
       stroke(255);
❼      float speed = dist(pmouseX, pmouseY, mouseX, mouseY);
❽      strokeWeight(speed);
❾      if (speed < 50) line(pmouseX, pmouseY, mouseX, mouseY);
       OscMessage myMessage = new OscMessage("AndroidData");
       myMessage.add(mouseX);
       myMessage.add(mouseY);
       oscP5.send(myMessage, remoteLocation);
     }
   }

   void oscEvent(OscMessage theOscMessage) {
     if (theOscMessage.checkTypetag("ii"))
     {
       x =  theOscMessage.get(0).intValue();
       y =  theOscMessage.get(1).intValue();
     }
   }
```

Here are the steps we take to change the draw() and oscEvent() methods from
the previous sketch code, on page 134:

❶ Create a new OSC connection on port 12001 to avoid conflicts with the
   previous sketch code, on page 134, which runs an OSC connection on port
   12000.

❷ Calculate the speed of the remote mouse, which we'll use for the stroke
   weight.

❸ Define a stroke weight for the line drawing sent from the desktop via OSC.
   It is determined by the mouse speed and calculated from the difference
   between the previous to the current mouse position using the dist() method.

❹ Draw a line from the previous mouse position stored in px and py to the
   current mouse position's x and y, received via OSC.

❺ Assign the current horizontal mouse position x to the previous position
   px once we are done drawing.

❻ Assign the current vertical mouse position y to the previous position py
   once we are done drawing.

❼ Calculate the speed of the fingertip moving across the screen using the distance dist() from the previous position (pmouseX, pmouseY) to the current position (mouseX, mouseY).

❽ Set the stroke weight for the line drawing on the Android to the fingertip's speed.

❾ Draw a line from the previous to the current finger position. Prevent large strokes and jumps when we resume drawing at a different part of the touch screen interface.

We moved a port number higher compared to the previous sketch so that the number would not conflict with the already established connection there. An OSC conflict with an already established connection on a specific port would be reported to the Processing console like this:

```
❮ ERROR @ UdpServer.start()  IOException, couldnt create new DatagramSocket
@ port 12000 java.net.BindException: Address already in use
```

If we stopped the app that occupies the port, we can reuse that port number. To stop a sketch, hold down the home button on the Android device and swipe the app horizontally to close it, or choose Settings → Manage Apps → Wi-FiDataExchangeAndroid → Force Stop.

Because we've moved to port number 12001 for this sketch, we won't run into a conflict. Let's go ahead and test the app now.

Run the Android App

Load the sketch for the Android and run it on the device. When the app launches, the console reports that we are running an OSC server on port 12001:

```
❮ UdpServer.run() UdpServer is running @ 12001
```

When you move your finger across the touch screen surface, you draw white lines in different thicknesses, depending on how fast you are going.

The Android sketch is now complete, and we can move on to the PC sketch so that we have two devices that can doodle collaboratively.

Program the PC

Now let's work on the PC sketch. As mentioned earlier, the Android and desktop sketch involved in this virtual canvas project are identical; we only need to make sure the IP address matches the remote Android device. Let's take a look at the following code snippet, where only the IP address differs from the Android sketch.

Networking/WiFiDataExchangePCDrawing/WiFiDataExchangePCDrawing.pde

```
void setup() {
  size(480, 800);
  oscP5 = new OscP5(this, 12001);
❶ remoteLocation = new NetAddress("10.0.1.41", 12001);
  background(78, 93, 75);
}
```

To enable a graphical output on the PC, we add the following single line of code.

❶ Adjust the IP address as a parameter in the NetAddress object remoteLocation to match the Android IP.

Now we are ready to doodle and communicate both ways.

Run the PC App

Let's go ahead and run the sketch on the desktop PC. The Android sketch is already running. If you draw with your mouse in the display window on the desktop, you will cause white lines to appear on the screen whose weight increases the faster you draw.

Now let's go back to the Android and draw on its touch screen surface while keeping an eye on the desktop window. Notice that the lines you draw "locally" appear in white, while those that appear "remotely" are in black. Keep doodling using either the desktop or the Android, and you should see the same image you draw on one device appear in reverse colors on the other, as shown in Figure 25, *Networked drawing app*, on page 141. Black and white marks perpetually override each other as we keep doodling.

You've exchanged data between the Android and a desktop PC using Wi-Fi; now is a good time to test OSC communication between two Android devices using Wi-Fi. For this, you'll need to go find a second Android device.

Run the Sketch on a Pair of Androids

Now that you have located a second Android device—let's call it Android 2—you can go ahead and confirm that you are able to send OSC messages between a pair of Android devices as well. Let's make sure again that you are on the correct network with the second device, and choose Settings → "Wireless & networks." Write down the IP address of the second device. With the IP addresses of both devices ready, open the sketch code, on page 141, that we've already loaded onto the first device.

Adjust the IP address for remoteLocation to match Android 2, and run the sketch on Android 1. The app starts up and Android 1 is ready. Repeat the steps on the other device, adjusting the IP address to match Android 1 and running the sketch on Android 2.

You've mastered networking Android devices using Wi-Fi. Now let's explore a slightly more advanced networking app, where we work with an extended set of OSC messages to develop a simple marble-balancing game for two devices.

6.6 Network a Pair of Androids for a Multiplayer Game

For this project, we are going to build on the previous sketch, in which we connected two Android devices using Wi-Fi and OSC. Let's build a simple multiplayer game where each player uses an Android device to tilt a marble toward a selected target, as illustrated in Figure 26, *Multiplayer balancing game*, on page 145. Instead of a scenario in which one player controls the outcome on a single device, two devices will share a virtual game board whose orientation reflects the actions of the two players. One player influences the tilt of the other's game board, and vice versa.

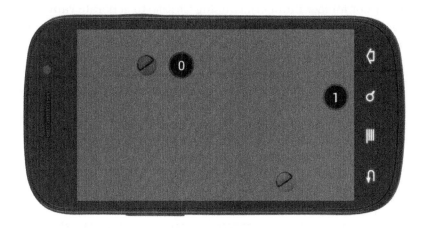

Figure 26—Multiplayer balancing game Played with two Android devices, two players compete in navigating individual marbles to the targets on a shared board, where the orientation of both devices influence each other.

To make the marbles for this game look three-dimensional, we'll load an image that provides us with the image texture we need for the desired effect. We'll use Processing's PImage class again to store the image.[12] We can load .gif, .jpg, .tga, and .png images using the loadImage(). We are going to use a PNG-formatted

---

12. http://processing.org/reference/PImage.html

image because it supports a transparent background.[13] With a transparent background, the image will appear to float on the surface of the game board without the background color showing up as a rectangle as the marble moves across it. PImage also offers us a tint() method, which we can use to create two differently colored marbles from one image.

The sketch we are going to build is identical on both devices with the exception of the value assigned to the variable remoteAddress, which points to the other Android device. This time we'll send a few more values via OSC compared with the earlier code, on page 141—seven instead of three, including the position of the marble, its speed, the position of each target, and the score for each player. OSC allows us to mix the data types we send within one message, so we'll send four floating point values followed by three integers and determine a valid OSC message using the checkTypetag(ffffiii) method.

To assign random positions to the marbles and targets when the app starts up, we'll use Processing's random() method.[14] It generates random floating point numbers every time the method is called. We can use it with one parameter (floating point or integer number), causing random() to generate values ranging from zero to that number. We can also use it with two parameters, making random() return values ranging from the first to the second number parameter.

Let's take a look:

Networking/MultiplayerBalance/MultiplayerBalance.pde

```
import oscP5.*;
import netP5.*;
import ketai.sensors.*;

OscP5 oscP5;
KetaiSensor sensor;
NetAddress remoteLocation;
float x, y, remoteX, remoteY;
float myAccelerometerX, myAccelerometerY, rAccelerometerX, rAccelerometerY;
int targetX, targetY, remoteTargetX, remoteTargetY;
int score, remoteScore;
float speedX, speedY = .01;
PImage marble;
String remoteAddress = "10.0.1.44";  //Customize!
void setup() {
  sensor = new KetaiSensor(this);
  orientation(PORTRAIT);
  textAlign(CENTER, CENTER);
  textSize(36);
```

---

13. http://en.wikipedia.org/wiki/Portable_Network_Graphics
14. http://processing.org/reference/random_.html

```
      initNetworkConnection();
      sensor.start();
      strokeWeight(5);
      imageMode(CENTER);
❶     marble = loadImage("marble.png");
      init();
   }

   void draw() {
      background(78, 93, 75);
      // Targets
      fill (0);
      stroke(0, 60, 0);
      ellipse(targetX, targetY, 70, 70);
      stroke (60, 0, 0);
      ellipse(remoteTargetX, remoteTargetY, 70, 70);
      noStroke();
      fill(255);
      text(score, targetX, targetY);
      text(remoteScore, remoteTargetX, remoteTargetY);
      // Remote Marble
❷     tint(120, 0, 0);
❸     image(marble, remoteX, remoteY);
      // Local Marble
❹     speedX += (myAccelerometerX + rAccelerometerX) * 0.1;
      speedY += (myAccelerometerY + rAccelerometerY) * 0.1;

      if (x <= 25+speedX || x > width-25+speedX) {
❺        speedX *= -0.8;
      }
      if (y <= 25-speedY || y > height-25-speedY) {
         speedY *= -0.8;
      }
❻     x -= speedX;
      y += speedY;
      tint(0, 120, 0);
      image(marble, x, y);
      // Collision
      if (dist(x, y, targetX, targetY) < 10) {
         score++;
         background(60, 0, 0);
         init();
      }
   }

   void oscEvent(OscMessage theOscMessage) {
❼     if (theOscMessage.checkTypetag("ffffiii"))
      {
         remoteX = theOscMessage.get(0).floatValue();
         remoteY = theOscMessage.get(1).floatValue();
```

```
    rAccelerometerX = theOscMessage.get(2).floatValue();
    rAccelerometerY = theOscMessage.get(3).floatValue();
    remoteTargetX = theOscMessage.get(4).intValue();
    remoteTargetY = theOscMessage.get(5).intValue();
    remoteScore = theOscMessage.get(6).intValue();
  }
}

void onAccelerometerEvent(float _x, float _y, float _z)
{
  myAccelerometerX = _x;
  myAccelerometerY = _y;
  OscMessage myMessage = new OscMessage("remoteData");
  myMessage.add(x);
  myMessage.add(y);
  myMessage.add(myAccelerometerX);
  myMessage.add(myAccelerometerY);
  myMessage.add(targetX);
  myMessage.add(targetY);
  myMessage.add(score);
  oscP5.send(myMessage, remoteLocation);
}

void initNetworkConnection()
{
  oscP5 = new OscP5(this, 12000);
  remoteLocation = new NetAddress(remoteAddress, 12000);
}
void init() {
  x = int(random(25, width-25));
  y = int(random(25, height-25));
  targetX = int(random(25, width-35));
  targetY = int(random(25, height-35));
}
```

Here's what we are working with for the balancing game.

❶ Load a marble image from the sketch data folder using loadImage().

❷ Tint the remote marble red to distinguish the two players. The tint() method is applied to the marble.png image, drawn next.[15]

❸ Draw the tinted marble image at the remote position (remoteX, remoteY).

❹ Calculate the horizontal marble speed speedX by adding the horizontal accelerometer values of both devices, called myAccelerometerX and rAccelerometerX. Reduce the speed by multiplying the accelerometer sum by a factor of 0.1. Do the same for the vertical direction in the following line.

———————————

15. http://processing.org/reference/tint_.html

❺ Bounce the marble off the screen edge whenever its distance from the edge is less then 25 pixels, which happens to equal half the diameter of the marble image. Consider the speedX, and dampen the speed at every bounce, reducing it to 80% (0.8) of the previous speed. Do the same for the *y*-axis next.

❻ Update the horizontal position x of the local marble.

❼ Look for a package of four floating point numbers followed by three integers, and parse the message to assign values for the remote position (remoteX and remoteY), the remote accelerometer values (rAccelerometerX and rAccelerometerY), the remote target position (remoteTargetX and remoteTargetY), and the remote score (remoteScore).

❽ Add all the local marble positions (x and y), the local accelerometer values (myAccelerometerX and myAccelerometerY), the local target (targetX and targetY), and the local score to the OSC message (myMessage), and send it to the other device.

❾ Initialize the local marble position and target position to appear randomly on the screen.

Now let's test the game.

Run the App

To run the game, let's first check the IP addresses on both of the Android devices we'll be using so that we can adjust the remoteAddress variable in the sketch for each Android device.

Connect the first Android device (Android 1) to the desktop computer via USB and load the MultiPlayerBalance sketch into Processing. Locate the remoteAddress variable in the code; we'll adjust this in a moment.

Now look up the IP address of the second Android device (Android 2), which is currently not connected via USB cable. Navigate to Settings → "Wireless & networks" on the device, and tap the Wi-Fi network the device is connected to. The IP address assigned to the device is shown on the bottom of the list. Write it down; it's the IP address for Android 2.

Now go back to the Processing sketch and adjust the IP address for remoteAddress to match the IP address (for Android 2) that you've just looked up.

Run the sketch on Android 1, which is already connected via USB cable. When the sketch is launched on the device, disconnect Android 1 and connect Android 2. We'll repeat those steps for the other device.

With Android 2 connected via USB cable, locate remoteAddress in the code so we can adjust the IP address again. Look up the IP address of Android 1 now, which is currently not connected via USB cable. Write it down.

Go back to the Processing code and adjust the IP address for remoteAddress to match the IP address (of Android 1) that you've just looked up.

Run the sketch on Android 2, which is already connected via USB cable. When the sketch launches on the device, we are ready to play.

Grab a friend and hand over one device. Now hold the device as level as possible to balance the green (local) marble toward its target, shown with a green stroke. Your friend is pursuing the same objective, which makes the balancing act more difficult as it probably interferes with the path of your marble toward the target. Once you've hit the target, or vice versa, the score increases and the game restarts. You can see score updates immediately when the target is reached. Enjoy your game!

This two-player game concludes our explorations into wireless networking using Wi-Fi networks.

6.7 Wrapping Up

You've mastered the exchange of data across devices within a Wi-Fi network. You've learned how to package diverse data types into OSC messages, send them across wireless local area networks, and unpack them on the other side. You've got devices talking to each other, which you can now easily expand into other application contexts, including making the Android a remote control for other devices on the network.

But if we don't have access to a Wi-Fi network and we'd like to exchange data with other Android devices directly, peer-to-peer, what can we do? All fourth-generation Android devices are equipped with Bluetooth, so in the next chapter we'll take a look at this short-distance wireless technology, and we'll also explore an emerging peer-to-peer networking standard known as Wi-Fi Direct. Then, in the following chapter, we'll explore near field communication, the emerging short-range wireless standard for contactless payment and smart cards. When you're done, you'll be an Android networking pro.

CHAPTER 7

Peer-to-Peer Networking Using Bluetooth and Wi-Fi Direct

In this chapter, we'll give peer-to-peer (P2P) networks the attention they deserve. We've mastered the exchange of data between Android devices using Wi-Fi. Now it's time to end our dependence on wireless infrastructure. Popular services such as Skype and BitTorrent are only two examples that use peer-to-peer technology.[1] However, the concept of P2P communication doesn't stop with telephony or file sharing and has little do with copyright.

P2P networking has several advantages. First of all, it's free. We don't require a carrier network or access to Wi-Fi infrastructure, and we won't be restricted by data quotas. P2P still works if wireless infrastructure is unavailable or overwhelmed due to high demand, for instance. It uses less power due to its short range and can help protect privacy because information remains decentralized. And finally, information flows directly from one device to the other—we can control the information flow and choose whether data is saved or retained.

P2P communication between two devices doesn't preclude us from also reaching out to web or cloud servers. For example, if we are connected P2P while we are on the move, we can update an online database as soon as a carrier network becomes available. Both networking paradigms can coexist and complement each other. P2P has the advantage that it can reliably provide us with instantaneous feedback across devices due to the very small lag time, and it provides the transmission rates that are crucial for some multiuser or multiplayer apps.

---

1. http://en.wikipedia.org/wiki/Peer-to-peer

The most common way to implement P2P exchanges of data between Android devices is to use Bluetooth, which is available on all Android devices shipping today. We'll start by building a remote cursor app, where we visualize the cursor position of two devices connected via Bluetooth. Then we'll build a peer-to-peer survey app that lets us create a poll for multiple users. Connected via Bluetooth, users pick answers from a common multiple choice questionnaire displayed on their device screens. Individual answers are gathered and visualized in real time, giving each user immediate feedback on the collective response and the distribution of answers as they accumulate.

Then we'll move on to Wi-Fi Direct, an emerging peer-to-peer networking standard where each device can serve as the Wi-Fi access point for the network. We'll revisit the remote cursor app and modify it to use Wi-Fi Direct so that we can directly compare its performance to Bluetooth. Wi-Fi Direct is designed to provide a higher bandwidth and better network range than Bluetooth. To get started, let's first take a look at the main classes we'll use in this chapter.

7.1 Introducing Short-Range Networking and UI Classes

For the apps we'll develop in this chapter, we'll use the following networking and UI classes from the Ketai library:

KetaiBluetooth[2] A Ketai class for working with Bluetooth on Android devices[3]—the class contains the necessary methods for Bluetooth discovery, pairing, and communication using the popular Bluetooth standard

KetaiWiFiDirect[4] A Ketai class to simplify working with Wi-Fi Direct on Android devices[5]—the class contains the necessary methods for Wi-Fi Direct peer discovery and data exchange. In a Wi-Fi Direct network, every Wi-Fi Direct–enabled device can serve as the access point for the other devices in the Wi-Fi network.

KetaiOSCMessage[6] A Ketai class that is identical to the oscP5 library's OscMessage class we worked with in Section 6.3, *Using the Open Sound Control Networking Format*, on page 129, with the difference being that it allows us to create KetaiOSCMessage using a byte array—it makes some private methods in OscMessage public so we can use it for Bluetooth communication.

---

2. http://ketai.googlecode.com/svn/trunk/ketai/reference/ketai/net/bluetooth/KetaiBluetooth.html
3. http://developer.android.com/guide/topics/wireless/bluetooth.html
4. http://ketai.googlecode.com/svn/trunk/ketai/reference/ketai/net/wifidirect/KetaiWiFiDirect.html
5. http://developer.android.com/guide/topics/wireless/wifip2p.html
6. http://ketai.googlecode.com/svn/trunk/ketai/reference/ketai/net/KetaiOSCMessage.html

KetaiList[7] A Ketai UI class that makes it easier to work with the native Android ListView widget—this class contains methods to populate, display, refresh, and retrieve strings from a selected list item. A KetaiList can be created using a String array or a String ArrayList.[8]

KetaiKeyboard[9] A class included in the Ketai UI package that allows us to toggle the Android software keyboard on and off without importing additional Android UI classes

We'll start with Bluetooth because it's the most ubiquitous peer-to-peer technology. Let's take a closer look at the Bluetooth methods that Ketai provides.

7.2 Working with the KetaiBluetooth Class

Besides the usual start() and stop() methods, KetaiBluetooth provides the following methods for discovering, pairing, and connecting Bluetooth devices:

onBluetoothDataEvent() Returns data sent via Bluetooth, including the device name where it originated as a String (useful when more than one Bluetooth device is connected) and the Bluetooth data as byte[] array

makeDiscoverable() Makes a Bluetooth device discoverable for 300 seconds

discoverDevices() Scans for discoverable Bluetooth devices

getDiscoveredDeviceNames() Returns a list of all Bluetooth devices found within range of the Bluetooth radio

connectToDeviceByName() Connect to a device using its assigned Bluetooth name

broadcast() Writes data to all connected Bluetooth devices

getPairedDeviceNames() Provides a list of devices that have been successfully paired with the Android device—paired devices can reconnect automatically if they are discoverable and within range, and they do not need to repeat the pairing process.

Now that we've seen the classes and methods that we'll use to build apps in this chapter, let's now take a closer look at Bluetooth, the most ubiquitous peer-to-peer standard.

---

7.   http://ketai.googlecode.com/svn/trunk/ketai/reference/ketai/ui/KetaiList.html

8.   http://processing.org/reference/ArrayList.html

9.   http://ketai.googlecode.com/svn/trunk/ketai/reference/ketai/ui/KetaiKeyboard.html

7.3 Introducing Bluetooth

Every Android device ships with a Bluetooth radio. It is a popular communication standard used for consumer electronics, health and wellness devices, PC peripherals, sports and fitness equipment, and smart home appliances, and it is typically found in wireless game controllers, headsets, keyboards, printers, and heart rate sensors, to name a few.[10] Because it is so ubiquitous, it will remain an important protocol even as new networking standards emerge.

The standard is managed by the Bluetooth Special Interest Group, which includes more than sixteen thousand member companies. "Bluetooth" refers to a tenth-century Danish king who united dissonant tribes into a single kingdom. The implication is that Bluetooth has done the same for the device and accessory market, uniting communication protocols into one universal standard.[11]

Bluetooth uses short-wavelength radio frequencies of 2400–2480 MHz and allows us to transfer data within a range of about 30 feet. It requires relatively little power and rarely experiences interference from other devices. But before we can transfer data, we must first *pair* the devices involved.[12] Once we've done that successfully, the Android stores a list of known devices, which we can use to reconnect them without pairing them again. If we already know the unique 48-bit address of the Bluetooth device to which we'd like to connect, we can skip the pairing process entirely.

If the Bluetooth radio is powered on, any Bluetooth-enabled device can send an inquiry to initiate a connection. If a device is discoverable, it sends information about itself to other Bluetooth devices within reach, including its own device name, allowing the devices to pair and exchange data securely. If we send data between Android devices, pairing and acceptance of the connection by the device owner is required for security reasons.

Let's now connect two Android devices via Bluetooth.

7.4 Working with the Android Activity Life Cycle

When we launch a Processing sketch as an app on the Android, we create an Android *activity* ready for us to interact via the touch screen interface.[13] We typically don't need to deal with the activity life cycle on the Android because

---

10. http://www.bluetooth.com/Pages/market.aspx
11. http://en.wikipedia.org/wiki/Bluetooth
12. http://en.wikipedia.org/wiki/Bluetooth#Pairing.2FBonding
13. http://developer.android.com/reference/android/app/Activity.html

Processing takes care of it for us.[14] To activate Bluetooth (and later NFC), we need to initialize the Bluetooth object we'll be working with at the very beginning of the activity life cycle.

When a new app or activity starts up, Android adds it to the stack of activities already running and places it on top of the stack to run in the foreground. The previous activity goes in the background and will come to the foreground again when the current activity exits.

We can summarize the four states an activity can take like this:

- The activity is active and running in the foreground on top of the stack.

- The activity lost focus because another non-fullscreen activity runs on top of the activity.

- The activity stopped because another activity is covering it completely.

- The paused or stopped activity is killed to make memory available for the active activity.

When an activity goes though this life cycle, Android provides the following callback methods for us to use. When the activity starts up, Android calls the following:

onCreate()[15]   Called when the activity is starting

onStart()   Called after onCreate() when the activity starts up—if the activity is already running, onRestart() is called before onStart().

onResume()   Called after onStart() when the activity becomes visible

After onResume(), the activity is running in the foreground and active. If we launch another activity, Android calls these methods:

onPause()   Called when another activity comes in the foreground

onStop()   Called after onPause() when the activity is no longer visible

onDestroy()   Called after onStop() when the activity is finishing or destroyed by the system

Enabling Bluetooth

To work with Bluetooth for the Bluetooth apps we'll create in this chapter, we will need to launch a new activity to initialize our Bluetooth right at the beginning when the activity starts up using onCreate(). Once Bluetooth is active,

---

14. http://developer.android.com/reference/android/app/Activity.html#ActivityLifecycle

15. http://developer.android.com/reference/android/app/Activity.html#onCreate%28android.os.Bundle%29

this activity returns to us the Bluetooth object we need via onActivityResult(),[16] which is called when the app starts up immediately before onResume() in the activity life cycle.[17] We'll look at the code to enable Bluetooth in more detail in this code, on page 162.

For the projects in this book, we'll need to deal with the life cycle only for Bluetooth and NFC. We'll work more with the activity life cycle in *Enable NFC and Bluetooth in the Activity Life Cycle*, on page 198, where we initiate NFC and Bluetooth. For all other apps, we can let Processing handle the life cycle. Future versions of Processing might allow libraries to work with lifecycle callback methods, so we don't need to include such code inside the sketch.

7.5 Connect Two Android Devices via Bluetooth

In the following sketch, we'll work with three tabs. The main tab, BluetoothCursors, contains our usual setup() and draw() methods and global variables. The second tab, EnableBluetooth, contains code that is necessary to enable Bluetooth on startup, registering our Bluetooth class when the so-called Android activity is created (this step might not be necessary in future versions of Processing).[18] Processing allows us to not dive too deep into the Android application life cycle, and we'll try to keep it that way. The third tab, called UI, contains all the code we'll use for GUI elements like menus, an Android list to select Bluetooth devices, and the software keyboard to enter user input. When the sketch is complete, we'll get a screen similar to the one shown in Figure 27, *Bluetooth Cursors app*, on page 157.

The code needs to facilitate the Bluetooth pairing process as follows: We start by making both Androids discoverable for Bluetooth by listing discovered devices. Then we choose the device to connect to from the list of discovered devices (you might be surprised to see what shows up). Finally, we pair and connect the devices to transfer the data via OSC, which we've already used in Section 6.3, *Using the Open Sound Control Networking Format*, on page 129. We'll need to confirm the Bluetooth connection in a popup window because we will be connecting the devices for the first time.

We'll use the Android software keyboard to discover other Bluetooth devices, make the device itself discoverable, connect to another device, list already paired devices, and show the current Bluetooth status. To work with the keyboard, we'll use the KetaiKeyboard class. And to show and pick discoverable

---

16. http://developer.android.com/reference/android/app/Activity.html#onActivityResult%28int,%20int,%20android.content.Intent%29

17. http://developer.android.com/reference/android/app/Activity.html#onResume%28%29

18. http://developer.android.com/reference/android/app/Activity.html

Figure 27—Bluetooth Cursors app. The illustration shows the local (white) and the remote (red) mouse pointer positions, marked as ellipses on the screen. The software keyboard is made visible using the keyboard tab shown at the top. Also shown are the Bluetooth and Interact tabs, which we use to interact with the cursors.

Bluetooth devices to connect to, we'll use the KetaiList class, making it easy for us to work with a native Android list without importing additional packages.

Working with a KetaiList

We can create a KetaiList object using either a String array or a String ArrayList.[19] Because an ArrayList stores a variable number of objects and we have a variable number of discoverable Bluetooth devices to connect to, it's the better choice for us here. We can easily add or remove an item dynamically in an ArrayList, and because we work with Bluetooth device names in our sketch, we'll create an ArrayList of type String.

19. http://processing.org/reference/ArrayList.html

Andreas Schlegel has updated his excellent ControlP5 UI library (as of 09/2012) to also work with the Android mode in Processing 2,[20] making it a great tool to develop all custom aspects of UI elements, such as controllers, lists, sliders, buttons, and input forms. Although the UI elements do not use Android's native UI classes, ControlP5 elements can be fully customized to match the look and feel of your app while still maintaining consistency with the Android's UI style guide.[21]

Let's get started with the main tab of our BluetoothCursors sketch.

P2P/BluetoothCursors/BluetoothCursors.pde

```
❶ import android.os.Bundle;
❷ import android.content.Intent;

   import ketai.net.bluetooth.*;
   import ketai.ui.*;
   import ketai.net.*;
   import oscP5.*;

❸ KetaiBluetooth bt;

❹ KetaiList connectionList;
❺ String info = "";
   PVector remoteCursor = new PVector();
   boolean isConfiguring = true;
   String UIText;

   void setup()
   {
     orientation(PORTRAIT);
     background(78, 93, 75);
     stroke(255);
     textSize(24);

❻   bt.start();

❼   UIText = "[b] - make this device discoverable\n" +
       "[d] - discover devices\n" +
       "[c] - pick device to connect to\n" +
       "[p] - list paired devices\n" +
       "[i] - show Bluetooth info";
   }

   void draw()
   {
     if (isConfiguring)
```

---

20. http://sojamo.de/libraries/controlP5
21. http://developer.android.com/design/style

```
    {
⑧    ArrayList<String> devices;
      background(78, 93, 75);

      if (key == 'i')
⑨       info = getBluetoothInformation();
      else
      {
        if (key == 'p')
        {
          info = "Paired Devices:\n";
⑩         devices = bt.getPairedDeviceNames();
        }
        else
        {
          info = "Discovered Devices:\n";
⑪         devices = bt.getDiscoveredDeviceNames();
        }

        for (int i=0; i < devices.size(); i++)
        {
⑫         info += "["+i+"] "+devices.get(i).toString() + "\n";
        }
      }
      text(UIText + "\n\n" + info, 5, 90);
    }
    else
    {
      background(78, 93, 75);
      pushStyle();
      fill(255);
      ellipse(mouseX, mouseY, 20, 20);
      fill(0, 255, 0);
      stroke(0, 255, 0);
⑬    ellipse(remoteCursor.x, remoteCursor.y, 20, 20);
      popStyle();
    }

    drawUI();
  }

  void mouseDragged()
  {
    if (isConfiguring)
      return;

⑭  OscMessage m = new OscMessage("/remoteMouse/");
    m.add(mouseX);
    m.add(mouseY);
```

```
⑮    bt.broadcast(m.getBytes());
     // use writeToDevice(String _devName, byte[] data) to target a specific device
     ellipse(mouseX, mouseY, 20, 20);
   }

⑯ void onBluetoothDataEvent(String who, byte[] data)
   {
     if (isConfiguring)
       return;

⑰   KetaiOSCMessage m = new KetaiOSCMessage(data);
     if (m.isValid())
     {
       if (m.checkAddrPattern("/remoteCursor/"))
       {
⑱       if (m.checkTypetag("ii"))
         {
           remoteCursor.x = m.get(0).intValue();
           remoteCursor.y = m.get(1).intValue();
         }
       }
     }
   }

⑲ String getBluetoothInformation()
   {
     String btInfo = "Server Running: ";
     btInfo += bt.isStarted() + "\n";
     btInfo += "Device Discoverable: "+bt.isDiscoverable() + "\n";
     btInfo += "\nConnected Devices: \n";

⑳   ArrayList<String> devices = bt.getConnectedDeviceNames();
     for (String device: devices)
     {
       btInfo+= device+"\n";
     }

     return btInfo;
   }
```

Here are the steps we need to take.

❶ Import the os.bundle Android package containing the onCreate() method we need to initialize Bluetooth.

❷ Import the os.bundle Android package containing the onCreate() method we need to initialize Bluetooth.

❸ Create a KetaiBluetooth type variable, bt.

❹ Create a KetaiList variable that we'll use to select the device to connect to.

❺ Create a String variable, info, to store changing status messages that we want to output to the Android screen.

❻ Start the bt Bluetooth object.

❼ Provide instructions for connecting to the other device using the keyboard.

❽ Create an ArrayList of type String to store the Bluetooth device, devices.

❾ Retrieve a Bluetooth status update and assign it to our info variable for screen output when we press i on the keyboard.

❿ Get a list of paired devices and assign it to the devices ArrayList to update the KetaiList when we press the p on the keyboard.

⓫ Get a list of discovered devices and assign it to the devices ArrayList to update the KetaiList when we press d on the keyboard.

⓬ Append each Bluetooth device entry in devices to our info text output, converting each individual ArrayList item into human-readable text using the toString() method.

⓭ Use the x and y components of the remoteCursor PVector, which stores the remote cursor location, and draw an ellipse at the exact same *x* and *y* location.

⓮ Create a new OSC message m to add our mouseX and mouseY cursor position to.

⓯ Broadcast the OSC message containing the cursor position to all connected devices using the OSC broadcast() method. Alternatively, we can use write-ToDevice(String _devName, byte[] data) to send the message to only one specific device.

⓰ Receive the byte[] array when the new Bluetooth data is sent from the remote device.

⓱ Receive the data as an OSC message.

⓲ Check if the OSC message contains two integer values for the mouse *x* and *y* position. We've also checked if the OSC message is valid and if the message we've sent contains the label "remoteCursor."

⓳ Return a String containing Bluetooth status info, including if Bluetooth isStarted() and isDiscoverable(), as well as the individual names of connected Bluetooth devices.

⓴ Get a list of all connected Bluetooth devices using getConnectedDeviceNames().

We've completed the crucial components of our sketch in setup() and draw(). To enable Bluetooth when the app starts up, we'll need to work with the activity life cycle as described in Section 7.4, *Working with the Android Activity Life Cycle*, on page 154. We'll put the code to enable Bluetooth into the tab named EnableBluetooth. Let's take a look.

P2P/BluetoothCursors/EnableBluetooth.pde

```
❶ void onCreate(Bundle savedInstanceState) {
     super.onCreate(savedInstanceState);
❷   bt = new KetaiBluetooth(this);
   }

   void onActivityResult(int requestCode, int resultCode, Intent data) {
❸   bt.onActivityResult(requestCode, resultCode, data);
   }
```

These are the steps we need to take to enable Bluetooth.

❶ Use the Android onCreate() method to initialize our Bluetooth object. The method is called when the activity is starting.

❷ Initialize the Bluetooth object bt when the activity is created.

❸ Return the bt object to the sketch using onActivityResult(), called right before onResume() in the activity life cycle.

We looked at the required onCreate() and onActivityResult() methods to initialize Bluetooth at the beginning of the activity.

Programming the UI

Now let's return to the part of the code that is responsible for all the UI elements, which we'll put in the UI tab of the sketch. It takes care of GUI elements and keyboard menu items.

Because the Bluetooth pairing process requires us to select a device from a whole list of discovered devices (you'll probably be surprised by how many Bluetooth devices are broadcasting around you), we'll use a KetaiList to simplify the selection process. We'll also need the keyboard to make menu selections during the pairing process, and we'll use the KetaiKeyboard class to toggle the keyboard on and off. For the KetaiList, we'll use the onKetaiListSelection() method to capture when the user picks an item from the list. And to show and hide the KetaiKeyboard, we'll work with the toggle() method.

Here are the steps to programming the UI.

P2P/BluetoothCursors/UI.pde

```
// UI methods

void mousePressed()
{
  if (mouseY <= 50 && mouseX > 0 && mouseX < width/3)
❶    KetaiKeyboard.toggle(this);
  else if (mouseY <= 50 && mouseX > width/3 && mouseX < 2*(width/3)) //config button
❷    isConfiguring=true;
  else if (mouseY <= 50 && mouseX >  2*(width/3) && mouseX < width) // draw button
  {
    if (isConfiguring)
    {
      background(78, 93, 75);
      isConfiguring=false;
    }
  }
}

void keyPressed() {
  if (key =='c')
  {
    //If we have not discovered any devices, try prior paired devices
    if (bt.getDiscoveredDeviceNames().size() > 0)
❸      connectionList = new KetaiList(this, bt.getDiscoveredDeviceNames());
    else if (bt.getPairedDeviceNames().size() > 0)
❹      connectionList = new KetaiList(this, bt.getPairedDeviceNames());
  }
  else if (key == 'd')
❺    bt.discoverDevices();
  else if (key == 'b')
❻    bt.makeDiscoverable();
}

void drawUI()
{
❼  pushStyle();
  fill(0);
  stroke(255);
  rect(0, 0, width/3, 50);

  if (isConfiguring)
  {
    noStroke();
    fill(78, 93, 75);
  }
  else
    fill(0);

  rect(width/3, 0, width/3, 50);
```

```
  if (!isConfiguring)
  {
    noStroke();
    fill(78, 93, 75);
  }
  else
  {
    fill(0);
    stroke(255);
  }
  rect((width/3)*2, 0, width/3, 50);
  fill(255);
```
⑧ `  text("Keyboard", 5, 30);`
⑨ `  text("Bluetooth", width/3+5, 30);`
⑩ `  text("Interact", width/3*2+5, 30);`
```
  popStyle();
}
```

⑪ `void onKetaiListSelection(KetaiList connectionList)`
```
{
```
⑫ `  String selection = connectionList.getSelection();`
⑬ `  bt.connectToDeviceByName(selection);`
⑭ `  connectionList = null;`
```
}
```

Let's take a look at the steps.

❶ Toggle the Android's software keyboard using toggle(). Make the KetaiKeyboard visible if it's hidden; hide it if it's visible.

❷ Set the boolean variable isConfiguring to true so we can switch to the Bluetooth configuration screen and for the pairing process.

❸ Assign the list of paired Bluetooth devices to the KetaiList connectionList, given there are paired devices.

❹ Assign the list of discovered Bluetooth devices to the KetaiList connectionList using the String array returned by bt.getDiscoveredDeviceNames(), given there are discovered devices.

❺ Discover Bluetooth devices using discoverDevices() when we press d on the software keyboard.

❻ Make the device discoverable using the makeDiscoverable() method.

❼ Save the current style settings using pushStyle() to preserve the stroke, text size, and alignment for the UI elements. Use the method in combination with popStyle() to restore the previous style settings.

❽ Draw the Keyboard UI tab.

❾ Draw the Bluetooth UI tab.

❿ Draw the Interact UI tab.

⓫ Call the onKetaiListSelection() event method when a user selects an item from the KetaiList.

⓬ Get the String that the user picked from the KetaiList.

⓭ Connect to the selected Bluetooth device using the connectToDeviceByName() method.

⓮ Remove all items from the list by setting the connectionList object to null.

Now let's test the app.

Run the App

Let's set the correct Android permissions before we run the sketch. Open the Android Permission Selector as we've done previously (see Section 4.4, *Setting Sketch Permissions*, on page 75), and check the following permissions:

- BLUETOOTH
- BLUETOOTH ADMIN
- INTERNET

Now connect your first device to your workstation with a USB cable and run the sketch. When the app is compiled, all three tabs in the sketch, BluetoothCursors, EnableBluetooth, and UI, will be compiled into one app. You will see our Bluetooth tab active and the menu options displayed on the screen. Before we interact, let's install the app on our second Android device.

Disconnect your first device from the USB port, connect your second Android, and install the identical BluetoothCursors sketch on the device. The sketch launches, and we are ready to pair the two devices.

On your first device (currently disconnected from USB), show the software keyboard by pressing the Keyboard tab. Then press b on the keyboard. If Bluetooth is turned off for your device (Settings → Bluetooth), you will be prompted to allow Bluetooth, as shown below. Otherwise the device will become discoverable for 300 seconds.

```
Android 1
[b] - make this device discoverable
[d] - discover devices
[c] - pick device to connect to
[p] - list paired devices
[i] - show Bluetooth info
```

⇒ **b**

❰ Alert:
An app on your phone wants to
make your phone discoverable
by other Bluetooth devices for
300 seconds. Allow?

⇒ **Yes**

Now switch to your second device (currently connected to USB), and follow
the process of discovering devices. Pick the name of the first Android device:

❰ Android 2

⇒ **d**

❰ Discovered Devices
[0] Nexus S

⇒ **c**

⇒ **Nexus S**

❰ Android 1
Bluetooth pairing Request

⇒ **pair**

❰ Android 2

⇒ **p**

❰ Paired Devices
[0] Nexus S

⇒ **i**

❰ Sever Running: true
Device Discoverable: true

Connected Devices:
Nexus S (78:47:1D:B6:20:48)

When your screen output looks like what's shown above, the Bluetooth server
is running on your second device and you have your first device show up in
the list of connected devices. You are now ready to interact.

Press the Interact screen tab on both devices. You'll see a white dot for the
local cursor and a red one for the remote one. As you move your finger over
the screen surface of one Android device, observe the other device and see
how the red dot moves magically to that position.

Congratulations! You've established a data connection between two Android
devices using Bluetooth. Now it all depends on your Bluetooth antenna, which
should reach a distance of about thirty feet. If you have a friend nearby to
test this, try it out. Otherwise, it will not be possible to observe how the connection goes out of range.

The process of discovering and pairing Bluetooth devices can seem cumbersome. However, Bluetooth can't just accept an incoming connection without confirmation for good security reasons. Once paired, we can reconnect automatically by picking the device address again from the list of paired devices. This is a sketch refinement you can try. If you'd like to "unpair" previously paired devices on your Android, tap the device name under Settings → Bluetooth → Paired Devices, and choose Unpair.

We will implement this remote cursor's app using Wi-Fi Direct later in this chapter on page 183, and you can then compare how the two standards perform in terms of update rate and wireless range.

Since you've mastered peer-to-peer networking using Bluetooth, let's build on our Bluetooth skills and create a survey app for multiple Bluetooth users.

7.6 Create a Survey App Using Bluetooth

We'll now move on to the chapter project, which is a survey app for multiple users using Bluetooth networking. Such an app is useful for teaching, decision-making, and learning assessments. We'll build on our Bluetooth skills and put them into practice. We'll learn how to send different data types via OSC over Bluetooth, share numeric data across devices in real time, and learn how to work with custom Processing classes.

For this survey app, we'll broadcast a number of questions that you can imagine as text slides shared by multiple users. All survey participants respond to the questions through each person's individual device by picking one out of three answers from a multiple choice list. We'll tally the responses in real time and send an update to all peer devices as illustrated in Figure 28, *Bluetooth survey app*, on page 168, giving each user instantaneous feedback on the survey as it unfolds.

There are many examples of survey and polling applications that are available online. They typically use proprietary online databases or a dedicated hardware infrastructure. Virtually no app exists using peer-to-peer connectivity on mobile devices—let's change that. Let's go ahead and write a survey app using some of the code we've already created for the remote cursor app in Section 7.5, *Connect Two Android Devices via Bluetooth*, on page 156.

For this survey app, we'll work with four tabs for this sketch: the main tab, which we'll name BluetoothSurvey, the EnableBluetooth tab, which is identical to the tab with the same name on page 162, a Question tab for a custom Processing class we'll write to take care of our Q & A, and a slightly modified version of the UI tab, which we developed on page 163.

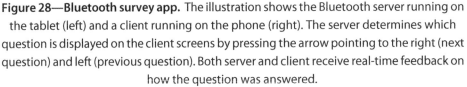

Figure 28—Bluetooth survey app. The illustration shows the Bluetooth server running on the tablet (left) and a client running on the phone (right). The server determines which question is displayed on the client screens by pressing the arrow pointing to the right (next question) and left (previous question). Both server and client receive real-time feedback on how the question was answered.

Our approach is as follows. We'll write a sketch that we'll load onto every device participating in the survey. This way we can distribute the app without making adjustments for each individual device. The app needs to figure out whether it serves as the Bluetooth server for the other devices or connects as a client. As participants, we then send different messages to the other devices using OSC (Section 6.3, *Using the Open Sound Control Networking Format*, on page 129), for example, to request the current question, to submit an answer, or to get an update on the statistics. We'll give each OSC message a dedicated label, which we can then use to determine what to do when an OSC event occurs. When we receive an OSC message, we check its label using checkAddr-Pattern(), and depending on what pattern we detect, we can respond accordingly.

Program the BluetoothSurvey Main Tab

Let's take a look at our main tab, which contains the following methods: setup(), draw(), onBluetoothDataEvent(), getBluetoothInformation(), loadQuestions(), requestQuestions(), and findQuestion().

P2P/BluetoothSurvey/BluetoothSurvey.pde

```
import android.os.Bundle;
import android.content.Intent;

import ketai.net.bluetooth.*;
import ketai.ui.*;
import ketai.net.*;
import oscP5.*;

KetaiBluetooth bt;

KetaiList connectionList;
String info = "";
boolean isConfiguring = true;
String UIText;
color clientColor = color(112, 138, 144);
color serverColor = color(127);

boolean isServer = true;

ArrayList<Question> questions = new ArrayList<Question>();
ArrayList<String> devicesDiscovered = new ArrayList();
Question currentQuestion;
int currentStatID = 0;
Button previous, next;

void setup()
{
  orientation(PORTRAIT);
  background(78, 93, 75);
  stroke(255);
  textSize(24);
  rectMode(CORNER);
  previous = new Button("previous.png", 30, height/2);
  next = new Button("next.png", width-30, height/2);

  bt.start();
  if (isServer)
    loadQuestions();

  UIText =  "[m] - make this device discoverable\n" +
    "[d] - discover devices\n" +
    "[c] - connect to device from list\n" +
    "[p] - list paired devices\n" +
```

```
      "[i] - show Bluetooth info";

    KetaiKeyboard.show(this);
}

void draw()
{
  if (isConfiguring)
  {
    ArrayList<String> devices;

    if (isServer)
      background(serverColor);  //green for server
    else
      background(clientColor); //grey for clients

    if (key == 'i')
      info = getBluetoothInformation();
    else
    {
      if (key == 'p')
      {
        info = "Paired Devices:\n";
        devices = bt.getPairedDeviceNames();
      }
      else
      {
        info = "Discovered Devices:\n";
        devices = bt.getDiscoveredDeviceNames();
      }

      for (int i=0; i < devices.size(); i++)
      {
        info += "["+i+"] "+devices.get(i).toString() + "\n";
      }
    }
    text(UIText + "\n\n" + info, 5, 90);
  }
  else
  {
    if (questions.size() < 1)
      requestQuestions();

    if (questions.size() > 0 && currentQuestion == null)
      currentQuestion = questions.get(0);

    if (isServer)
      background(serverColor);
    else
      background(clientColor);
```

❸

```
      pushStyle();
      fill(255);
      stroke(255);
      ellipse(mouseX, mouseY, 20, 20);
      if (currentQuestion != null)
        currentQuestion.display(25, 100);
❹    //        text(currentQuestion.toString(), 75, 75);  //
      popStyle();
    }
    drawUI();
    broadcastStats();
  }

  void onBluetoothDataEvent(String who, byte[] data)
  {
    //   but allows construction by byte array
    KetaiOSCMessage m = new KetaiOSCMessage(data);
    if (m.isValid())
    {
      print(" addrpattern: "+m.addrPattern());

      //handle request for questions
❺    if (m.checkAddrPattern("/poll-request/"))
      {
        if (isServer)
        {
          int lastID =  m.get(0).intValue();

          for (int j = 0; j < questions.size(); j++)
          {
            Question q = questions.get(j);

            if (q.id <= lastID)
              continue;

❻          OscMessage msg = new OscMessage("/poll-question/");
            msg.add(q.id);
            msg.add(q.question);
            msg.add(q.answer1);
            msg.add(q.answer2);
            msg.add(q.answer3);
            bt.broadcast(msg.getBytes());
          }
        }
      }
❼    else if (m.checkAddrPattern("/poll-question/"))
      {
        if (isServer)
          return;
```

```
          //id, question, choice a, choice b, choice c
 (8)      if (m.checkTypetag("issss"))
          {
            int _id = m.get(0).intValue();
            println("processing question id: " + _id);

            //we already have this question...skip
            if (findQuestion(_id) != null)
              return;

 (9)        Question q = new Question(
            m.get(0).intValue(),
            m.get(1).stringValue(),
            m.get(2).stringValue(),
            m.get(3).stringValue(),
            m.get(4).stringValue());
            questions.add(q);
          }
        }
 (10)   else if (m.checkAddrPattern("/poll-answer/"))
        {
          if (!isServer)
            return;
          //question id + answer
 (11)     if (m.checkTypetag("ii"))
          {
            Question _q = findQuestion(m.get(0).intValue());
            if (_q != null)
            {
              println("got answer from " + who + " for question " +
                m.get(0).intValue() + ", answer: " + m.get(1).intValue());
 (12)         _q.processAnswerStat(m.get(1).intValue());
              OscMessage msg = new OscMessage("/poll-update/");
              println("sending poll update for question " + _q.id + "-" +
                _q.total1 + "," + _q.total2 + "," + _q.total3);
              msg.add(_q.id);
              msg.add(_q.total1);
              msg.add(_q.total2);
              msg.add(_q.total3);
              bt.broadcast(msg.getBytes());
            }
          }
        }
        //update answer stats
 (13)   else if (m.checkAddrPattern("/poll-update/") && !isServer)
        {
          //question id + 3 totals
 (14)     if (m.checkTypetag("iiii"))
          {
            int _id = m.get(0).intValue();
```

```
        Question _q = findQuestion(_id);
        if (_q != null)
        {
          println("got poll update for question " +
            _id + " vals " + m.get(1).intValue() + ", " +
            m.get(2).intValue() + "," + m.get(3).intValue());

          _q.updateStats(m.get(1).intValue(),
          m.get(2).intValue(),
          m.get(3).intValue());
        }
      }
    }
    else if (m.checkAddrPattern("/poll-current-question/") && !isServer)
    {
      int targetQuestionId =  m.get(0).intValue();
      Question q = findQuestion(targetQuestionId);
      if (q != null)
        currentQuestion = q;
    }
  }
}

String getBluetoothInformation()
{
  String btInfo = "BT Server Running: ";
  btInfo += bt.isStarted() + "\n";
  btInfo += "Device Discoverable: "+bt.isDiscoverable() + "\n";
  btInfo += "Is Poll Server: " + isServer + "\n";
  btInfo += "Question(s) Loaded: " + questions.size();
  btInfo += "\nConnected Devices: \n";

  ArrayList<String> devices = bt.getConnectedDeviceNames();
  for (String device: devices)
  {
    btInfo+= device+"\n";
  }
  return btInfo;
}

void loadQuestions()
{
  String[] lines;
  lines = loadStrings("questions.txt");

  if (lines != null)
  {
    for (int i = 0; i < lines.length; i++)
    {
      Question q = new Question(lines[i]);
```

```
        if (q.question.length() > 0)
        {
          q.id = i+1;
          questions.add(q);
        }
      }
    }
  }
}

void requestQuestions()
{
  //throttle request
  if (frameCount%30 == 0)
  {
    int lastID = 0;

    if (questions.size() > 0)
    {
      Question _q = questions.get(questions.size()-1);
      lastID = _q.id;
    }

    OscMessage m = new OscMessage("/poll-request/");
    m.add(lastID);
    bt.broadcast(m.getBytes());
  }
}

Question findQuestion(int _id)
{
  for (int i=0; i < questions.size(); i++)
  {
    Question q = questions.get(i);
    if (q.id == _id)
      return q;
  }
  return null;
}

void broadcastStats()
{
  if (!isServer)
    return;

  if (frameCount%60 == 0)
  {
    if ( currentStatID > 0 && currentStatID <= questions.size())
    {
      Question _q = findQuestion(currentStatID);
      if (_q != null)
```

```
      {
        println("sending poll update for question " + _q.id + "-" +
          _q.total1 + "," + _q.total2 + "," + _q.total3);
        OscMessage msg = new OscMessage("/poll-update/");
        msg.add(_q.id);
        msg.add(_q.total1);
        msg.add(_q.total2);
        msg.add(_q.total3);
        bt.broadcast(msg.getBytes());
        currentStatID++;
      }
    }
    else {
      if (questions.size() > 0)
        currentStatID = questions.get(0).id;
    }
    sendCurrentQuestionID();
  }
}
void sendCurrentQuestionID() {
  if (currentQuestion == null)
    return;
  OscMessage msg = new OscMessage("/poll-current-question/");
  msg.add(currentQuestion.id);
  bt.broadcast(msg.getBytes());
}
```

These are the main steps we need to take to implement the survey app.

❶ Create an ArrayList called questions, which we'll use to store objects of the custom Question class we'll write to store questions and corresponding answers.

❷ Store the current question in a variable, currentQuestion, which is presented on all devices simultaneously for the survey.

❸ Set the currentQuestion to the first question in the questions ArrayList.

❹ Present the currentQuestion on the screen as formatted output String, using our custom toString() method in the Question class.

❺ Check if the OSC message we receive via onBluetoothDataEvent() contains the label "poll-request."

❻ Create a new OscMessage msg with the label "poll-question" for each object in our questions ArrayList, add the question and answers stored in the Question object to the OSC message, and broadcast() the message to all connected users.

❼ Check if we received an OSC message labeled "poll-question."

❽ Check if the OSC message labeled "poll-question" contains an integer followed by four String values, if we are connected as a client.

❾ Create a new Question object based on the received integer and String data.

❿ Check if the received OSC message is labeled "poll-answer."

⓫ Check if the "poll-answer" message contains two integer values if we are the server app.

⓬ Find the corresponding question to the answer we've received and process the answer, adding to the tally of responses.

⓭ Check if the OSC message is labeled "poll-update."

⓮ Check if the OSC message labeled "poll-update" contains four integer values.

⓯ Update the poll statistic for the question we've received via OSC by updating the total number of responses for each answer.

⓰ Load the questions from the questions.txt flat file located in the data folder of the sketch using loadStrings() if we operate as the server.[22] loadStrings() loads each line of the text file as an item in the String array lines. If we are connected as a client, we receive the questions peer-to-peer from the server.

⓱ add() the Question object to the questions ArrayList.

⓲ Request question if we don't have any in our questions ArrayList. Retry every thirtieth frame, or once a second, at a default frameRate of 30 fps.

⓳ Find the corresponding question to the received answer ID in the questions ArrayList method.

⓴ When the custom method broadcastStats() is called and the device is serving as the Bluetooth server, send an update with all totals to all connected client devices using an OSC message labeled "poll-update."

Program the Question Tab

Let's now work on our questions and answers. We'll build a custom Processing class called Question that can take care of multiple questions and the corresponding answers for us.[23] To make the number of questions we can work with flexible, we've already set up an ArrayList for the questions variable. Each

---

22. http://processing.org/reference/loadStrings_.html
23. http://processing.org/reference/class.html

question comes with three possible answers, which belong to a specific question; that's why it's best we work with a custom class.

A *class* is a composite of data stored in variables and methods. If we use a custom class, we can keep the Q & A data together in one object that consists of the actual question, three answers, three totals, and the answer given by the individual participant. We can also write a couple of methods that help us keep track of the totals for each answer and return the statistic back to us for a text output.

Now let's take a look at the Question class, which gets its own tab in the sketch.

P2P/BluetoothSurvey/Question.pde

```
// Question Class

❶ class Question
   {
     int id=0;
     String question="";
     String answer1, answer2, answer3="";
     int total1, total2, total3 = 0;
     int myAnswer, correctAnswer;

❷   Question(String _row)
     {
❸     String[] parts = split(_row, '\t');
       if (parts.length == 4)
       {
         question = parts[0];
         answer1 = parts[1];
         answer2 = parts[2];
         answer3 = parts[3];
       }
     }

❹   Question(int _id, String q, String a1, String a2, String a3)
     {
       id = _id;
       question = q;
       answer1 = a1;
       answer2 = a2;
       answer3 = a3;
     }

❺   void updateStats(int s1, int s2, int s3)
     {
       total1 = s1;
       total2 = s2;
```

```
      total3 = s3;
   }
⑥  void processAnswerStat(int _answer)
   {
     if (_answer == 1)
       total1++;
     else if (_answer == 2)
       total2++;
     else if (_answer == 3)
       total3++;
   }

   void setAnswer(int _answer)
   {
     myAnswer = _answer;
     processAnswerStat(_answer);
   }

⑦  float getAnswerStat(int _answer)
   {
     if (_answer == 1)
       return total1;
     else if (_answer == 2)
       return total2;
     else if (_answer == 3)
       return total3;
     return 0;
   }

⑧  void saveResults()
   {
     String line = question + "\t" +
       answer1 + "\t" + total1 + "\t";
     line += answer2 + "\t" + total2 + "\t" +
       answer3 + "\t" + total3;
   }

   boolean isAnswered()
   {
     if (myAnswer == 0)
       return false;
     return true;
   }

⑨  void display(int x, int y)
   {
     pushStyle();
     pushMatrix();
     translate(x, y);
     if (myAnswer == 0  && !isServer)
```

```
  {
    text(id+") " + question + "\n\n" +
      "[1] " + answer1 + "\n" +
      "[2] " + answer2 + "\n" +
      "[3] " + answer3, 0, 0);
  }
  else
  {

    float total = total1+total2+total3;

    //avoid div by 0
    if (total == 0)
      total = 1;

    float lineheight = textAscent()+textDescent();
    lineheight = 20;
    text( id+") " + question, 0, 0);

    textAlign(LEFT, TOP);
    translate(0, lineheight*2);

    text(answer1 + " (" + nf((total1/total)*100, 2, 2) + " %) ", 0, 0);
    translate(0, lineheight*1.5);
    rect(0, 0, map((total1/total)*100, 0, 100, 0, width-150), lineheight-5);
    translate(0, lineheight*1.5);

    text(answer2 + " (" +nf( (total2/total)*100, 2, 2 ) + " %) ", 0, 0);
    translate(0, lineheight*1.5);
    rect(0, 0, map((total2/total)*100, 0, 100, 0, width-150), lineheight-5);
    translate(0, lineheight*1.5);


    text(answer3 + " (" +nf( (total3/total)*100, 2, 2) + " %) ", 0, 0);
    translate(0, lineheight*1.5);
    rect(0, 0, map((total3/total)*100, 0, 100, 0, width-150), lineheight-5);
    translate(0, lineheight*2.5);

    if (isServer)
      text("Number of Answers for this question: " + total, 0, 0);
  }
  popMatrix();
  popStyle();
  }
}
```

Let's take a closer look at the Question class variables and methods.

❶ Create a custom Processing class called Question. The class definition does not take parameters.

❷ Create the constructor for the Question class, taking one String parameter _row.

❸ Split the String, which contains one row of questions.txt. Use the tab character, \t, as a delimiter to split() the string.[24]

❹ Add a second constructor for Question, taking five parameters instead of a String like the first constructor does. Custom classes can be overloaded with multiple constructors to accommodate multiple types of parameters, here an integer for the ID, followed by a String for the question, followed by three String values for the answers.

❺ Update the totals for each answer when we receive an answer from a participant.

❻ Process the statistic for each answer (how many times each answer has been picked compared to the total number of answers).

❼ Get the statistic for each answer.

❽ Save each answer and its statistic.

❾ Return the String output presented on the screen. If no answer has been given yet on the device, show the question and the multiple choice answers; otherwise, show the statistics as well.

Now it's time modify the UI tab.

Program the UI Tab

We need to make few adjustments to the UI tab to modify it for our survey app based on the previous code on page 163. Most of it is redundant and otherwise called out.

P2P/BluetoothSurvey/UI.pde
```
// UI methods
void mousePressed() {
  if (mouseY <= 50 && mouseX > 0 && mouseX < width/3)
    KetaiKeyboard.toggle(this);
  else if (mouseY <= 50 && mouseX > width/3 && mouseX < 2*(width/3))
    isConfiguring=true;
  else if (mouseY <= 50 && mouseX >  2*(width/3) && mouseX < width &&
    bt.getConnectedDeviceNames().size() > 0)
  {
    if (isConfiguring) {
      background(127);
      isConfiguring=false;
```

---

24. http://processing.org/reference/split_.html

```
      }
    }

    if (bt.getConnectedDeviceNames().size() > 0)  {
      if (currentQuestion == null)
        return;
      if (previous.isPressed() && isServer) //previous question
      {
        if (findQuestion(currentQuestion.id-1) != null)
          currentQuestion = findQuestion(currentQuestion.id-1);
        sendCurrentQuestionID();
      }
      else if (next.isPressed()  && isServer) //next question
      {
        if (findQuestion(currentQuestion.id+1) != null)
          currentQuestion = findQuestion(currentQuestion.id+1);
        else
          requestQuestions();
        sendCurrentQuestionID();
      }
    }
  }

  void keyPressed() {
    if (!isConfiguring && !isServer) {
      if (currentQuestion != null && !currentQuestion.isAnswered())
        if (key == '1') {
          currentQuestion.setAnswer(1);
          OscMessage m = new OscMessage("/poll-answer/");
          m.add(currentQuestion.id);
          m.add(1);
          bt.broadcast(m.getBytes());
        }
        else if (key == '2') {
          currentQuestion.setAnswer(2);
          OscMessage m = new OscMessage("/poll-answer/");
          m.add(currentQuestion.id);
          m.add(2);
          bt.broadcast(m.getBytes());
        }
        else if (key == '3') {
          currentQuestion.setAnswer(3);
          OscMessage m = new OscMessage("/poll-answer/");
          m.add(currentQuestion.id);
          m.add(3);
          bt.broadcast(m.getBytes());
        }
    }
    else if (key =='c') {
      if (bt.getDiscoveredDeviceNames().size() > 0)
```

```
      connectionList = new KetaiList(this, bt.getDiscoveredDeviceNames());
    else if (bt.getPairedDeviceNames().size() > 0)
      connectionList = new KetaiList(this, bt.getPairedDeviceNames());
  }
  else if (key == 'd')
    bt.discoverDevices();
  else if (key == 'm')
    bt.makeDiscoverable();
}
```

Here are the changes we've made to the UI tab.

❶ Jump to the previous question by decrementing the ID for currentQuestion.

❷ Jump to the next question by incrementing the ID for currentQuestion.

❸ Send an OSC message called "poll-answer" if we press 1 on the keyboard. The message contains the current question ID followed by the answer 1.

❹ Send an OSC message called "poll-answer" if we press 2 that contains the current question ID followed by the answer 2.

❺ Send an OSC message called "poll-answer" if we press 3 that contains the current question ID followed by the answer 3.

Now it's time to test the app.

Run the App

Run the app on the Android device you've currently connected via USB. When the app is compiled, disconnect that device and run it on the other device. If you have a third (or fourth) device available, load the sketch onto as many Android devices as you'd like to test with.

Now follow the steps we took earlier in *Run the App*, on page 165, to connect two devices via Bluetooth for the remote cursor app.

Finally, press the Survey tab and answer your first question. Press the left and right arrows to move through the questions. Respond to the questions using the software keyboard and notice how the statistics change as you punch in 1, 2, and 3.

You've completed a survey app for multiple Bluetooth devices, where we've been diving deep into the peer-to-peer networking process. Although very ubiquitous, Bluetooth has its limitations in terms of transmission bandwidth and range.

Less ubiquitous than Bluetooth but more powerful in terms of bandwidth and range, is the emerging Wi-Fi Direct P2P networking standard. Let's take a look at the final networking standard we'll discuss in this chapter, which is also fairly easy to work with.

7.7 Working with Wi-Fi Direct

Wi-Fi Direct was introduced in Android 4.0 (API level 14) to enable Android devices to connect directly to each other via Wi-Fi without a fixed Wi-Fi access point. Each device in a Wi-Fi Direct network can serve as an access point for any of the other devices in the network. Like Bluetooth, Wi-Fi Direct allows us to discover Wi-Fi Direct devices and connect to them if confirmed by the user. Compared to Bluetooth, Wi-Fi Direct offers a faster connection across greater distances and is therefore the preferred networking protocol for multiplayer games or multiuser applications, when every connected device supports Wi-Fi Direct.

In many ways, Wi-Fi Direct is very familiar to us when it comes to allowing devices to connect to each other. We've also worked with Wi-Fi already and sent OSC messages over the wireless local area network in Chapter 6, *Networking Devices with Wi-Fi*, on page 127. When we use Wi-Fi Direct, we combine the P2P aspects and pairing process of Bluetooth with the ease of use of Wi-Fi.

Wi-Fi Direct is currently supported on a few of the newest Android devices, so the following section may describe operations that are not possible on your device just yet. But because it's a powerful standard, we'll discuss it now and compare it to Bluetooth's wireless peer-to-peer performance using our earlier remote cursor sketch code, on page 158.

Let's take a look at the KetaiWi-FiDirect class first,[25] which makes working with Android's Wi-Fi Direct features an easy task.[26] For this sketch, we'll work with the following KetaiWi-FiDirect methods:

connectToDevice()   Connects to a specific Wi-Fi Direct–enabled device

getConnectionInfo()   Gets the status of the Wi-Fi Direct connection

getIPAddress()   Gets the IP address of a specified Wi-Fi Direct device

getPeerNameList()   Returns the list of connected Wi-Fi Direct devices

Now, let's go ahead and implement the remote cursor app using Wi-Fi Direct.

7.8 Use Wi-Fi Direct to Control Remote Cursors

We've already implemented the remote cursors app earlier in this chapter in Section 7.5, *Connect Two Android Devices via Bluetooth*, on page 156. In order

---

25. http://ketai.googlecode.com/svn/trunk/ketai/reference/ketai/net/wifidirect/KetaiWiFiDirect.html

26. http://developer.android.com/guide/topics/wireless/wifip2p.html

to compare Wi-Fi Direct to Bluetooth, we'll implement the same remote cursor app, replacing its Bluetooth peer-to-peer networking functionality with Wi-Fi Direct. Large portions of the code are identical to the Bluetooth version of the sketch shown on page 158 and on page 163, so we will focus only on the code that we'll change from Bluetooth to Wi-Fi Direct.

Using Wi-Fi Direct, we'll be able to use the OSC protocol again to send data to remote devices, as we've already done in Section 6.4, *Network an Android with a Desktop PC*, on page 131.

Modify the Main Tab

P2P/WiFiDirectCursors/WiFiDirectCursors.pde

```
① import ketai.net.wifidirect.*;
  import ketai.net.*;
  import ketai.ui.*;
  import oscP5.*;
  import netP5.*;

② KetaiWiFiDirect direct;
  KetaiList connectionList;
  String info = "";
  PVector remoteCursor = new PVector();
  boolean isConfiguring = true;
  String UIText;

③ ArrayList<String> devices = new ArrayList();
④ OscP5 oscP5;
⑤ String clientIP = "";

  void setup()
  {
    orientation(PORTRAIT);
    background(78, 93, 75);
    stroke(255);
    textSize(24);

⑥   direct = new KetaiWiFiDirect(this);

    UIText =  "[d] - discover devices\n" +
      "[c] - pick device to connect to\n" +
      "[p] - list connected devices\n" +
      "[i] - show WiFi Direct info\n" +
⑦     "[o] - start OSC Server\n";
  }

  void draw()
  {
    background(78, 93, 75);
```

```
    if (isConfiguring) {
      info="";
      if (key == 'i')
❽       info = getNetInformation();
      else if (key == 'd') {
        info = "Discovered Devices:\n";
❾       devices = direct.getPeerNameList();
        for (int i=0; i < devices.size(); i++)
        {
          info += "["+i+"] "+devices.get(i).toString() + "\t\t"+devices.size()+"\n";
        }
      }
      else if (key == 'p')  {
        info += "Peers: \n";
      }
      text(UIText + "\n\n" + info, 5, 90);
    }
    else {
      pushStyle();
      noStroke();
      fill(255);
      ellipse(mouseX, mouseY, 20, 20);
      fill(255, 0, 0);
      ellipse(remoteCursor.x, remoteCursor.y, 20, 20);
      popStyle();
    }
    drawUI();
  }

  void mouseDragged() {
    if (isConfiguring)
      return;

    OscMessage m = new OscMessage("/remoteCursor/");
    m.add(pmouseX);
    m.add(pmouseY);

    if (oscP5 != null) {
      NetAddress myRemoteLocation = null;

      if (clientIP != "")
        myRemoteLocation = new NetAddress(clientIP, 12000);
      else if (direct.getIPAddress() != KetaiNet.getIP())
        myRemoteLocation = new NetAddress(direct.getIPAddress(), 12000);

      if (myRemoteLocation != null)
        oscP5.send(m, myRemoteLocation);
    }
  }
```

```
    void oscEvent(OscMessage m) {
⑩    if (direct.getIPAddress() != m.netAddress().address())
⑪      clientIP = m.netAddress().address();
      if (m.checkAddrPattern("/remoteCursor/")) {
        if (m.checkTypetag("ii")) {
          remoteCursor.x = m.get(0).intValue();
          remoteCursor.y = m.get(1).intValue();
        }
      }
    }
⑫ String getNetInformation()
    {
      String Info = "Server Running: ";
      Info += "\n my IP: " + KetaiNet.getIP();
      Info += "\n initiator's IP:  " + direct.getIPAddress();
      return Info;
    }
```

Let's take a look at the steps we took to change our remote cursor app to use Wi-Fi Direct.

❶ Import the Ketai library's Wi-Fi Direct package.

❷ Create a variable direct of the type KetaiWiFiDirect.

❸ Create an ArrayList for discovered Wi-Fi Direct devices.

❹ Create a OscP5-type variable, oscP5, as we've used already in Chapter 6, *Networking Devices with Wi-Fi*, on page 127.

❺ Create a String variable to hold the client IP address.

❻ Create the WiFiDirect object, direct.

❼ Include a keyboard menu item o to start the OSC server

❽ Get the Wi-Fi Direct network information.

❾ Get the list of connected Wi-Fi Direct peer devices.

❿ Check if the Wi-Fi Direct server IP address is different from our device IP, which means we are connecting as a client.

⑪ Set the clientIP variable to the device IP address, since we've determined we are connecting as a client to the Wi-Fi Direct network.

⑫ Get the Wi-Fi Direct information, including our IP address and the server's IP address.

For the UI, we won't change very much compared to the previous UI code, on page 163. Let's take a look.

Modify the UI Tab

Now it's time to see what's needed to modify the UI tab to support Wi-Fi direct. We'll need to adjust the discover key (d) to call the Wi-Fi Direct discover() method and the info key (i) to get the Wi-Fi Direct connection info using getConnection-Info(). Also, we need to introduce an OSC key (o) to the menu, allowing us to start OSC networking now over Wi-Fi Direct.

```
P2P/WiFiDirectCursors/UI.pde
// UI methods
void mousePressed() {
  //keyboard button -- toggle virtual keyboard
  if (mouseY <= 50 && mouseX > 0 && mouseX < width/3)
    KetaiKeyboard.toggle(this);
  else if (mouseY <= 50 && mouseX > width/3 && mouseX < 2*(width/3)) //config button
  {
    isConfiguring=true;
  }
  else if (mouseY <= 50 && mouseX >  2*(width/3) && mouseX < width) { // draw button
    if (isConfiguring) {
      isConfiguring=false;
    }
  }
}
void keyPressed() {
  if (key == 'c') {
    if (devices.size() > 0)
      connectionList = new KetaiList(this, devices);
  }
  else if (key == 'd') {
❶    direct.discover();
     println("device list contains "  + devices.size() + " elements");
  }
  else if (key == 'i')
❷    direct.getConnectionInfo();
  else if (key == 'o') {
    if (direct.getIPAddress().length() > 0)
❸      oscP5 = new OscP5(this, 12000);
  }
}
```

Now let's see what we adjusted for the UI tab of the Wi-Fi Direct remote cursor sketch.

❶ Discover Wi-Fi Direct devices if we press d on the keyboard.

❷ Get the Wi-Fi Direct information.

❸ Initialize the OSC connection on port 1200.

Everything looks quite familiar from the Bluetooth version of this sketch. The difference is that we are connecting and sending OSC messages like we've done in Chapter 6, *Networking Devices with Wi-Fi*, on page 127.

Now let's test the app.

Run the App

Run the app on your Wi-Fi Direct–enabled Android device. Disconnect the USB cable, and run the app on your second Wi-Fi Direct device. Press d on the keyboard to discover Wi-Fi Direct devices. Then press c to show the list of discovered devices and pick your second device. You need to allow the Wi-Fi Direct connection request. Once you do, press the Interact tab on both devices and move your finger across the screen. Notice how quickly both cursors respond; there seems to be no noticeable delay, and the motion is continuous at a high frame rate.

Compare the performance of the Wi-Fi Direct remote cursor app to the Bluetooth remote cursor app we've installed earlier. You can observe that Wi-Fi Direct performs better. Now grab a friend and put the connection range to the test for both flavors of the remote cursor sketch and see which one has the better range.

This concludes our explorations in the world of peer-to-peer networking. Now you are independent of networking infrastructure and ready to program your multiuser and multiplayer apps for users within close proximity.

7.9 Wrapping Up

We've learned that we don't need Wi-Fi/3G/4G infrastructure to interact with other Android users. We can write a range of apps that use peer-to-peer principles. We've learned about Bluetooth discovery, pairing, connecting, and exchanging data. We've learned that Wi-Fi Direct uses a similar discovery process as Bluetooth but it provides more bandwidth and greater connection distances.

With a range of networking projects under our belt, it's time now to move on to another emerging standard, near field communication, or NFC, which allows us not only to interact with other NFC-enabled Android devices but also with NFC tags embedded in stickers, posters, objects, or point-of-sale payment systems.

CHAPTER 8

Using Near Field Communication (NFC)

Now that we've learned how to create peer-to-peer networks using Bluetooth and Wi-Fi Direct, it's time for us to dive into a more user-friendly method for connecting Android devices and sharing data. *Near field communication* (NFC) is an emerging short-range wireless technology designed for zero-click transactions and small data payloads. In a zero-click transaction between Android devices, you simply touch them back-to-back—that's it. For instance, we can invite a friend to join a multiplayer game or exchange contact information simply by touching our devices.

Using NFC, we can also exchange images, apps, and other data between devices without first pairing them—a feature that Google calls *Android Beam*. Beam is Android's trademark for NFC when the protocol is used for device-to-device communication. It was introduced with the release of Ice Cream Sandwich and is now a standard feature with all new Android devices. Google began promoting Beam with the release of Jelly Bean. When two unlocked Android devices facing back-to-back are brought near each other, Beam pauses the app that is currently running in the foreground and waits for us to confirm the NFC connection by tapping the screen. We'll use Android Beam's NFC features for the peer-to-peer networking app we'll write in this chapter.

With a maximum range of about four centimeters—slightly less than the length of a AA battery—NFC's reach is limited when compared to that of Bluetooth or Wi-Fi Direct, providing a first level of security. One shortcoming of the technology is that it's fairly slow and not designed for large data payloads. We can use it, however, to initiate a higher-bandwidth connection, for instance via Bluetooth, which we'll do later in this chapter.

Because NFC is quick and user-friendly, it promises to revolutionize the point-of-sale (POS) industry, which has been monetized by services such as Google

Wallet and other merchandise services promoting NFC.[1] For example, we can pay for a purchase at a MasterCard PayPass or Visa payWave terminal or read an NFC tag embedded in a product. Most Android smart phones shipped in the US today, and some tablets like the Nexus 7, come with NFC built in.

In addition to simplifying device interaction, NFC also promises to bridge the worlds of bits and atoms seamlessly, enabling us to interact with physical objects that have NFC chips embedded in them, also known as *tags*. Tags are RFID chips that contain NFC-formatted data. They can be mass produced for less than a dollar each and can store a small amount of data, often in the form of a URL that points to a website with more information.[2] Most tags are read-only, some can be written to, and some can even be programmed.

In this chapter, we'll first use NFC to initiate a P2P connection between two Android devices by simply touching them back-to-back. Then we'll use that connection to send an increasingly detailed camera preview from one device to another, introducing us also to recursion as a programming concept. At the end of this chapter we'll be writing apps to read and write NFC tags. If you don't have an NFC tag at hand, you can get them at your local (online) store.

Let's take a closer look at the NFC standard first.

8.1 Introducing NFC

Near field communication can be used to exchange data between any pair of NFC equipped devices. When we develop peer-to-peer apps for mobile devices, zero-click interaction via NFC is the key to effortless networking via Bluetooth or Wi-Fi Direct. Support for NFC was first added to Android in 2011 with the release of Ice Cream Sandwich,[3] and although the technology is not yet ubiquitous, most Android phones and some tablets sold in the US today ship with it.

With NFC, we don't need to make a device discoverable, compare passcodes, or explicitly pair it with another because we establish the NFC network simply by touching one device to another. Only the deliberate back-to-back touch of two devices will trigger an NFC event. Simply walking by a payment reader or getting close to another device on a crowded bus is not sufficient. Front-to-front contact between devices won't do the trick either. Only when both devices are within four centimeters of each other will a connection result.

---

1. http://www.google.com/wallet/
2. http://en.wikipedia.org/wiki/Uniform_resource_identifier
3. http://developer.android.com/guide/topics/nfc/index.html

NFC is high frequency (HF) RFID technology operating at 13.56 MHz.[4] It's a subset of RFID, but near field communication overcomes many of the security and privacy concerns that businesses and individuals have expressed about the use of RFID,[5] which was reflected in the RFID mandates implemented in 2005 by Walmart and the United States Department of Defense for their global supply chains.[6] RFID does not have a range limitation, but NFC does.

NFC tags are passive devices and don't require batteries. They get their power through *induction* from a powered NFC device such as an Android phone or tablet. Induction occurs when a conductor passes through a magnetic field, generating electric current. If an NFC tag (conductor) comes close to the magnetic coil embedded in a powered NFC device (magnetic field), an electric current is induced in the tag, reflecting radio waves back to the NFC device (data). Because the tags lack power and only reflect the radio waves emitted by an NFC device, they are also referred to as *passive* tags.

NFC tags come in different shapes and sizes and are roughly between the size of a quarter and a business card, as shown here:

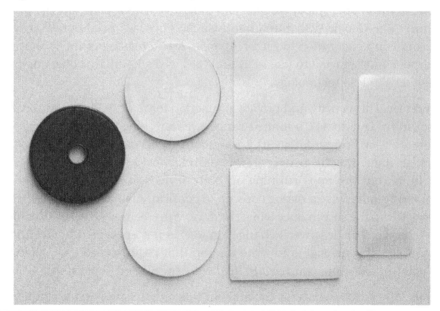

Figure 29—NFC tags. Different types of tags with different form factors: (from left to right) a heat resistant token, round and square stickers, and a machine washable tag

---

4.   http://en.wikipedia.org/wiki/Rfid
5.   http://en.wikipedia.org/wiki/Radio-frequency_identification#Privacy
6.   http://www.rfidjournal.com/article/articleview/607/1/1/

NFC tags carry small amounts of data, typically between 40 bytes or characters and 1 kilobyte. Because of this limited amount of usable memory, tags are commonly used to store a URL that points to more information online.

Android devices respond to HF RFID tags because they are using the same radio frequency that NFC uses. For example, when you touch your biometric passport, the RFID tag inside the book from your library, the tag from your last marathon attached to your shoe, or a tagged high-end product or piece of clothing, your Android signals with a beep that it has encountered a tag. This doesn't mean that we can successfully decipher such an RFID tag. The information stored on your ID card, passport, PayPass, or payWave card is encrypted. What's more, RFID tags embedded in products typically store inventory IDs that don't comply with the NFC specification,[7] which means we can't decipher the tag.

However, it is possible for our NFC-enabled Android phone or tablet to emulate an HF RFID tag, which is the reason we can use the Android to pay at a Pay-Pass or payWave terminal. Because the PayPass and payWave tag content is proprietary and encrypted, we also can't simply write a point-of-sale app of our own—like Google Wallet and bank-issued apps, we need to comply with the proprietary encryption to get a response. An increasing number of transit authorities have started to use RFID and NFC as well and are collecting fares using this wireless technology.

The first level of security and privacy protection for near field communication is proximity. Due to NFC's limited range, we don't need to make our device discoverable or browse for nearby Bluetooth devices. When we use NFC to exchange data directly between two Android devices, the second level of security is that the apps running on both devices must be running in the foreground—otherwise a dialog pops up to confirm. Also, when we use Beam, we need to tap the screen once while the devices are near each other to confirm the exchange. The data we exchange via NFC is not encrypted by default on the Android. If your goal is to write an app that requires security, like your own point-of-sale app, you need to deal with encryption separately.

We'll use the KetaiNFC class for the apps in this chapter, making it simpler for us to work with Android's NFC package. Let's take a look at the KetaiNFC class next.

---

7.   http://www.nfc-forum.org/aboutnfc/interop/

8.2 Working with the KetaiNFC Class and NDEF Messages

KetaiNFC allows us to easily access the NFC methods of Android's nfc package from within a Processing sketch.[8] It allows us to receive NFC events and read and write tags in the NFC Data Exchange Format (NDEF), the official specification defined by the NFC Forum.[9] Android implements this data format with the Ndef class, which provides methods for us to read and write NdefMessage data on NFC tags. An NdefMessage can contain binary data (NdefMessage(byte[])) or NdefRecord objects (NdefMessage(NdefRecord[]).[10] An NdefRecord object contains either MIME-type media, a URI, or a custom application payload.[11] NdefMessage is the container for one or more NdefRecord objects.

We'll use the KetaiNFC class to write NDEF data. Depending on the data type provided to write(), it will create the corresponding NdefMessage for us accordingly. For the projects in this chapter, we'll use the following NFC methods:

write()[12] A Ketai library method to write a text String, URI, or byte[] array—depending on the datatype provided to write() as a parameter, it sends an NFC message formatted in that datatype.

onNFCEvent() An event method returning NDEF data of different types, such as a text String or byte array—depending on the datatype returned, onNFCEvent() can be used to respond differently depending on the NDEF message returned.

Let's get started by creating a peer-to-peer connection using NFC.

8.3 Share a Camera Preview Using NFC and Bluetooth

The idea of this project is to allow two or more individuals to quickly join a peer-to-peer network using NFC and Bluetooth. NFC is a good choice because it reduces the number of steps users must complete to create a network. We'll take advantage of the user-friendly NFC method to pair devices and rely on the NFC-initiated higher-bandwidth Bluetooth network to handle the heavy lifting.

Our sketch will use a recursive program to send an increasingly accurate live camera image from one Android device to another. Once we've paired the two devices via NFC, we'll begin with a camera preview that consists of only one

---

8. http://developer.android.com/reference/android/nfc/package-summary.html

9. http://www.nfc-forum.org/specs/spec_list/

10. http://developer.android.com/reference/android/nfc/NdefMessage.html

11. http://developer.android.com/reference/android/nfc/NdefRecord.html

12. http://ketai.googlecode.com/svn/trunk/ketai/reference/ketai/net/nfc/KetaiNFC.html#write(java.lang.String)

large "pixel," which we'll draw as a rectangle in our program. Each time we tap the screen on the remote device, we will increase the resolution of the transmitted camera preview by splitting each pixel of the current image into four elements, as illustrated in Figure 30, *Broadcast pixels using NFC and Bluetooth*. In the next level, each of those pixels is split again into four, and so on—exponentially increasing the preview resolution until the image becomes recognizable. The color is taken from the corresponding pixel of the camera preview pixel located exactly in the area's center.

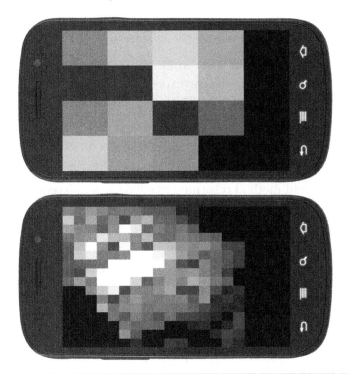

Figure 30—Broadcast pixels using NFC and Bluetooth. Touching NFC devices back-to-back initiates the Bluetooth connection, starting a two-directional pixel broadcast. The camera preview is then sent from one device to the other and displayed there. The top image shows the sampled camera image after two taps, the bottom image after four.

When we run the app on the networked Androids, we will get a sense of how much data we can send via Bluetooth and at what frame rate. We'll revisit concepts from previous chapters where we worked with a live camera preview, Chapter 5, *Using Android Cameras*, on page 93, and sent Bluetooth messages, Chapter 7, *Peer-to-Peer Networking Using Bluetooth and Wi-Fi Direct*, on page 151, now using NFC to initiate the network.

Generate a Low-Resolution Preview

Let's go ahead and work on the main tab of our sketch, where we'll put our camera code, and write a function to generate images of the camera preview at higher and higher resolutions. The program works by repeatedly calling itself, a technique known to programmers as *recursion*.[13] This technique allows us to iterate through the image until we reach a number of divisions that we'll set beforehand with a variable we'll name divisions. Setting a limit is important since the recursion would otherwise continue forever, eventually "freezing" the app. Let's name the recursive function interlace(). Each time it runs when we tap the screen, it will split each pixel in the current image into four new pixels.

The interlace() method we'll create works with the divisions parameter to control how many recursions will be executed. We'll start with a divisions value of 1, for one division. Each time we tap the screen, divisions will increase to 2, 3, and so on, which will also increase the level parameter in our interlace() method. There we are using level to check that it has a value greater than 1 before recursively calling the interlace() method again to split each pixel into four.

In the main tab we also import the Ketai camera package, which is familiar to us from Chapter 5, *Using Android Cameras*, on page 93. We'll create a KetaiCamera object that we'll name cam. The cam object will read the image each time we receive a new frame from the camera.

For this sketch, we'll use the following tabs to organize our code:

NFCBTTransmit Contains the main sketch, including our setup() and draw() methods, along with the interlace() method for recursively splitting the camera preview image. It also contains a mousePressed() method to increase the global variable divisions, used as a parameter for interlace(), and a keyPressed method that allows us to toggle the local camera preview on and off.

ActivityLifecycle Contains all the methods we need to start NFC and Bluetooth correctly within the activity life cycle. We require a call to onCreate() for launching Bluetooth, onNewIntent() to enable NFC, and onResume() to start both NFC and Bluetooth.

Bluetooth A tab for the two Bluetooth methods, send() and onBluetoothDataEvent(), to send Bluetooth messages and receive others in return.

---

13. http://en.wikipedia.org/wiki/Recursion_%28computer_science%29

NFC The tab that contains the setupNFC() method to create the NFC object we
     are working with and the onNFCEvent() method that launches the Bluetooth
     connection when we received the other device's Bluetooth ID via NFC.

We'll create each of those tabs step by step and present the code for each
component separately in the following sections.

Let's first take a look at our main tab.

NFC/NFCBTTransmit/NFCBTTransmit.pde

```
import android.content.Intent;
import android.app.PendingIntent;
import android.content.Intent;
import android.os.Bundle;

import ketai.net.*;
import oscP5.*;
import netP5.*;

import ketai.camera.*;
import ketai.net.bluetooth.*;
import ketai.net.nfc.*;

KetaiCamera cam;

❶ int divisions = 1;
   String tag="";

   void setup()
   {
     orientation(LANDSCAPE);
     noStroke();
     frameRate(10);
     background(0);
❷    rectMode(CENTER);
     bt.start();
     cam = new KetaiCamera(this, 640, 480, 15);
     ketaiNFC.beam("bt:"+bt.getAddress());
   }

   void draw()
   {
     if (cam.isStarted())
❸      interlace(cam.width/2, cam.height/2, cam.width/2, cam.height/2, divisions);

     if ((frameCount % 30) == 0)
       ketaiNFC.beam("bt:"+bt.getAddress());
   }

❹ void interlace(int x, int y, int w, int h, int level)
```

```
  {
    if (level == 1)
    {
⑤    color pixel = cam.get(x, y);
⑥    send((int)red(pixel), (int)green(pixel), (int)blue(pixel), x, y, w*2, h*2);
    }

    if (level > 1) {
⑦    level--;
⑧    interlace(x - w/2, y - h/2, w/2, h/2, level);
      interlace(x - w/2, y + h/2, w/2, h/2, level);
      interlace(x + w/2, y - h/2, w/2, h/2, level);
      interlace(x + w/2, y + h/2, w/2, h/2, level);
    }
  }

  void onCameraPreviewEvent()
  {
    cam.read();
  }

  void mousePressed()
  {
    if (!cam.isStarted())
      cam.start();

⑨  divisions++;
  }
```

Here are the steps we need to recursively process the live camera image.

❶ Set the initial number of divisions to 1, showing one fullscreen rectangle.

❷ Center the rectangle around the horizontal and vertical location where it is drawn, using rectMode().

❸ Call the recursive function with starting values for each parameter, starting in the center of the camera preview.

❹ Use the following parameters for interlace(): horizontal position x, vertical position y, rectangle width w, rectangle height h, and the number of divisions.

❺ Get the pixel color at the defined x and y location in the camera preview image from the pixel located in the exact center of each rectangular area we use for the low-resolution preview.

❻ Send the pixel data using our user-defined function send().

❼ Decrease the limit variable by 1 before recalling the recursive function. Decrease this variable and call the function only if the limit is greater than 1 to provide a limit.

❽ Call interlace() recursively from within itself using a new location and half the width and height of the previous call as parameters.

❾ Increment the number of divisions when tapping the screen.

Now that we are done with our coding for the camera and the recursive program to create a higher-and-higher resolution image preview, let's create the code we need to activate NFC and Bluetooth in the activity life cycle.

Enable NFC and Bluetooth in the Activity Life Cycle

To use NFC and Bluetooth, we need to take similar steps in the activity life cycle as we've done for our Bluetooth peer-to-peer app. In Section 7.4, *Working with the Android Activity Life Cycle*, on page 154, we looked at the callback methods called during an activity life cycle. For this project, we need tell Android that we'd like to activate both NFC and Bluetooth. Let's put the life-cycle code for the activity into an ActivityLifecycle tab.

At the very beginning of the life cycle, onCreate(), we'll launch KetaiBluetooth by initiating our KetaiBluetooth object, and we'll tell Android that we intend to use NFC. We do so using an *intent*,[14] which is a data structure to tell Android that an operation needs to be performed. For example, an intent can launch another activity or send a result to a component that declared interest in it. Functioning like a kind of glue between activities, an intent binds events between the code in different applications. We need an Intent to launch NFC.

When NFC becomes available because our activity is running in the foreground on top of the activity stack, we get notified via onNewIntent(), because we asked for such notification with our intent in onCreate(). This is where we tell Android that we use the result of the returned intent with our ketaiNFC object, launching NFC in our sketch. An activity is always paused before receiving a new intent, and onResume() is always called right after this method.

When Bluetooth is available as the result of the Bluetooth activity we launched onCreate() while instantiating KetaiBluetooth, the connection is handed to us via onActivityResult(), which we then assign to our bt object.

Finally, onResume(), we start our Bluetooth object bt and instantiate our NFC object ketaiNFC.

---

14. http://developer.android.com/reference/android/content/Intent.html

Let's take a look at the actual code for ActivityLifecycle.

NFC/NFCBTTransmit/ActivityLifecycle.pde

```
① void onCreate(Bundle savedInstanceState) {
     super.onCreate(savedInstanceState);
     bt = new KetaiBluetooth(this);
     ketaiNFC = new KetaiNFC(this);
     ketaiNFC.beam("bt:"+bt.getAddress());
   }

② void onNewIntent(Intent intent)
   {
    if (ketaiNFC != null)
        ketaiNFC.handleIntent(intent);
   }

③ void onActivityResult(int requestCode, int resultCode, Intent data)
   {
    bt.onActivityResult(requestCode, resultCode, data);
   }

④ void exit() {
     cam.stop();
   }

   //Stop BT when app is done...
⑤ void onDestroy()
   {
     super.onDestroy();
     bt.stop();
   }
```

We need these steps to initiate NFC and Bluetooth correctly within the activity life cycle.

❶ Instantiate the Bluetooth object bt to start a Bluetooth activity. Register the NFC intent when our activity is running by itself in the foreground using FLAG_ACTIVITY_SINGLE_TOP.

❷ Receive the NFC intent that we declared in onCreate(), and tell Android that ketaiNFC handles it.

❸ Receive the Bluetooth connection if it started properly when we initiated it in onCreate().

❹ Release the camera when another activity starts so it can use it.

❺ Stop Bluetooth and the camera when the activity stops.

All of this happens right at the beginning when our sketch starts up. The callback methods we are using require some getting used to. Because NFC and Bluetooth launch in separate treads or activities from our sketch—and not sequentially within our sketch—we need the callback methods to get notified when the Bluetooth activity and the NFC intent have finished with their individual tasks.

And because we depend on the successful delivery of the NFC payload for our Bluetooth connection, we need to use those callback methods and integrate them into the activity life cycle of our sketch. Processing and Ketai streamline many aspects of this programming process; when it comes to peer-to-peer networking between Android devices, we still need to deal with those essentials individually.

Now let's move on to the NFC tab, where we put the NFC classes and methods.

Add the NFC Code

We don't need much code to import NFC and make the KetaiNFC class available to the sketch. When we receive an NFC event using onNFCEvent(), we take the Bluetooth address that has been transferred as a text String and use it to connect to that device using connectDevice().

Let's take a look at the code.

NFC/NFCBTTransmit/NFC.pde
```
KetaiNFC ketaiNFC;

❶ void onNFCEvent(String s)
  {
    tag = s;
    println("Connecting via BT to " +s.replace("bt:", ""));
❷   bt.connectDevice(s.replace("bt:", ""));
  }
```

Here are the NFC steps we take.

❶ Receive the String from the NFC event using the onNFCEvent() callback method.

❷ Connect to the Bluetooth address we've received, removing the prefix "bt:" first.

Finally, let's take a look at the Bluetooth tab.

Add the Bluetooth Code

In the Bluetooth tab, we import the necessary Ketai Bluetooth and OSC package to send the Bluetooth messages. Let's use a custom function called send() to assemble the OSC message, sending out the color, location, and dimension of our pixel.

If we receive such a pixel from the networked Android via onBluetoothDataEvent(), we unpack the data contained in the OSC message and draw our pixel rectangle using a custom function, receive().

Let's take a look at the code.

NFC/NFCBTTransmit/Bluetooth.pde

```
PendingIntent mPendingIntent;
KetaiBluetooth bt;
OscP5 oscP5;

void send(int r, int g, int b, int x, int y, int w, int h)
{
❶  OscMessage m = new OscMessage("/remotePixel/");
   m.add(r);
   m.add(g);
   m.add(b);
   m.add(x);
   m.add(y);
   m.add(w);
   m.add(h);

❷  bt.broadcast(m.getBytes());
}

❸ void receive(int r, int g, int b, int x, int y, int w, int h)
{
   fill(r, g, b);
   rect(x, y, w, h);
}

void onBluetoothDataEvent(String who, byte[] data)
{
   KetaiOSCMessage m = new KetaiOSCMessage(data);
   if (m.isValid())
   {
     if (m.checkAddrPattern("/remotePixel/"))
     {
❹      if (m.checkTypetag("iiiiiii"))
       {
               receive(m.get(0).intValue(), m.get(1).intValue(),
               m.get(2).intValue(), m.get(3).intValue(),
               m.get(4).intValue(), m.get(5).intValue(), m.get(6).intValue());
       }
     }
   }
}
```

Here are the steps we take to send and receive OSC messages over Bluetooth.

❶ Add individual values to the OscMessage m.

❷ Send the byte data contained in the OSC message m via Bluetooth using broadcast().

❸ Receive individual values sent via OSC, and draw a rectangle in the size and color determined by the received values.

❹ Check if all seven integers in the OSC message are complete before using the values as parameters for the receive() method.

Now with our recursive program, camera, NFC, and Bluetooth code completed, it's time to test the app.

Run the App

Before we run the app, we need to set two permissions. Open the Permission Selector from the Sketch menu and select CAMERA and INTERNET.

Now browse to the sketch folder and open AndroidManifest.xml in your text editor, where you'll see that those permissions have been set. Add NFC permissions so the file looks something like this:

NFC/NFCBTTransmit/AndroidManifest.xml
```xml
<?xml version="1.0" encoding="UTF-8"?>
<manifest xmlns:android="http://schemas.android.com/apk/res/android"
android:versionCode="1" android:versionName="1.0" package="">
  <uses-sdk android:minSdkVersion="10"/>
  <application android:debuggable="true" android:icon="@drawable/icon"
  android:label="">
    <activity android:name="">
      <intent-filter>
        <action android:name="android.intent.action.MAIN"/>
        <category android:name="android.intent.category.LAUNCHER"/>
      </intent-filter>
    </activity>
  </application>

<uses-permission android:name="android.permission.BLUETOOTH"/>
  <uses-permission android:name="android.permission.BLUETOOTH_ADMIN"/>
  <uses-permission android:name="android.permission.CAMERA"/>
  <uses-permission android:name="android.permission.INTERNET"/>
  <uses-permission android:name="android.permission.NFC" />
</manifest>
```

Run the app on the device that is already connected to the PC via USB. When it launches, disconnect and run the app on your second Android device. Now it's time for the moment of truth—touch both devices back-to-back and confirm the P2P connection.

You should see a colored rectangle on each display, taken from the camera preview of the other device. If you move your camera slightly, you'll recognize that its color is based on a live feed. Tap each screen to increase the resolution and observe what happens on the other device, then tap again. Each new division requires more performance from the devices as the number of pixels we send and display increases exponentially.

Keep tapping and you will observe how the app slows as the size of the data payload increases.

Now that we've learned how to send a Bluetooth ID via NFC Beam technology to another device, let's move on to reading and writing NFC tags.

8.4 Read a URL from an NFC Tag

Moving on to the world of NFC tags, our sketches will get significantly shorter. Tags come in different shapes and sizes, as illustrated in Figure 29, *NFC tags*, on page 191, and they mostly store a few dozen characters, which is why most tags contain a URL pointing to a website. For this first app, we'll create a sketch that can read NFC tags.

Because we are dealing mostly with URLs, let's also include some Processing code that lets us open the link in the device browser. We'll check if it is a valid URL before we launch the browser. When we launch our sketch on the device, the app will wait for an NFC event to occur, which will be triggered when we touch the tag with the device. We'll also want to display the tag's content on the device, as shown in Figure 31, *Read an NFC tag*, on page 204.

Enable NFC

To get started, let's enable NFC using the now familiar activity lifecycle methods we used in the previous sketch. All the lifecycle code we need to enable NFC goes into our EnableNFC tab.

This tab is identical to *Enable NFC and Bluetooth in the Activity Life Cycle*, on page 198, with the exception that we don't have to start up Bluetooth as well. Let's take a look at the code.

NFC/NFCRead/EnableNFC.pde
```
PendingIntent mPendingIntent;

void onCreate(Bundle savedInstanceState) {
  ketaiNFC = new KetaiNFC(this);
  super.onCreate(savedInstanceState);
```

Figure 31—Read an NFC tag. When you approach the NFC tag with the Android device, it outputs the collected text/URL on the display. Tapping the screen will take you to the URL saved on the tag.

```
  mPendingIntent = PendingIntent.getActivity(this, 0, new Intent(this,
  getClass()).addFlags(Intent.FLAG_ACTIVITY_SINGLE_TOP), 0);
}

void onNewIntent(Intent intent) {
  if (ketaiNFC != null)
    ketaiNFC.handleIntent(intent);
}
```

Now let's move on to our main sketch, NFCRead.

Add the Main Tab

Now that we've set up everything so NFC can start up properly, let's take a look at the main tab, where we read the tag. When we receive an NFC event that includes a text String, we then use Processing methods to clean the String, check if it's a valid URL, and link to the browser. We use trim() to remove whitespace characters from the beginning and the end of the String.[15] Then we can use the resulting String directly with Processing's link() method, which opens the browser and shows the website stored on the tag. To check if it's a valid URL, we use the indexOf() method,[16] which tests if a substring is embedded in a string. If it is, it returns the index position of the substring, and if not, it returns -1.

---

15. http://processing.org/reference/trim_.html
16. http://processing.org/reference/String_indexOf_.html

Here is the code.

```
NFC/NFCRead/NFCRead.pde
import android.app.PendingIntent;
import android.content.Intent;
import android.os.Bundle;

import ketai.net.nfc.*;

String tagText = "";
KetaiNFC ketaiNFC;

void setup() {
  ketaiNFC = new KetaiNFC(this);
  orientation(LANDSCAPE);
  textSize(36);
  textAlign(CENTER, CENTER);
}

void draw() {
  background(78, 93, 75);
  text("Tag:\n"+ tagText, width/2, height/2);
}

void onNFCEvent(String txt) {
  tagText = trim(txt);
}

void mousePressed() {
  if (tagText.indexOf("http://") == 0)
    link(tagText);
}
```

❶ Specify how to display the content of the tag stored in tagText on the device display.

❷ Receive a String from the tag when the device touches it and an NFC event occurs.

❸ Assign a clean version of the String to tagText after removing whitespace characters from the beginning and end using trim().[17]

❹ Receive a String from the tag when the device touches it and an NFC event occurs.

❺ Jump to the link stored on the tag using link(). Follow the link in the device browser when tapping the screen, given there is text stored on the tag.

---

17. http://processing.org/reference/trim_.html

Before we run the sketch, we'll again need to make sure that we have the appropriate NFC permissions.

Set NFC Permissions

Because NFC permissions are not listed in Processing's Android Permissions Selector, where we usually make our permission selections (Section 4.4, *Setting Sketch Permissions*, on page 75), we need to modify AndroidManifest.xml directly to enable NFC. Processing typically takes care of creating this file for us when we run the sketch, based on the selection(s) we've made in the Permission Selector, and it re-creates the file every time we change our permission settings. Also, when we make no permission selections at all, Processing creates a basic manifest file inside our sketch folder.

Since we are already editing the Android manifest file manually, let's jump ahead and also add an intent filter that launches our app when a tag is discovered.[18] This way, NFCRead will start when the app is not yet running and resume when it is running in the background.

Let's take a look at the sketch folder and see if AndroidManifest.xml already exists inside it. Open the sketch folder by choosing Sketch → Show Sketch Folder. You should see two Processing source files in the folder for this sketch, one named EnableNFC and the other NFCRead.

Now to create a manifest, return to Processing and choose Android → Sketch Permissions from the menu. Although we won't find an NFC check box in there, it will still create an AndroidManifest.xml template for us that we can modify.

To modify the manifest, navigate to the sketch folder and open AndroidManifest.xml. Make your changes to the manifest so it looks like the following .xml code.

NFC/NFCRead/AndroidManifest.xml
```
<?xml version="1.0" encoding="utf-8"?>
<manifest xmlns:android="http://schemas.android.com/apk/res/android"
          package=""
          android:versionCode="1"
          android:versionName="1.0">
  <uses-sdk android:minSdkVersion="9" />
❶ <uses-permission android:name="android.permission.NFC" />
  <application android:label=""
                android:icon="@drawable/icon"
                android:debuggable="true">
    <activity android:name="">
        <intent-filter>
❷           <action android:name="android.nfc.action.TECH_DISCOVERED"/>
```

---

18. http://developer.android.com/guide/components/intents-filters.html

```
            </intent-filter>
            <intent-filter>
❸              <action android:name="android.nfc.action.NDEF_DISCOVERED"/>
            </intent-filter>
            <intent-filter>
❹              <action android:name="android.nfc.action.TAG_DISCOVERED"/>
              <category android:name="android.intent.category.DEFAULT"/>
            </intent-filter>
      </activity>
    </application>
  </manifest>
```

In the manifest .xml, we take the following steps.

❶ Set NFC permission.

❷ Have the app look for a tag.

❸ Make Android look for an NDEF tag.

❹ If an NDEF tag is discovered and the app is not already running in the foreground, make the activity the default.

Now that the appropriate NFC permissions are in place, let's run the app.

Run the App

Run the app on the device. When it starts up, our tagText String is empty. You can tap the screen but nothing happens, because we don't yet have a link to jump to.

Now approach your tag with the back of your device. A few centimeters before you touch the tag, you will hear a beep, which signals that an NFC event has occurred. The URL stored on the tag should now appear on your display (Figure 31, *Read an NFC tag*, on page 204). If you have another one, try the other tag and see if it has a different URL.

Now that you've successfully read NFC tags, it's time to learn how to write them as well, either to add your own URL or to change the NDEF message on there.

8.5 Write a URL to an NFC Tag

The NFC device built into the Android can also write to NFC tags. Most tags you get in a starter kit can be repeatedly rewritten. So if you'd like to produce a small series of NFC-enabled business cards, provide a quick way to share information at a fair booth, or create your own scavenger hunt with NFC stickers, you can write tags with your Android.

Let's build on our previous sketch and add a feature to do that. The app must still be able to read a tag to confirm that our content has been successfully written. To write tags, let's use the software keyboard to type the text we want to send as a String to the tag, as illustrated in Figure 32, *Read and write NFC tags*, on page 208. If we mistype, we need the backspace key to delete the last character in our String. Once we've completed the String, let's use the ENTER key to confirm and write() the tag. The transmission to write the actual tag is then completed when we touch the tag. Finally, when we come in contact with the tag again, we read its content.

Figure 32—Read and write NFC tags. Use the keyboard to input a URL and press Enter. The string will then be written to the tag on contact.

Let's introduce a variable called tagStatus to provide us with some onscreen feedback during this process. The sketch itself is structured identically to our previous example on page 205. We'll keep the EnableNFC tab and the permissions we set for AndroidManifest.xml.

Let's take a look at the main tab.

```
NFC/NFCWrite/NFCWrite.pde
import android.app.PendingIntent;
import android.content.Intent;
import android.os.Bundle;
import ketai.net.nfc.*;
import ketai.ui.*;

KetaiNFC ketaiNFC;

String tagText = "";
```

```
② String tagStatus = "Tap screen to start";

  void setup() {
    if (ketaiNFC == null)
      ketaiNFC = new KetaiNFC(this);
    orientation(LANDSCAPE);
    textAlign(CENTER, CENTER);
    textSize(36);
  }

  void draw() {
    background(78, 93, 75);
③   text(tagStatus + " \n" + tagText, 0, 50, width, height-100);
  }

  void onNFCEvent(String txt) {
    tagText = trim(txt);
    tagStatus = "Tag:";
  }

  void mousePressed() {
④   KetaiKeyboard.toggle(this);
    tagText = "";
    tagStatus = "Type tag text:";
⑤   textAlign(CENTER, TOP);
  }

  void keyPressed() {
⑥   if (key != CODED)
    {
      tagStatus = "Write URL, then press ENTER to transmit";
⑦     tagText += key;
    }
⑧   if (key == ENTER)
    {
⑨     ketaiNFC.write(tagText);
      tagStatus = "Touch tag to transmit:";
      KetaiKeyboard.toggle(this);
      textAlign(CENTER, CENTER);
    }
⑩   else if (keyCode == 67)
    {
⑪     tagText = tagText.substring(0, tagText.length()-1);
    }
  }
```

Let's take a look at the steps we need to take to write a tag.

❶ Import the Ketai user interface package to show and hide Android's software keyboard.

❷ Declare a variable tagStatus to give us feedback on the text input and writing status.

❸ Show the tag status and the current text input to write to the tag.

❹ Toggle the Android software keyboard to type the text String.

❺ Adjust the display layout to TOP-align vertically so we can accommodate the software keyboard.

❻ Check if the key press is CODED.

❼ Add the last character typed on the software keyboard to the tagText String.

❽ Check if the Enter key is pressed on the keyboard.[19]

❾ Prepare writing the content of the tagText variable to the tag on contact using write().

❿ Check if the coded backspace button 67 is pressed on the software keyboard to remove the last character in tagText.

⓫ Remove the last character in the tagText String using the String method substring() and length(). Determine the current length() of the String and return a substring() from the first character 0 to the next-to-last character.

Run the App

Run the app on the device and follow the instruction on the display. Start by tapping the screen, which will cause the software keyboard to appear. Type your text. If you mistype, you can correct it using the backspace button. When you are done, finish up by tapping the Enter key. Now the device is ready to write to the tag. Touch the tag with the back of the device, and if the sketch is operating properly, you should hear a beep, which indicates the device has found and written to the tag. Touch the tag again to read what's now on it. That's it!

Now that we've completed both reading and writing tags, we know how easy this kind of interaction is to do and we've got an idea of how useful it can be.

8.6   Wrapping Up

With all those different networking techniques under your belt, you've earned the networking badge of honor. Now you'll be able to choose the right networking method for your mobile projects. You already know how to share data

---

19. http://processing.org/reference/key.html

with a remote device and you've mastered peer-to-peer networking for those that are nearby. You've seen how near field communication can be used to initiate a peer-to-peer connection between two devices and to read NFC tags. Each of these highly relevant mobile concepts complement each other and can be combined—making for a whole lot of apps you can build.

Now that we've seen how to share all kinds of data between networked devices, it's time to take a closer look at the databases and formats we can use both locally and remotely.

Part IV

Working with Data

CHAPTER 9

Working with Data

Sooner or later, we'll need to be able to store and read data. To keep track of user choices and settings, we need to write data into a file or database stored on the Android device. We can't always rely on a carrier or network connection to read and write data from the Web or the Cloud, so we require a repository on the Android device; that way we can stop the app or reboot the phone without losing data and provide continuity between user sessions. Users expect mobile devices to seamlessly integrate into their daily routines and provide them with information that is relevant to their geographic and time-specific context. Entire books have been dedicated to each section in this chapter. As we create the chapter projects, we'll try our best to remain focused on the Android specifics when we are working with data and to explore only those formats and techniques you're most likely to use.

Processing has received a major upgrade to its data features, which were compiled into a comprehensive Table class. The Table class allows us to read, parse, manipulate, and write tabular data in different datatypes. With Processing 2.0, Ben Fry, one of its principal authors, has now integrated the methods and techniques from his seminal *Visualizing Data [Fry08]* into the Processing core, making it easier for us to visually explore data.

Using the Table class, we'll be visualizing tab- and comma-separated data in no time. We'll learn how to work with private and public data storage on the Android, keeping data accessible only for our app, and alternatively share it with other apps via Android's external storage. We'll read data from the internal and external storage and write data into tab-separated value files stored on the Android.

To demonstrate how sensors, stored data, and Processing techniques for displaying data can be combined, we'll create an app that acquires real-time earthquake data and displays the result. The app will read, store, and show all reported earthquakes worldwide during the last hour using the data access techniques you'll learn in this chapter and data collected by the US Environmental Protection Agency (EPA). For the project, we'll make use of the Location code introduced in Chapter 4, *Using Geolocation and Compass*, on page 69. In a second step, we'll refine the earthquake app to indicate when new earthquakes are reported using timed device vibrations.

In the following chapter of this two-part introduction to data, we'll work with SQLite, the popular relational database management system for local clients like the Android and used by many browsers and operating systems. It implements the popular Structured Query Language (SQL) syntax for database queries, which we can use to access data that we've stored locally on our device. We'll first get SQLite running with a simple sketch and learn how to use SQL queries to retrieve data from one or more tables, and then we'll use it to capture, store, browse, and visualize sensor values. These are the tools we'll need to write some more ambitious data-driven projects.

Let's first take a closer look at data, data storage, and databases.

9.1 Introducing Databases

To autocomplete the words that users type, guess a user's intent, or allow users to pick up where they have left off requires that our apps work with files and databases; there is simply no alternative. For example, when we pull up a bookmark, check a score, or restore prior user settings, we read data that we've written earlier into a local file or database. Data is essential for mobile apps because both time and location are ubiquitous dimensions when we use our Android devices, and it requires additional considerations when we develop, compared to desktop software. We expect our mobile apps to also be functional when cellular or Wi-Fi networks are unavailable. In such a scenario, apps typically rely on the data that has been saved in prior sessions, which typically get updated when a network becomes available.

Whether they are stored in tabular files or as object-oriented records, databases generally share one characteristic—structured data in the form of text and numbers, separated into distinct categories, or *fields*. The more specific the fields, the better the results and sorts the database can deliver. As we know, for example, dumping all of our receipts into one shoebox is not the kind of database structure an accountant or financial advisor would recommend: labeled files and folders are far more efficient and searchable.

Recommending which type of organization, or *data architecture*, is the best for a particular task goes beyond the scope of this book. It's the subject of numerous anthologies (such as *Visualizing Data [Fry08]*),[1] which do a great job of breaking down appropriate table relations, data types, and queries. We're going to limit the scope of our exploration to tab- and comma-separated values (TSV and CSV) because they are easy to use and very common, and we'll balance it with the more powerful SQLite data management system, providing us with more complex queries and the most widely deployed data management system out there.

The most common structural metaphor for representing a database is a table (or a couple of them). Known to us from spreadsheets, a table uses columns and rows as a data structure. Columns, also known as fields, provide the different categories for a table; rows contain entries in the form of numbers and text that always adhere to the structure provided by the columns.

Processing provides us with a Table class that lets us read, parse, manipulate, and write tabular data, which we'll be using throughout the chapter. It's a very useful class that is built into Processing's core and provides us with methods akin to what we'd expect from a database. However, it is used as an object stored in memory only until we explicitly write the contents to a file.

9.2 Working with the Table Class and the File System

Throughout this chapter, we'll work with Processing's Table class, and particularly with the following methods:

Table	A comprehensive Processing class to load, parse, and write data in different file formats—it provides similar methods that we'd find in a database.
getRowCount()	A Table method, which returns the number of rows or entries inside a table
getInt(), getLong(), getFloat(), getDou-ble(), getString()	A series of Table methods to retrieve the different value types from a specified row and column provided to the methods as two parameters separated by comma
addRow()	A Table method to add a new row to the table
writeTSV()	A Table method to write a .tsv file to a specified location in the file system, provided to the method as a parameter
Environment[2]	An Android class that provides access to environment variables such as directories

---

1. http://search.oreilly.com/?q=database
2. http://developer.android.com/reference/android/os/Environment.html

File[3]	A Java method to create a file path to a specified location in the file system
URL[4]	A Java class for a Uniform Resource Locator, a pointer to a resource on the Web
BufferedReader[5]	A Java class that reads text from a character-input stream and buffers them so we can read individual characters as complete text—we use it in this chapter to make sure we've received all the comma-separated values stored in our online data source.
InputStreamReader[6]	A Java class reading a bytes stream and decoding the data into text characters
sketchPath()	A Processing method returning the file path to the sketch in the file system—if we run our sketch on the Android device, it returns the path to the app's location within Android's file system.
KetaiVibrate()[7]	A Ketai class giving access to the built-in device vibration motor
vibrate()[8]	A KetaiVibrate method to control the built-in device vibration motor—this can be used without parameters for a simple vibration signal, a duration parameter in milliseconds, or an array of numbers that trigger a pattern of vibrations, vibrate(long[] pattern, int repeat).

Since we are writing to the device's file system in this chapter, let's take a look at the options we have.

9.3 Working with Android Storage

The Android device is equipped with the following storage types, which are available to our apps for saving data. We can keep our data private or expose it to other applications, as we've done deliberately in Section 5.5, *Snap and Save Pictures*, on page 104, to share images we took.

Internal Storage This is used to store private data on the device memory. On the Android, files we save are saved by default to internal storage and are

---

3. http://docs.oracle.com/javase/1.4.2/docs/api/java/io/File.html
4. http://docs.oracle.com/javase/6/docs/api/java/net/URL.html
5. http://docs.oracle.com/javase/1.4.2/docs/api/java/io/BufferedReader.html
6. http://docs.oracle.com/javase/1.4.2/docs/api/java/io/InputStreamReader.html
7. http://ketai.googlecode.com/svn/trunk/ketai/reference/ketai/ui/KetaiVibrate.html
8. http://ketai.googlecode.com/svn/trunk/ketai/reference/ketai/ui/KetaiVibrate.html

private, which means other applications cannot access the data. Because they are stored with our application, files saved to internal storage are removed when we uninstall an app. We'll use the internal storage in Section 9.6, *Save User Data in a TSV File*, on page 226.

External Storage All Android devices support a shared external storage that we can use to store files. The external storage can be a removable SD card or a nonremovable storage medium, depending on your Android device's make and model. If we save a file to external storage, other applications can read the file and users can modify or remove it in the USB mass storage mode when we connect the device to the desktop via USB. In 4.1 Jelly Bean or earlier versions of Android, we need to be careful when writing essential data there for the app to run, and we can't use it for any data we need to keep private. Since 4.2 Jelly Bean, Android provides a READ_EXTERNAL_STORAGE permission for protected read access to external storage. In the Settings menu on the Android device, a new developer option called Protect USB storage allows us to activate a read-access restriction and test this new permission option for protected read access to external storage.[9]

SQLite Databases SQLite support on the Android provides us with a simple database management tool for our local storage, both internal and external, which we'll explore in the next chapter, Chapter 10, *Using SQLite Databases*, on page 245.

Network Connections We've explored the possibility of working with a web server for stored data already in Section 4.9, *Find a Significant Other (Device)*, on page 86, which is an option for files that do not have to be readily available for our app to run. This is not a good option for user preferences, as we can't rely on a carrier or Wi-Fi network to reach the server.

Cloud Services Cloud services are becoming increasingly popular and are another option for extending the storage capabilities of Android devices. Google's Cloud platform,[10] for instance, provides SDKs to integrate the Cloud into your apps alongside a Google Cloud Messaging service to send a notification to your Android device if new data has been uploaded to the Cloud and is available for download.[11] Also, Google Drive provides an SDK to integrate Google's document and data storage service into our apps.[12]

---

9. http://developer.android.com/guide/topics/data/data-storage.html
10. http://cloud.google.com/try.html
11. http://developer.android.com/guide/google/gcm/
12. https://developers.google.com/drive/integrate-android-ui

We'll focus on Android's internal storage in this chapter. Let's get started and use the Table class now to read data from a tab-separated file.

9.4 Read a Tab-Separated Grocery List

Let's get started by working with a familiar list, a grocery list for our favorite pasta recipe, which we'll display on the device screen. Let's color-code the ingredients based on where we have to go to get them. We'll work with tab-separated values stored in a text file called groceries.txt, which is located in the data folder of our sketch. The file contains eleven items saved into individual rows, each row containing the amount, unit, item, and source for each ingredient on our list, separated by a tab character. The first row contains the labels for each column, which we'll keep for our reference but not display on the Android screen, as shown in Figure 33, *Reading groceries items from a tab-separated data file*, on page 220.

Figure 33—Reading groceries items from a tab-separated data file. The eleven items we need for this favorite pasta recipe are listed, color-coded by source (cyan for "market" and orange for "store").

To implement this sketch, we'll use Processing's Table class for loading and parsing the file's contents row by row. When we initialize our Table object in setup(), we provide a file path to our data as a parameter, and Table object will take care of loading the data contained in the file for us. The grocery items and amounts contained in the groceries.txt file each use one row for one entry, separated by a new line ("\n") character. A tab separates the amount from the volume unit, item description, and the source where we'd like to get it.

Let's look at the text file containing our grocery items, which are saved into individual rows and separated by tabs.

Data/DataReadGroceries/data/groceries.txt
```
amount  unit      item      source
1       pound     flour     store
6       pcs       eggs      market
0.5     tablespoon          salt      store
        some      cold water
2       pcs       onions    market
1       stick     butter    market
1/4     pound     Gruyere cheese    store
1/4     pound     Emmental cheese   store
1       bunch     chives    market
        taste     salt      store
        taste     pepper    store
```

Now let's take a look at our code.

Data/DataReadGroceries/DataReadGroceries.pde
```
Table groceries;

void setup()
{
①  groceries = new Table(this, "groceries.txt");
   textSize(24);
②  rectMode(CENTER);
③  textAlign(CENTER, CENTER);
   noStroke();
④  noLoop();
   background(0);
⑤  int count = groceries.getRowCount();

   for (int row = 1; row < count; row++) {
⑥    float rowHeight = height/count;
⑦    String amount = groceries.getString(row, 0);
⑧    String unit = groceries.getString(row, 1);
⑨    String item = groceries.getString(row, 2);

⑩    if (groceries.getString(row, 3).equals("store")) {
⑪      fill(color(255, 110, 50));
     }
```

```
      else if (groceries.getString(row, 3).equals("market")) {
        fill(color(50, 220, 255));
      }
      else {
        fill(127);
      }
⑫    rect(width/2, rowHeight/2, width, rowHeight);
      fill(255);
⑬    text(amount + " " + unit + " " + item, width/2, rowHeight/2);
⑭    translate(0, rowHeight);
    }
}
```

Here are the steps we take to read our text file and display the grocery list.

❶ Load groceries.tsv by providing the file name as a parameter to the Table object groceries.

❷ Set the rectangle drawing mode to CENTER so that the x and y location of the rectangle specifies the center of the rectangle instead of the default upper left corner.

❸ Center the text labels for our rows horizontally and vertically within our text area.

❹ Do not loop the sketch (by default it loops 60 times per second), because we are not updating the screen and do not interact with the touch screen interface. This optional statement saves us some CPU cycles and battery power; the sketch produces no different visual output if we don't use this statement.

❺ Count the number of rows contained in colors and store this number in count—used also to position the rectangles.

❻ Calculate the rowHeight of each color rectangle by dividing the display height by the number of rows in the file.

❼ Get the text string from column 0 that contains the amount using getString().

❽ Get the text string from column 1 that contains the measurement unit.

❾ Get the item description from column 2, unit.

❿ Check if the location stored in column 3 matches "store."

⑪ Check if the location stored in column 3 matches "market."

⑫ Draw a rectangle with the fill color c horizontally centered on the screen and vertically moved down by half a rowHeight.

⓭ Output the text label for each named color centered within the row rectangle.

⓮ Move downward by one rowHeight using translate().

Let's now move on to reading comma-separated values from a text file.

9.5 Read Comma-Separated Web Color Data

In the next sketch, we'll work with hexadecimal values of web colors and juxtapose them with their official name from the HTML web specification. Our data source contains comma (",") separated values (CSV), which we read from the file stored in the data directory of our sketch. The CSV file contains sixteen rows, each containing two values separated by a comma. The first value contains a String that is one of the named colors in the W3C's HTML color specification.[13] The second value contains a text String that represents the hexadecimal value (or "hex value," for short) of that named color. When we juxtapose a text description with its color in a list of individually labeled swatches, our sketch will display a screen like that shown in Figure 34, *Reading comma-separated color values*, on page 224. To distribute each swatch vertically, we use the translate() method we've implemented already in Section 4.8, *Find Your Way to a Destination*, on page 83.[14]

Hexadecimal is a numbering system with a base of 16. Each value is represented by symbols ranging 0..9 and A..F (0, 1, 2, 3, 4, 5, 6, 7, 8, 9, A, B, C, D, E, F)—sixteen symbols that each represent one hexadecimal value. Two hex values combined can represent decimal numbers up to 256 (16 times 16)—the same number we use to define colors in other Processing color modes such as RGB and HSB (see Section 2.2, *Using Colors*, on page 21).

In most programming languages, hexadecimal color values are typically identified by a hash tag (#) or the prefix 0x. The hex values stored in column 1 of our file contains a # prefix. We need to convert the text String representing the hex color in the first column into an actual hex value we can use as a parameter for our fill() method. For that, we use two Processing methods, substring() and unhex(),[15] to bring the hex value into the correct format, and then we convert the String representation of a hex number into its equivalent integer value *before* applying it to fill().

---

13. www.w3.org/MarkUp/Guide/Style

14. http://processing.org/reference/translate_.html

15. http://processing.org/reference/String_substring_.html and http://processing.org/reference/unhex_.html.

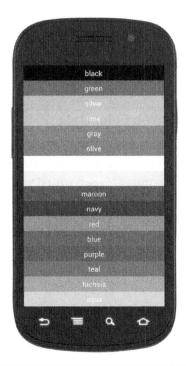

Figure 34—Reading comma-separated color values. Sixteen named colors from the HTML specification are stored in a .csv file and juxtaposed with their hexadecimal color value.

The substring() method allows us to remove the # prefix, and unhex() allows us to convert String into hex. The unhex() method expects a hexadecimal color specified by eight hex values, the first two (first and second) defining the alpha value or transparency; the next two (third and fourth), red; then the next two (fifth and sixth), green; and finally the last two values (seventh and eighth), the blue value of that color. When we read the color from the file, we'll prepend "FF" so we get fully opaque and saturated colors.

Let's first take a peek at the color data we copy into colors.csv.

Data/DataRead/data/colors.csv

```
black,#000000
green,#008000
silver,#C0C0C0
lime,#00FF00
gray,#808080
olive,#808000
white,#FFFFFF
yellow,#FFFF00
maroon,#800000
```

```
navy,#000080
red,#FF0000
blue,#0000FF
purple,#800080
teal,#008080
fuchsia,#FF00FF
aqua,#00FFFF
```

Open the file in your text editor and copy the file into your sketch's data folder. The file contents are fairly easy for us to grasp, as the file only contains two columns and sixteen rows. Our approach would be the same if we faced a .csv file containing fifty columns and one thousand rows. Note that there are no spaces after the commas separating the values, as this would translate into a whitespace contained in the value following the comma.

Now let's take a look at our Processing sketch.

Data/DataRead/DataRead.pde
```
Table colors;

void setup(){
❶  colors = new Table(this, "colors.csv");

   textSize(24);
   rectMode(CENTER);
   textAlign(CENTER, CENTER);
   noStroke();
   noLoop();
   int count = colors.getRowCount();

   for (int row = 0; row < count; row++) {
❷    color c =  unhex("FF"+colors.getString(row, 1).substring(1));
     float swatchHeight = height/count;
❸    fill(c);
     rect(width/2, swatchHeight/2, width, swatchHeight);
     fill(255);
     text(colors.getString(row, 0), width/2, swatchHeight/2);
     translate(0, swatchHeight);
   }
}
```

Here are the steps we take to load and parse the data.

❶ Load the text file containing colors as comma-separated values.

❷ Define a hex color from the String contained in column 1 after removing the # prefix using substring() and prepending "FF" for a fully opaque alpha channel.

❸ Set the fill() color for the color rectangle to the hex color we've retrieved from the text file.

Now that you know how it works, let's run the app.

Run the App

When our sketch runs, the colors.csv file will be included as a resource and installed with our app on the device. You'll see the sixteen named colors in HTML as individual swatches filling up the screen. Because we haven't locked orientation() in this sketch, the display will change its orientation depending on how we hold the device. We've implemented the position and alignment of the swatches in a variable manner based on the current display's width and height, so the sketch will scale to any orientation or display size on our Android phone or tablet.

Now that we know how to read data from a file, let's now move ahead and read and write tab-separated values.

9.6 Save User Data in a TSV File

In this project, we'll learn how to save user data. We'll implement a simple drawing sketch that allows us to place a sequence of points on the Android touch screen. When we press a key on the device, the resulting drawing doodle consisting of individual points is saved to the app folder on the Android device.

Using the menu button on the device as a trigger, we'll write each horizontal and vertical position x and y into a text file using tab-separated values. To keep track of how many points we've saved into our file, we'll output our row count on the display as well. If we pause or close the app and come back later, the points we've saved will be loaded into the sketch again, and we can continue where we left off. If we add to the drawing and press the menu button again, the new points will be appended to our data.tsv file and saved alongside our previous points.

We'll revisit the simple drawing concepts from Section 2.1, *Introducing the Android Touch Screen*, on page 18, and Section 6.5, *Share Real-Time Data*, on page 140, and use the mouseX and mouseY location of our fingertip to continuously draw points on the screen, as shown in Figure 35, *Write data to an Android*, on page 228. Using Java's File class, we'll also learn about Android storage and file paths, because we are creating a .tsv file inside our app. This file will only be available for our app and not be usable by other locations, keeping the data private.

In terms of working with data, we'll start this time from scratch. We won't be copying an existing data source into the sketch's data folder. Instead we'll create data via the touch screen interface and write it into a file located in our sketch folder. This time, we use tab-separated values and save the data into a data.tsv file.

There is no significant difference between the two delimiters.[16] Instead of a comma, TSV uses a tab (\t) to separate values. The most important thing to consider when choosing between the two formats is this: if you use comma-separated values, you cannot have entries that include a comma in a text string, and if you use tab-separated values, you cannot have entries that use tabs without changing the table structure and making it impossible to parse the file correctly.

You can modify CSV and TSV text files in any text editor, and your operating system might already open it up with your default spreadsheet software. I personally have an easier time deciphering tab-separated values because tabs lay out the columns in a more legible way, which is why I prefer TSV. The Table class can handle, read, and write either format equally well, so from a technical perspective, it really doesn't make much of difference how we store our data.

To implement this sketch, we'll revisit the handy PVector class we already used in Section 3.6, *Display Values from Multiple Sensors*, on page 49, to store value pairs in a vector. When we worked with an existing file earlier, we were certain that the .csv file exists. Now when we run the sketch for the first time, the data.tsv file we'll be using to store our data won't exist yet, and we'll need to create one using Processing's Table method writeCSV(). To check if data.tsv exists from a prior session, we'll use the try catch construct typically used in Java to catch exceptions that would cause our app to crash.[17] We use it in our sketch to check if data.tsv already exists within our app. If we are trying to load the file when it does not exist the first time around, we'll receive an exception, which we can use to create the file.

To draw, we'll use Processing's mouseDragged() method again, called every time we move our finger by one or more pixels while tapping the screen. This means that we will add new points to our table only when we move to a new position. The point count we display at the top of the screen will give us some feedback whenever we've added a new point to the list. To save the points to the Android's internal storage, press one of the device buttons.

---

16. http://www.w3.org/2009/sparql/docs/csv-tsv-results/results-csv-tsv.html
17. http://wiki.processing.org/w/Exceptions

Let's take a look at the sketch.

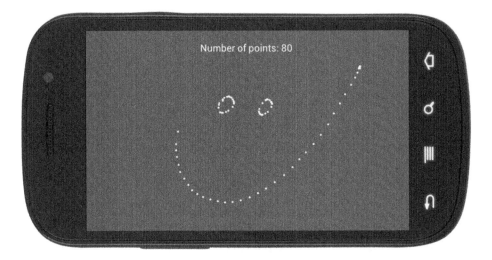

Figure 35—Write data to an Android. The illustration shows a total of eighty data points drawn on the touch screen, stored in the points PVector array, and saved to the Android storage in a file called data.tsv when we press a button.

Data/DataWrite/DataWrite.pde

```
① Table tsv;
② ArrayList<PVector> points = new ArrayList<PVector>();
  void setup()
  {
    orientation(LANDSCAPE);
    noStroke();
    textSize(24);
    textAlign(CENTER);
③   try {
④     tsv = new Table(new File(sketchPath("")+"data.tsv"));
    }
⑤   catch (Exception e) {
⑥     tsv = new Table();
    }
    for (int row = 1; row < tsv.getRowCount(); row++)
    {
⑦     points.add(new PVector(tsv.getInt(row, 0), tsv.getInt(row, 1), 0));
    }
  }

  void draw()
  {
    background(78, 93, 75);
```

```
    for (int i = 0; i < points.size(); i++)
    {
⑧    ellipse(points.get(i).x, points.get(i).y, 5, 5);
    }
    text("Number of points: " + points.size(), width/2, 50);
}

void mouseDragged()
{
⑨  points.add(new PVector(mouseX, mouseY));
    String[] data = {
⑩    Integer.toString(mouseX), Integer.toString(mouseY)
    };
⑪  tsv.addRow();
⑫  tsv.setRow(tsv.getRowCount()-1, data);
}

void keyPressed()
{
⑬  tsv.writeTSV(new File(sketchPath("")+"data.tsv"));
}
```

We take the following steps to create a new Table, add points to it, and save those points into a file.

❶ Create a new variable called tsv of type Table.

❷ Create a PVector ArrayList called points to store the *x* and *y* location of a finger-tip.

❸ Try reading the data.tsv file from the Android sketch folder, if it exists.

❹ Create the tsv Table object using a parameter. For the parameter, use Java's File class and Processing's sketchPath() for the file path, which the Table class will attempt to load—causing an exception that the file doesn't exist.

❺ Catch the java.io.FileNotFoundException, which you can see in the console if the data.tsv file doesn't exist at the defined location.

❻ Create a new tsv Table object without a parameter if it's the first time we run the sketch and the data.tsv file doesn't exist.

❼ Parse the tsv Table object row by row and add a new PVector to our points ArrayList for every record in our data.tsv file. Do nothing if getRowCount() returns 0.

❽ Parse the points ArrayList and draw a five-pixel-wide and -high ellipse() for each item using the PVector's x and y components for the *x* and *y* location.

⑨ Add a new PVector to the points ArrayList when a new mouseDragged() event is triggered.

⑩ Create a String array called data containing two String values using Java's toString() method to convert the mouseX and mouseY values into a text string.

⑪ Add a row to the Table object using the addRow() Table method.

⑫ Set the last row in the Table object to the String array data.

⑬ Using writeTSV(), write our tsv Table object to the data.tsv file inside our app at the sketchPath() location on the Android. Trigger the method using keyPressed(), which will detect if we press any menu button or key on the keyboard.

We won't need to give the sketch permission to access the Android's internal storage because we are writing to the memory allocated for our app. Let's run the code.

Run the App

When the app starts up, use your finger and doodle on the screen. It leaves behind a trace of points drawn sixty times per second. Each time, we set the point position using mouseX and mouseY and add the point to our PVector array, making the point count go up.

Press MENU to save all point coordinates to internal storage. Now let's test whether we've written our data successfully by closing and restarting our app.

Press the HOME key to go back to the home screen. Now press and hold the HOME button to open the recent app screen, showing DataWrite alongside other apps you've launched recently.

To close the DataWrite app or any app that's running, swipe the app icon horizontally left or right, and it will close. Let's reopen the DataWrite app now to see if our points are still there by navigating to the apps installed on the device using the Apps button.

Reopen the app. The sketch launches, showing all the previously saved points we've doodled. Great, you've built an app that stored data on the Android device.

Now that you've learned how to write data to the app using a specified location in internal storage, it's time to explore how to share data with other apps using Android's external storage.

9.7 Write Data to External Storage

Building on our previous code, on page 228, let's now make some modifications so we can write our data to the Android's external storage. This allows us to share files with other applications, as we've done when we worked with the camera and saved pictures to the external storage in Section 5.5, *Snap and Save Pictures*, on page 104. We can also copy our data to the desktop by mounting the device as USB mass storage.

The process of mounting the device as USB mass storage is inconsistent across devices and is manufacturer-specific. Some devices like the Nexus S offer to "Turn on USB storage" when you connect the device to the desktop via a USB cable. Other devices like the Galaxy S3 now require an app to launch the device as mass storage. Either way, Android devices typically offer such a feature, and we'll take a look at the data.tsv file once we've created it on the external storage.

To work with the file path to the external storage, we need to import Android's android.os.Environmentpackage,[18] which will give us access to the Environment class and its getExternalStorageDirectory() method, including the file path method getAbsolutePath(). We use both methods to create the path String for our sketch, writing to and reading from data.tsv on the external storage.

Let's take a look at the code snippet showing keyPressed(), where we only modify our file path for writing data.tsv to the external storage. The path for reading data.tsv is, and must be, identical.

```
Data/DataWriteExternal/DataWriteExternal.pde
void keyPressed()
{
  tsv.writeTSV(new File(
  Environment.getExternalStorageDirectory().getAbsolutePath() +
  "/data.tsv"));
}
```

❶ Use Android's Environment method getExternalStorageDirectory() to get the name of the external storage directory on the Android device, and use getAbsolutePath() to get the absolute path to that directory. Work with that path as a parameter for Java's File object, providing a File-type parameter for Processing's writeTSV() Table method, used to write the actual TSV file.

Let's test the app now.

---

18. http://developer.android.com/reference/android/os/Environment.html

Run the App

Before we can write to the external storage, we need to give the appropriate permission to do so in the Permissions Selector. Open the Android Permissions Selector, scroll to Write External Storage and check the permission box.

Now run the sketch on your device. It looks and behaves identically to the previous sketch shown in Figure 35, *Write data to an Android*, on page 228. Draw some points on the screen and save it by pressing any of the menu keys. The only difference here is that we save data.tsv now into the root of your Android's external storage directory.

Let's browse the external storage and look for our data.tsv file. Depending on your Android make and model, try unplugging the USB cable connecting your device and the desktop, and plug it back in. You should be prompted to "Turn on USB" storage. If this is the case, go ahead and confirm (on some devices, try browsing to Settings → "More..." on the Android and look for a USB mass storage option. Alternatively, look for the USB mass storage process recommended by your device manufacturer).

When you turn on USB storage, the device lets you know that some apps will stop; go ahead and OK that. Now move over to your desktop computer and browse to your USB mass storage medium, often called NO NAME if you haven't renamed it. Click on your mass storage device, and right there in the root folder, find a file called data.tsv.

Check data.tsv by opening it in your favorite text editor. You'll find two columns there neatly separated by a tab; in each row, you'll find a pair of integer values. This is perfectly sufficient for our project. More complex data projects typically require a unique identifier for each row, a row in one table to point to a specific record in another. We'll look into this when we are in Section 10.1, *Working with SQLite Databases*, on page 246, later in this chapter.

Now that we've learned how to use CSV and TSV data stored on the Android device, let's explore how to load comma-separated values from a source hosted online in the next project.

9.8 Visualize Real-Time Earthquake Data

Let's create an app to track earthquakes, putting our newly acquired data skills to work on a nifty data visualization project. The objective of the project is to visualize the location and magnitude of all of the earthquakes that have been reported worldwide during the last hour. We'll use live data hosted on the Environmental Protection Agency's website and visualize it as an animated map, shown in Figure 36, *Earthquakes reported worldwide during the last hour*, on page 234. The CSV data format that we'll work with again is typically available on governmental sites such as for the EPA or the US Census.[19]

When we take a look at the text data source containing comma-separated values, we can see the data structure shown below. The file linked here is a sample of the live online source, saved on July 24, 2012, which we'll use as a fallback in case we don't have an Internet connection. The first row contains the field labels.

```
Data/DataEarthquakes/data/eqs1hour_2012-07-24.txt
Src,Eqid,Version,Datetime,Lat,Lon,Magnitude,Depth,NST,Region
```

The actual data source we'll work with is hosted online:

http://earthquake.usgs.gov/earthquakes/catalogs/eqs1hour-M0.txt

Follow the link in your browser, and you'll see the current live CSV file consisting of comma-separated values. We won't need to use all of the fields in order to visualize the location and magnitude of each earthquake, but we will need Lat, Lon, and Magnitude.

To display the geographic location of each earthquake, we'll use an equirectangular projection world map,[20] which stretches the globe into a rectangular format. This allows us to translate the longitude and latitude values for each earthquake into an x and y location that we can display on our device screen. Such a projection maps the longitude meridians to regularly spaced vertical lines and maps latitudes to regularly spaced horizontal lines.[21] The constant intervals between parallel lines lets us overlay each earthquake's geolocation accurately in relation to the world map.

The map includes the complete range of longitude meridians from -180 to 180 degrees, but only a portion of the latitude degree spectrum—from -60 to 85 degrees instead of the usual -90 to 90 degrees. The poles are not included in the map, which are the most distorted portion of an equirectangular projection map. Because they are less populated and less frequently the source of earthquakes, they are also less relevant for our app, and we can use the map's pixel real estate for its more populated land masses.

To use our pixel real estate most effectively, we'll draw the world map full screen, covering the complete width and height of the Android screen and introducing some additional distortion to our data visualization due to the

---

19. http://www.census.gov/

20. http://commons.wikimedia.org/wiki/File:Timezones2008-GE.png

21. http://en.wikipedia.org/wiki/Equirectangular_projection

device's own aspect ratio. Because both the map and the location data scales depend on the display width and height, our information remains geographically accurate.

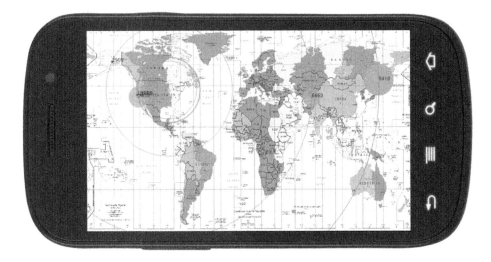

Figure 36—Earthquakes reported worldwide during the last hour. The device location is indicated by a green circle. Red circles indicate the locations of earthquakes reported within the hour—the size and pulse frequency indicate their magnitude.

Using a data file that is hosted online changes the way we load the file into Processing's Table class. Unlike our earlier examples, where we loaded the file from the Android's storage, we won't know ahead of time whether we can successfully connect to the file due to a very slow or an absent Internet connection, for instance. So we'll use the try catch construct we've seen in code, on page 228, again to attempt loading from the online source. If it fails, catch the exception and load a data sample stored in our sketch's data folder as a fallback.

Let's take a look at the code.

Data/DataEarthquakes/DataEarthquakes.pde

```
import ketai.sensors.*;

Table earthquakes, delta;

int count;
PImage world;
String src = "http://earthquake.usgs.gov/earthquakes/catalogs/eqs1hour-M0.txt";
```

```
   void setup()
   {
     location = new KetaiLocation(this);
     try {
②      earthquakes = new Table(this, src);
     }
     catch
       (Exception x) {
       println("Failed to open online stream reverting to local data");
③      earthquakes = new Table(this, "eqs1hour_2012-07-24.txt");
     }
     count = earthquakes.getRowCount();

     orientation(LANDSCAPE);
     world = loadImage("world.png");
   }

   void draw ()
   {
     background(127);
④    image(world, 0, 0, width, height);

     for (int row = 1; row < count; row++)
     {
⑤      float lon = earthquakes.getFloat(row, 5);
⑥      float lat = earthquakes.getFloat(row, 4);
⑦      float magnitude = earthquakes.getFloat(row, 6);
⑧      float x = map(lon, -180, 180, 0, width);
⑨      float y = map(lat, 85, -60, 0, height);
       noStroke();
       fill(0);
       ellipse(x, y, 5, 5);
⑩      float dimension = map(magnitude, 0, 10, 0, 100);
       float freq = map(millis()%(1000/magnitude),
⑪        0, 1000/magnitude, 0, magnitude*50);
⑫      fill(255, 127, 127, freq);
       ellipse(x, y, dimension, dimension);

       Location quake;
⑬      quake = new Location("quake");
       quake.setLongitude(lon);
       quake.setLatitude(lat);
⑭      int distance = int(location.getLocation().distanceTo(quake)/1609.34);
       noFill();
       stroke(150);
⑮      ellipse(myX, myY, dist(x, y, myX, myY)*2, dist(x, y, myX, myY)*2);
       fill(0);
⑯      text(distance, x, y);
     }
```

```
// Current Device location
noStroke();
float s = map(millis() % (100*accuracy/3.28), 0, 100*accuracy/3.28, 0, 127);
fill(127, 255, 127);
ellipse(myX, myY, 5, 5);
fill(127, 255, 127, 127-s);
ellipse(myX, myY, s, s);
println(accuracy);
}
```

Here are the steps we need to take to load and visualize the data.

❶ Define an src string containing the URL to the data source hosted online.

❷ Create a new Processing Table object called earthquakes using our BufferedReader Java input called in.

❸ Use the fallback local data source eqs1hour_2012-07-24.txt stored in the data folder of our sketch if the connection to the online source fails. The local file is a sample of the online source using the same data structure.

❹ Draw the world map fullscreen over the screen's width and height, with the upper left image corner placed at the origin.

❺ Get the longitude of the individual earthquake stored in each table row as a floating point number from the field index number 5, which is the sixth column in our data source.

❻ Get the latitude of the earthquake as a float from the field index number 4.

❼ Get the magnitude of the earthquake as a float from the field index number 6.

❽ Map the retrieved longitude value to the map's visual degree range (matching the Earth's degree range) of -180..180, and assign it to the horizontal position x on the screen.

❾ Map the retrieved latitude value to the map's visual degree range of 85..-60, and assign it to the vertical position y on the screen.

❿ Map the dimension of the red circles visualizing the earthquakes based on their individual magnitudes.

⓫ Calculate a blink frequency for the red circles based on the milliseconds (millis()[22]) passed since the app started, modulo 1000 milliseconds, resulting in a frequency of once per second, and then divide it by the earthquake's magnitude to blink faster for greater magnitudes.

---

22. http://processing.org/reference/millis_.html

⑫ Use the blink frequency variable freq to control the alpha transparency of the red ellipses with the RGB value color(255, 127, 127).

⑬ Create a new Android Location object "quake," and set it to the latitude and longitude of the individual earthquake.

⑭ Calculate the distance of the current device location stored in the KetaiLocation object, and compare it to the quake location stored in the Android object. Divide the resulting number in meters by 1609.34 to convert it to miles.

⑮ Draw a circle with a gray outline indicating the distance of the current location to the earthquake. Use Processing's distance method dist() to calculate the distance between both points on the screen, and draw an ellipse with a width and a height of double that distance.

⑯ Draw a text label indicating the distance from the current device location to the earthquake at the position of the earthquake on the screen.

⑰ Draw a slowly animated green circle to indicate the current device's location on the map. The pulse rate is one second for a 100-foot accuracy, or 0.1 seconds for a 10-foot accuracy.

Let's look at the Location tab next, which includes all the necessary code to determine the location of our device. It's very similar to our code, on page 74.

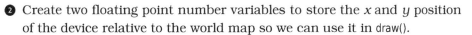
Data/DataEarthquakes/Location.pde

```
❶ KetaiLocation location;

   float accuracy;
❷ float myX, myY;

   void onLocationEvent(double lat, double lon, double alt, float acc)
   {
❸   myX = map((float)lon, -180, 180, 0, width);
❹   myY = map((float)lat, 85, -60, 0, height);
❺   accuracy = acc;
     println("Current Longitude: " + lon + " Longitude: " + lat);
   }
```

Here's what we need to do to determine our device location.

❶ Create a KetaiLocation variable named location.

❷ Create two floating point number variables to store the *x* and *y* position of the device relative to the world map so we can use it in draw().

❸ Map the lon value we receive from the Location Manager relative to the screen width.

Map the lat value we receive from the Location Manager relative to the screen height.

 Assign the accuracy value we receive from the Location Manager to the global accuracy variable, and use it for the blink rate of the green ellipse indicating the current device's location.

Let's test the app now.

Run the App

We need to make sure we set the correct Android permissions again to run this sketch. Not only do we need to select INTERNET from the Android Permission Selector under Sketch Permissions, we also need to check ANDROID_COARSE_LOCATION at least, or if we want to know it more accurately we check ANDROID_FINE_LOCATION as well. A couple of hundred feet matter less in this application, so the Fine Location is optional.

Run the sketch on your device. When it starts up, the app will try to connect to the data source online. If your device doesn't have a connection to the Internet, it will catch the exception ("Failed to open online stream reverting to local data") and load a sample stored as a fallback inside our data folder.

Your device might not have an updated coarse location available, so it might take a couple of seconds until the green circle moves into the correct location on the world map; the gray concentric circles are tied to the (green) device location and indicate the distance to each individual earthquake.

Try Another Source

Try another source from the EPA's catalog,[23] where you can find CSV files containing other earthquake data using the same file structure we've seen earlier in the code, on page 233.

Replace the src text string with this URL:

http://earthquake.usgs.gov/earthquakes/catalogs/eqs7day-M2.5.txt

Now rerun the code. Looking at the seven-day-period visualization, you can see how vibrant our planet is, even though we've limited the scope of the application to earthquakes of magnitude 2.5 and higher. In terms of their physical impact, experts say earthquakes of magnitude 3 or lower are almost imperceptible, while earthquakes of magnitude 7 and higher can cause serious damage over large areas.[24]

---

23. http://earthquake.usgs.gov/earthquakes/catalogs/

24. http://en.wikipedia.org/wiki/Earthquake

Because the comma-separated data structure of this seven-day-period data file is identical to the one we used earlier in the last hour, we don't have to do anything else besides replace the source URL. The app loads the additional data rows containing the earthquake data and displays it independent of how many earthquakes are reported, as shown in Figure 37, *Earthquakes reported worldwide during the last seven days.*

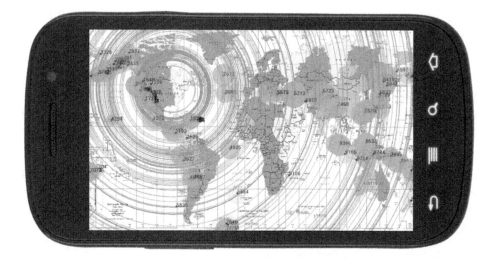

Figure 37— Earthquakes reported worldwide during the last seven days. Only earthquakes with a magnitude of 2.5 and higher are included in this data source.

Let's now refine the earthquake app using a feature that we're quite familiar with—device vibration.

9.9 Add Vibes to the Earthquake App

How much we know and care about earthquakes and the alert systems that are used to warn people about them probably depends on where you live and what kind of incident history your area has. Clearly the earthquake app we've developed so far has educational value and is not designed as a warning system. Wouldn't it be great, though, if we could keep the app running and receive a notification when a new earthquake incident is reported? Maybe, but we have neither the time nor the attention span to keep looking at our device screen, so let's use a very familiar feedback device built into our Android, the tiny DC motor that makes it vibrate.

We can take this quite literal translation from Earth's vibrations to device vibrations quite far, as we can control the duration of each device's vibrations and can even use a vibration pattern. So let's refine our earthquake app by mapping each individual earthquake magnitude to an individual vibration duration and the number of earthquakes to the number of vibrations. Furthermore, we can continue to check the online data source for reports of new earthquakes and vibrate the device each time a new one appears. We won't modify the visual elements of the app any further, but we'll focus on manipulating the audio-tactile response from the vibration motor built into the device to give us the effect we want.

To refine our app in this way, we can work with KetaiVibrate, which gives us straightforward access to the device's vibration motor. We'll also need an additional Processing Table object so we can compare our data to the data received from the live data source and add new quakes to the earthquakes Table when we determine they have occurred.

Let's take a look at the code, focusing on the vibrate() and update() methods that provide the functionality we're looking for. Besides the main tab, we'll use the Location tab we've seen already in the previous iteration of the app in the code, on page 237.

Data/DataEarthquakesShake/DataEarthquakesShake.pde
```
import ketai.sensors.*;
import ketai.ui.*;

Table history;
PImage world;
String src = "http://earthquake.usgs.gov/earthquakes/catalogs/eqs1hour-M0.txt";
❶ KetaiVibrate motor;
int lastCheck;

void setup()
{
  location = new KetaiLocation(this);
  try {
    history = new Table(this, src);
  }
  catch
    (Exception x) {
    println("Failed to open online stream reverting to local data");
    history = new Table(this, "eqs7day-M2_5_2012-08-14.txt");
  }
  orientation(LANDSCAPE);
  world = loadImage("world.png");
  lastCheck = millis();
```

```
❷   motor = new KetaiVibrate(this);
  }

  void draw () {
    background(127);
    image(world, 0, 0, width, height);

    if (history.getRowCount() > 0) {
      for (int row = 1; row < history.getRowCount(); row++) {
        float lon = history.getFloat(row, 5);
        float lat = history.getFloat(row, 4);
        float magnitude = history.getFloat(row, 6);
        float x = map(lon, -180, 180, 0, width);
        float y = map(lat, 85, -60, 0, height);

        noStroke();
        fill(0);
        ellipse(x, y, 5, 5);
        float dimension = map(magnitude, 0, 10, 0, 100);
        float freq = map(millis()%(1000/magnitude),
        0, 1000/magnitude, 0, magnitude*50);
        fill(255, 127, 127, freq);
        ellipse(x, y, dimension, dimension);

        Location quake;
        quake = new Location("quake");
        quake.setLongitude(lon);
        quake.setLatitude(lat);
        int distance = int(location.getLocation().distanceTo(quake)/1609.34);

        noFill();
        stroke(150);
        ellipse(myX, myY, dist(x, y, myX, myY)*2, dist(x, y, myX, myY)*2);
        fill(0);
        text(distance, x, y);
      }
    }
    // Current Device location
    noStroke();
    float s = map(millis() % (100*accuracy*3.28), 0, 100*accuracy*3.28, 0, 127);
    ellipse(myX, myY, 5, 5);
    fill(127, 255, 127, 127-s);
    ellipse(myX, myY, s, s);

❸   if (millis() > lastCheck + 10000) {
      lastCheck = millis();
      update();
    }
  }
```

```
    void vibrate(long[] pattern)
    {
④    if (motor.hasVibrator())
⑤      motor.vibrate(pattern, -1);
      else
        println("No vibration service available on this device");
    }

    void update()
    {
      println(history.getRowCount() + " rows in table before update" );

      ArrayList<Float> magnitudes = new ArrayList<Float>();
      Table earthquakes;

      try {
        earthquakes = new Table(this, src);
      }
      catch
        (Exception x) {
        println("Failed to open online stream, reverting to local data");
        earthquakes = new Table(this, "eqs7day-M2_5_2012-08-14.txt");
      }

      if (earthquakes.getRowCount() > 1)
⑥      for (int i = 1; i < earthquakes.getRowCount(); i++)
        {
          if (findInTable(history, 1, earthquakes.getString(i, 1)))
          {
            continue;
          }
          String[] rowString = earthquakes.getStringRow(i);
⑦        history.addRow();
⑧        history.setRow(history.getRowCount()-1, rowString);
          //Magnitude field is number 6
⑨        Float magnitude = new Float(earthquakes.getFloat(i, 6));
          magnitudes.add(magnitude);
          println("adding earthquake: " + earthquakes.getString(i, 1));
        }

⑩    long[] pattern = new long[2*magnitudes.size()];

      int j = 0;
      for (int k=0; k < pattern.length;)
      {
        pattern[k++] = 500;
        pattern[k++] = (long)(magnitudes.get(j) * 100);
        j++;
      }
```

```
⑪    motor.vibrate(pattern, -1);
     println(history.getRowCount() + " rows in table after update" );
   }

⑫ boolean findInTable(Table t, int col, String needle) {
     for (int k=0; k < t.getRowCount(); k++) {
⑬     if (needle.compareTo(t.getString(k, col)) == 0)
         return true;
     }
     return false;
   }
```

Let's take a look at the modifications we need to make to frequent updates and add vibration feedback to the earthquake app.

❶ Create a motor variable of type KetaiVibrate.

❷ Create the KetaiVibrate object motor.

❸ Check if the ten-second interval has expired.

❹ Check if the device has a vibration motor built in and available.

❺ Vibrate the device motor using the KetaiVibrate method vibrate() using the vibration pattern as the first parameter and "no-repeat" (-1) as the second parameter.

❻ Iterate through the earthquakes table; determine the number of rows contained in it using getRowCount().

❼ Add a new row into the history.

❽ Set the new row in the history table to the new entry found in the earthquakes table.

❾ Get the magnitude of the new entry we've found.

❿ Create an array of long numbers to be parsed into the vibrate() method as a duration pattern.

⑪ Call the vibrate method using the pattern we've assembled as an array of long numbers.

⑫ Create a boolean custom method to iterate through a table and find a specific String entry we call needle. Use the table name, the column index number we are searching in, and the needle as parameters for the method.

⑬ Iterate through the table t contents in column col, and compare the entry to the needle. Return true if we find a matching entry, and false if we don't.

Let's test the sketch.

Run the App

Run the sketch on your device. Visually, everything looks familiar. Every ten seconds the app is checking back to the EPA's server for updates. When the app detects a new earthquake, you'll hear the device vibrate briefly. A 2.5-magnitude earthquake results in a quarter-second vibration. If you receive two or more updates, you'll hear two or more vibrations.

When earthquakes disappear from the data source hosted by the EPA, we still keep them in our history Table. So for as long as the app is running, we'll accumulate earthquake records, and we show them all collectively on the world map.

This completes our earthquake app as well as our investigation in comma- and tab-separated data structures.

9.10 Wrapping Up

This concludes our examination of databases and tables, a highly relevant subject when developing mobile applications. You'll be able to read and write data to the Android into private and public directories and work with comma- and tab-separated values. This will allow you to save settings and application states so you can get your users started where you left off.

For more complex projects, where our interactions with the data become more complicated and our questions more detailed, we might need to work with a database, which gives us the crucial features to search, sort, and query the data we are working with. The most commonly used local database management system on mobile devices is SQLite, which we'll learn about in the next chapter.

CHAPTER 10

Using SQLite Databases

In this second part of our introduction to data, we'll work with SQLite, the popular relational database management system for local clients such as the Android, used also by many browsers and operating systems to store data. It implements the popular Structured Query Language (SQL) syntax for database queries, which we can use to access data stored locally on our Android device.

SQLite is a fairly simple and fast system, is considered very reliable, and has a small footprint that can be embedded in larger programs. It offers less fine-grained control over access to data than other systems like PostgreSQL or MySQL does, but it is simpler to use and administer, which is the main objective of the technology. It works very well as a file format for applications like Computer-Aided Design (CAD), financial software, and record keeping.[1] It is often used in cellphones, tablet computers, set-top boxes, and appliances because SQLite does not require administration or maintenance. This simple database management system can be used instead of disk files, like the tab- or comma-delimited text files we've worked with in Chapter 9, *Working with Data*, on page 215, replacing them with ad-hoc SQLite disk files.

In this chapter, we'll first get SQLite running with a simple sketch and learn how to use SQL queries to retrieve data from a SQLite table. Then we'll create an app that uses SQLite to capture accelerometer data from the sensor built into the Android. We'll use the recorded sensor values to create a time series visualization of the data. Finally, we'll query the data set we've recorded based on a certain device orientation we are looking for, and we'll highlight the sensor value that matches our query criteria.

---

1. http://www.sqlite.org/whentouse.html

Let's take a look at the classes and methods that allow us to use SQLite-databases for more complex data-driven apps.

10.1 Working with SQLite Databases

Now that we've seen most of Processing's Table features, it's time we take a look at the widely used SQLite database management system for local clients. It is based on the the popular Structured Query Language syntax for database queries and will look very familiar if you've worked with SQL before. Ketai gives us access to Android's SQLiteDatabase class and provides us with the essential methods we need to create, query, and update content in the database tables.

The Ketai KetaiSQLite class is what we need to create full-fledged local SQLite databases on the device. For the projects in this chapter, we'll use it to store a number of points that we'll create by tapping the touch screen interface, and later we'll use it to record accelerometer sensor data using the KetaiSensor class we've seen in Chapter 3, *Using Motion and Position Sensors*, on page 39. Let's get started by taking a look at the relevant Processing and Ketai methods we'll be working with throughout the chapter.

We'll create two SQLite projects, one to get us up and running with a few random values in a SQLite database. The next project will take advantage of the KetaiSensor class to capture accelerometer data directly into a SQLite database, which we'll browse and visualize on the Android display.

For the SQLite app we'll create in this chapter, we'll discuss SQL queries only very briefly. If you are unfamiliar with the language or would like to explore SQL queries further later on, you can find a more thorough reference online for the statements outlined next.[2]

Let's take a look at the KetaiSQLite class and SQLight basics.

10.2 Working with the KetaiSQLite Class

To use SQLite on the Android, we'll work with the following KetaiSQLite methods.

KetaiSQLite[3]   Ketai class for working with SQLite databases—it can be used to create a KetaiSQLite database or to load an existing database.

---

2. http://en.wikipedia.org/wiki/SQL
3. http://ketai.googlecode.com/svn/trunk/ketai/reference/ketai/data/KetaiSQLite.html

execute()[4]	KetaiSQLite method for executing a SQLite query to a database, which doesn't return data
query()[5]	KetaiSQLite method for sending a SQLite query to a database, returning data
getRecordCount()[6]	KetaiSQLite method returning all records in a specified table, using the table name as parameter
getDataCount()[7]	KetaiSQLite method returning all records in a database across all tables

Now let's take a look at the most important declarative SQL we'll use in our database project.[8]

CREATE[9]	SQL statement for creating a table in a database with specified fields and data types
INSERT[10]	SQL statement for creating a new row in a table
SELECT[11]	SQL statement to query a database, returning zero or more rows of data
WHERE[12]	SQL clause used in conjunction with a SELECT statement and expressions[13]
*	SQL wildcard that stands for "all" in a query
INTEGER, TEXT	SQL field data types
PRIMARY KEY	SQL statement to make a field the primary key
AUTOINCREMENT	SQL statement to make an integer field, which is typically also the primary key to automatically increment by one in order to be unique

Now let's get started with our first KetaiSQLite database.

---

4. http://ketai.googlecode.com/svn/trunk/ketai/reference/ketai/data/KetaiSQLite.html#execute(java.lang.String)

5. http://ketai.googlecode.com/svn/trunk/ketai/reference/ketai/data/KetaiSQLite.html#query(java.lang.String)

6. http://ketai.googlecode.com/svn/trunk/ketai/reference/ketai/data/KetaiSQLite.html#getRecord-Count(java.lang.String)

7. http://ketai.googlecode.com/svn/trunk/ketai/reference/ketai/data/KetaiSQLite.html#getDataCount()

8. http://en.wikipedia.org/wiki/Structured_Query_Language#Queries

9. http://www.sqlite.org/lang_createtable.html

10. http://www.sqlite.org/lang_insert.html

11. http://www.sqlite.org/lang_select.html

13. http://www.sqlite.org/lang_expr.html

12. http://www.sqlite.org/optoverview.html#where_clause

10.3 Implement a Data Table in SQLite

In the next project, we'll create a simple record-keeping sketch using the SQLite data management system, which can store a list of individual names and the IDs associated with them. Using text strings for the names we store and integer values for the associated IDs allows us to explore two different data types within the database. There is essentially no limit to the number of entries we can add to the SQLite table, besides the usual memory restrictions we have in Android's internal storage.

The goal of this SQLite project is to familiarize ourselves with the steps we need to follow to create a SQLite database, a new table inside the database, and data entries inside that table. To see whether we are successful, we'll output the contents of the table to the Android screen as shown in Figure 38, *Working with a SQLiteDatabase*, on page 248. We'll use the KetaiSQLite class for this project and the remaining projects of this chapter.

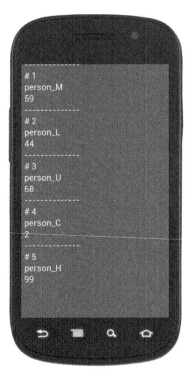

Figure 38—Working with a SQLiteDatabase. This screen output shows the initial five entries inserted in the data table. Each record contains a unique ID assigned by the database management system shown with a # prefix, a random name, and a random age.

To implement this SQLite sketch we'll first create a KetaiSQLite object, then create a new table called data using a CREATE TABLE statement, after that, INSERT data into the table, and finally, SELECT all the table contents to output it on the device screen. This is the most concise way to complete the necessary steps when we are working with a database.

To keep it simple, we'll populate the table only with values for two fields we call name and age. Besides those two fields, we'll also implement a field called _id, which is good practice: we should always use this to provide a unique identifier for each record. To keep each ID unique, we'll use SQL's AUTOINCREMENT feature, which takes care of incrementing the numeric integer ID each time we add a new record to the table. This ensures that all table rows have a number assigned to it, each unique throughout the table.

To create five sample entries inside the data SQLite table, we'll use a for() loop to generate a random name text String and a random age for the respective fields.

Note that we are neither using our familiar setup() nor the draw() method for this sketch. We don't need them here because we are writing a static sketch that executes our statements to create, populate, and display the database content, and that's it. In all those cases, we need to use setup() and draw() as we did in all the sketches we've developed so far.

Let's take a look at the code.

```
SQLite/SQLite/SQLite.pde
import ketai.data.*;
❶ KetaiSQLite db;
String output = "";
String CREATE_DB_SQL = "CREATE TABLE data (" +
"id INTEGER PRIMARY KEY AUTOINCREMENT, " +
"name TEXT, age INTEGER)";
orientation(PORTRAIT);
textSize(28);
❷ db = new KetaiSQLite( this);

if ( db.connect() ) {
❸   if (!db.tableExists("data"))
❹     db.execute(CREATE_DB_SQL);
❺   for (int i=0; i < 5; i++)
      if (!db.execute(
❻         "INSERT into data (`name`,`age`) " +
          "VALUES ('Person_" + (char)random(65, 91) +
          "', '" + (int)random(100) + "' )"
          )
          )
        println("error w/sql insert");
    println("data count for data table after insert: " +
```

```
⑦      db.getRecordCount("data"));

    // read all in table "table_one"
⑧    db.query( "SELECT * FROM data" );
⑨    while (db.next ())
    {
      output +="-------------\n";
⑩      output += "# " + db.getString("_id") + "\n";
      output += db.getString("name") + "\n";
      output += db.getInt("age") + "\n";
    }
  }
  background(78, 93, 75);
⑪  text(output, 10, 10);
```

We need to take the following steps to implement our SQLite database table.

❶ Define a KetaiSQLite variable called db.

❷ Create the db object of type KetaiSQLite.

❸ Check if the data table exists from a prior session; if not, create a new data table as defined in the query string CREATE_DB_SQL using three fields of type INTEGER, TEXT, and INTEGER for the respective fields _id, name, and age.

❹ Execute the SQL query to create the data table using the KetaiSQLite method execute().

❺ Loop five times to create five initial entries in the data table.

❻ INSERT values for the data table into the name and age fields using a random character suffix to make the "Person_" string unique (characters 65..90 represent A..Z in the ASCII character table[14]) and using a random integer number ranging 0..99 for age.

❼ Get the record count for the data table using KetaiSQLite's getRecordCount() method.

❽ Send a query to the database requesting all (*) records from the data table.

❾ Parse all records in the table using a while loop until there are no more to be found.

❿ Create an output String containing all records in the data.

⓫ Show the output text to give us feedback on the data table contents.

Let's run the sketch now.

---

14. http://en.wikipedia.org/wiki/ASCII

Run the App

Run the sketch on your device. You'll see five records similar to Figure 38, *Working with a SQLiteDatabase*, on page 248. To retrieve the individual entries of each record, we use the getString() and getInt() methods, which take the table's field names as parameters. If we use a field name that doesn't exist, the get-String() and getInt() methods will return 0. You can check this out by adding the following line of code to the output string.

```
output += db.getInt("foo") + "\n";   //doesn't exist, so we get '0'
```

If you are interested in working with an existing SQLite database, you can use the KetaiSQLite class to load it from the sketch data folder. You'd load the example.sqlite database as shown in the following code snippet.

```
KetaiSQLite db;
KetaiSQLite.load(this, "example.sqlite", "example");
db = new KetaiSQLite( this, "example");
```

You are now able to work with SQLite databases on the Android, which also lets you explore aspiring data-driven projects. Let's put the new skills in practice by creating a sketch that lets us record accelerometer sensor data to a SQLite database.

10.4 Record Sensor Data into a SQLite Database

To see how useful a database can be, let's go one step further and create an app that lets us record sensor data directly into a SQLite database table. We'll then use SQL queries to browse the sensor data we've recorded from the accelerometer and visualize the data on the Android screen as a time series.[15] A time series plots data points recorded at fixed intervals. For our example, we will record a data point every time we receive a new accelerometer value.

Alongside the accelerometer sensor values x, y, and z, we'll record time as *Unix time* (measured in milliseconds since January 1, 1970 UTC[16]) using Android's System method, currentTimeMillis().[17] This allows us to identify precisely at what time (and date) the data has been captured. The Unix time stamp will also serve as the unique ID in our data table. So for our data table, we'll need the following table structure and data types created by the following SQL query.

```
CREATE TABLE data ( time INTEGER PRIMARY KEY, x FLOAT, y FLOAT, z FLOAT)
```

---

15. http://en.wikipedia.org/wiki/Time_series
16. http://en.wikipedia.org/wiki/Unix_time
17. http://developer.android.com/reference/java/lang/System.html#currentTimeMillis%28%29

Let's look at each part of the SQL statement separately.

CREATE TABLE	The SQL keyword to create a table
data	The name we give the created table
time INTEGER PRIMARY KEY	Defines the first time field we'll create with the datatype INTEGER—the id field also functions as the PRIMARY KEY for the table. In a database that can use multiple tables that relate to each other, the primary key uniquely identifies each record in the table.
x	A field of type FLOAT that we use to store the value reported from the accelerometer's *x*-axis
y	A field of type FLOAT that we use to store the value reported from the accelerometer's *y*-axis
z	A field of type FLOAT that we use to store the value reported from the accelerometer's *z*-axis

Here's our approach to visualizing the time series data from the accelerometer sensor.

To display our time series on the screen, we'll work with a pair of variables called plotX and plotY, taking each of our data points and mapping it to the correct horizontal and vertical positions on the screen. We calculate plotX by using the record counter i to determine the total number of entries. We then use this number to spread the collected data over the full display width. We determine the vertical position plotY for each point by mapping each *x*, *y*, and *z* sensor value in relation to the display height.

Because the device reports a value equal to 1 g when it rests on the table (g-force equals 9.81 m/s^2, as we know from Section 3.5, *Display Values from the Accelerometer*, on page 46), let's use 2 g as the assumed maximum so we can move and shake the device and still show those higher values on the screen. Values of 0 g are shown centered vertically on the screen; positive values plot in the upper half of the display, and negative values in the bottom half.

Let's take a look at the code.

SQLite/DataCapture/DataCapture.pde
```
import ketai.data.*;
import ketai.sensors.*;

KetaiSensor sensor;
KetaiSQLite db;
boolean isCapturing = false;
```

```
    float G = 9.80665;
    String CREATE_DB_SQL =
①    "CREATE TABLE data ( time INTEGER PRIMARY KEY, x FLOAT, y FLOAT, z FLOAT);";

    void setup() {
      db = new KetaiSQLite(this);
      sensor = new KetaiSensor(this);
      orientation(LANDSCAPE);
      textAlign(LEFT);
      textSize(24);
      rectMode(CENTER);
      frameRate(5);
②    if ( db.connect() ) {
③      if (!db.tableExists("data"))
④        db.execute(CREATE_DB_SQL);
      }
      sensor.start();
    }

    void draw() {
      background(78, 93, 75);
      if (isCapturing)
        text("Recording data...\n(tap screen to stop)" +"\n\n" +
⑤          "Current Data count: " + db.getDataCount(), width/2, height/2);
      else
⑥      plotData();
    }

    void keyPressed() {
⑦      if (keyCode == BACK) {
        db.execute( "DELETE FROM data" );
      }
⑧      else if (keyCode == MENU) {
        if (isCapturing)
          isCapturing = false;
        else
          isCapturing = true;
      }
    }

    void onAccelerometerEvent(float x, float y, float z, long time, int accuracy) {
      if (db.connect() && isCapturing) {
        if (!db.execute(
⑨        "INSERT into data (`time`,`x`,`y`,`z`) VALUES ('" +
          System.currentTimeMillis() + "', '" + x + "', '" + y + "', '" + z + "')"
          )
        )
⑩        println("Failed to record data!" );
      }
    }
```

```
     void plotData() {
       if (db.connect()) {
         pushStyle();
         line(0, height/2, width, height/2);
         line(mouseX, 0, mouseX, height);
         noStroke();
⑪       db.query("SELECT * FROM data ORDER BY time DESC");
         int  i = 0;
⑫       while (db.next ())
         {
⑬         float x = db.getFloat("x");
           float y = db.getFloat("y");
           float z = db.getFloat("z");
           float plotX, plotY = 0;

           fill(255, 0, 0);
           plotX = map(i, 0, db.getDataCount(), 0, width);
           plotY = map(x, -2*G, 2*G, 0, height);
⑭         ellipse(plotX, plotY, 3, 3);
           if (abs(mouseX-plotX) < 1)
⑮           text(nfp(x, 2, 2), plotX, plotY);

           fill(0, 255, 0);
           plotY = map(y, -2*G, 2*G, 0, height);
⑯         ellipse(plotX, plotY, 3, 3);
           if (abs(mouseX-plotX) < 1)
             text(nfp(y, 2, 2), plotX, plotY);

           fill(0, 0, 255);
           plotY = map(z, -2*G, 2*G, 0, height);
⑰         ellipse(plotX, plotY, 3, 3);
           if (abs(mouseX-plotX) < 1)
           {
             text(nfp(z, 2, 2), plotX, plotY);
             fill(0);
             text("#" + i, mouseX, height);
           }
           i++;
         }
         popStyle();
       }
     }
```

Let's take a look at the steps we need to take to implement the sketch.

❶ Define a String called CREATE_DB_SQL containing the SQL query to create a new table called data. Use four columns, or fields (called time, x, y, and z) to store sensor data. Associate the data type INTEGER with the time field and make it the PRIMARY KEY, and use the datatype FLOAT for the sensor axis.

❷ Connect to the SQLite database that we've associated with the sketch when we created db.

❸ Create the data table if it doesn't already exist in the SQLite database, using the CREATE_DB_SQL String we've declared earlier.

❹ Send the table query CREATE_DB_SQL to the database using execute(), a method that doesn't return values but just executes a query.

❺ Give some feedback on the display while we are recording data points.

❻ Call the custom function plotData(), taking care of the data visualization.

❼ If the DELETE key is pressed, erase all content in the data table using a DELETE query, which leaves the table structure intact.

❽ Capture a MENU key event and use it to start and stop recording data.

❾ Use an INSERT SQL query to add a record into the data table every time we receive a sensor value via onAccelerometerEvent(). Use the Android System method currentTimeMillis() to request the current UTC time in milliseconds.

❿ If the insertion of the new record fails, print an error message to the console.

⓫ Use a SELECT SQL statement to request all entries from the data table, sorting them by the UTC field in descending order.

⓬ Use while() to parse through the data table for as long as the next() method returns TRUE and there are more entries to browse.

⓭ Get the x-axis value from the record using the getFloat() method with the field name x as the parameter. Do the same for the y- and z-axes.

⓮ Draw a red ellipse() at the location's horizontal position plotX.

⓯ Show the x value in a text label aligned with the ellipse if the horizontal position of the ellipse matches the horizontal finger position. Use the same approach for the y- and z-axes later on.

⓰ Draw the y-axis values using the same approach we took for x but with a green fill color.

⓱ Draw the z-axis values using the same approach we took for x and y but using a blue fill color.

Now let's run the app.

Run the App

Run the sketch on the device. When you run it for the first time, the SQLite data table will be created first. Press the menu key on the device to start recording accelerometer data. While you record sensor data, you'll see the record count increase. Press Menu again to stop the recording process.

You'll see a screen output similar to Figure 39, *Capturing sensor data in SQLite*, on page 257, showing the *x*-, *y*-, and *z*-axis values scattered as red, green, and blue dots around the vertical center representing 0. Positive g-force values are shown on the top half of the display, and negative values on the bottom.

You can continue adding points to the database by continuing to periodically press the Recent button. Once you reach a couple hundred points, you will note that it takes a bit longer to write and read the data. Our sensor reports values so fast that we record a couple hundred values into our SQLite database in just a few seconds. And because our database is stored on the device's SD card, the more values we've captured, the longer it will take to write.

You can reduce the number of entries into our database, for example, by recording only every other sensor value in onAccelerometerEvent(). Depending on your application, you can also write to the database at a reduced time interval. If you'd like to erase all data from the database, press the Back button. It triggers a DELETE query so we can start from scratch.

The process of creating tables and inserting and selecting data is in principle the same for any SQLite database project. Whether you have four or forty fields, a hundred or a thousand rows, this project can serve as a template for many of your data-driven Android projects.

Besides working with all the data in our database table, there is another important aspect of a database we need to explore—selecting data using a condition and returning only values that match that condition, which brings us to our next section.

10.5 Refine SQLite Results Using WHERE Clauses

Since we recorded data into a SQLite database, we can do much more with the data than parsing our data row by row. For example, KetaiSQLite methods can help us get the minimum and maximum values of a particular field in our table. This comes in very handy when we're displaying time-series graphs and want to distribute our data points evenly across a display in a way that takes full advantage of the available pixel real estate of each Android device.

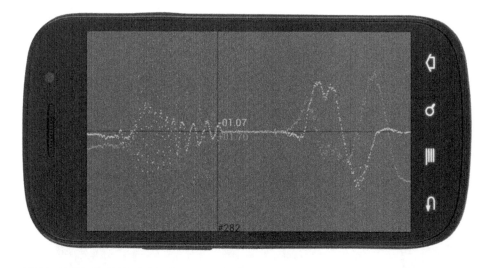

Figure 39—**Capturing sensor data in SQLite.** We visualize the recorded *x* (red), *y* (green), and *z* (blue) accelerometer values using SQLite entries, showing individual values and the record number (black) by moving a finger across the screen. On the left we see increasing device shakes and rest, and on the right, continuous device rotation.

Conditional SQL queries using WHERE clauses allow us to search table records that match a particular value we specify in our clause. It returns all rows for which the WHERE clause is true. WHERE clauses are often used with one of the following operators: =, <>, >, >=, <, <=, or LIKE.

For instance, adding WHERE x > 5 to our SELECT statement will only return records that have values greater than 5 in the x field of our data table. Similarly, we could request from the data table in our previous sketch code, on page 249, only the name of a person older than age 21. This way we can quickly implement many of the user-driven interactions we know from searching an online store for books only by a particular author, or shopping for merchandise from a particular brand.

Let's explore WHERE clauses based on the code we've just worked on to visualize sensor data stored in our SQLite database table we've called data. We'll leave the structure of the sketch intact but add a query that uses a WHERE clause to find only those records that match our condition.

As a condition for our WHERE clause, let's look for all the records that indicate the device is resting flat on the table (display pointing up). This is only the case if the *z*-axis shows a value of approximately 1 g, or +9.81, while the *x*- and y-axis values are close to 0. Let's use a white circle to indicate data points that match our condition, as shown in Figure 40, *Refining SQL queries using WHERE clauses.*

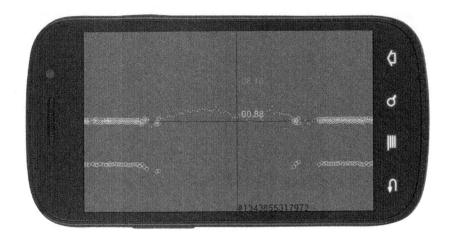

Figure 40—Refining SQL queries using WHERE clauses. Data points recorded when the Android remains flat and still are highlighted via white circles. The number on the bottom of the screen indicates the Unix time when the record was created.

We add the WHERE clause to the previous SELECT statement we've used. We are allowing values differing up to 1 m/s^2 from the value we are looking for.

```
SELECT * FROM data WHERE z > 8.81 AND abs(x) < 1 AND abs(y) < 1
```

Instead of the scheme we used in our previous sketch, let's specify time using the Unix time stored in the time field of the data table. This is more accurate because we don't receive sensor updates at an exact interval. Instead, we use the exact moment we've received new values in the form of a time stamp, and we use this time stamp to plot the data exactly when it occurred on our horizontal time axis. Essentially we are plotting each recorded data point proportional to the lowest (right) and highest (left) recorded time stamp. To correctly represent a Unix time value, we'll need thirteen digits. For that level of precision, we'll use the Java long datatype, a datatype that can handle long integers.[18] The map() method we've used throughout the book is not designed to handle such large integer values, so we simply build our helper method getLong() based on Processing's map() algorithm.

---

18. http://processing.org/reference/long.html

Let's look at the plotData() and mapLong() methods we are now working with, building on the code, on page 252.

SQLite/DataCaptureClause/DataCaptureClause.pde

```
void plotData()
{
  if (db.connect())
  {
    pushStyle();
    textAlign(LEFT);
    line(0, height/2, width, height/2);
    line(mouseX, 0, mouseX, height);
    noStroke();
    db.query("SELECT * FROM data");
❶  long myMin = Long.parseLong(db.getFieldMin("data", "time"));
❷  long myMax = Long.parseLong(db.getFieldMax("data", "time"));
    while (db.next ())
    {
❸    long t = db.getLong("time");
      float x = db.getFloat("x");
      float y = db.getFloat("y");
      float z = db.getFloat("z");
      float plotX = 0;
      float plotY = 0;

      fill(255, 0, 0);
❹    plotX = mapLong(t, myMin, myMax, 0, width);
      plotY = map(x, -2*G, 2*G, 0, height);
      ellipse(plotX, plotY, 3, 3);
      if (abs(mouseX-plotX) < 1)
        text(nfp(x, 2, 2), plotX, plotY);

      fill(0, 255, 0);
      plotY = map(y, -2*G, 2*G, 0, height);
      ellipse(plotX, plotY, 3, 3);
      if (abs(mouseX-plotX) < 1)
        text(nfp(y, 2, 2), plotX, plotY);

      fill(0, 0, 255);
      plotY = map(z, -2*G, 2*G, 0, height);
      ellipse(plotX, plotY, 3, 3);
      if (abs(mouseX-plotX) < 1)
      {
        text(nfp(z, 2, 2), plotX, plotY);
        fill(0);
❺      text("#" + t, mouseX, height);
      }
    }
    noFill();
    stroke(255);
```

```
db.query("SELECT * FROM data WHERE z > 8.81 AND abs(x) < 1 AND abs(y) < 1");
while (db.next ())
{
  long t = db.getLong("time");
  float x = db.getFloat("x");
  float y = db.getFloat("y");
  float z = db.getFloat("z");
  float plotX, plotY = 0;

  plotX = mapLong(t, myMin, myMax, 0, width);
  plotY = map(x, -2*G, 2*G, 0, height);
  ellipse(plotX, plotY, 10, 10);

  plotY = map(y, -2*G, 2*G, 0, height);
  ellipse(plotX, plotY, 10, 10);

  plotY = map(z, -2*G, 2*G, 0, height);
  ellipse(plotX, plotY, 10, 10);
}
popStyle();
}
}

// map() helper method for values of type long
float mapLong(long value, long istart, long istop, float ostart, float ostop) {
 return (float)(ostart + (ostop - ostart) * (value - istart) / (istop - istart));
}
```

Now let's see what changes we've made to our previous sketch code, on page 252.

❶ Get the minimum value of the time field in the data table using KetaiSQLite's getFieldMin() method. Use the datatype long to hold the returned thirteen-digit Unix time value.

❷ Get the maximum value of the time field in the data table using getFieldMax(). Use the datatype long to hold the time value.

❸ Parse the data, including the time field, which contains a long value that we store in the variable t.

❹ Calculate the plotX position of our data point based on the time value stored in data.

❺ Draw a text label for the data point's Unix time stamp.

❻ Use a WHERE clause that only returns results where the condition is true.[19]

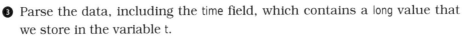

---

19. http://www.sqlite.org/optoverview.html#where_clause

❼ Draw a white circle around the data points that match the device's rest state.

❽ Define the user-defined method mapLong() as working identically to map() but handling values of datatype long.[20]

Now let's test our sketch.

Run the App

Run the sketch on the device, and you'll see it start up empty again, as no database table data exists in this modified sketch with a new name. When you start recording using your menu key, make sure to lay the device flat and let it rest in that position for a moment before you move it around a bit.

Now stop recording data. You'll see that the data points recorded at rest are highlighted by a white ring. Those data points that don't match our condition remain without a highlight. This means that our SQL query did the job, returning only the records that match z-axis values greater than +8.81 and x- and y-axis values smaller than 1 m/s^2.

You can try other WHERE clauses and see the same data highlighted differently, depending on the conditions and expressions you've used.

Working with SQLite databases is certainly not limited to sensor data. The tables we create can contain any type of numbers and text strings, making the projects in this chapter an ideal template to explore your other data-driven app ideas.

10.6 Wrapping Up

Working with local SQLite databases, you can now also develop your aspiring data-driven applications and take advantage of the powerful Structured Query Language to filter, search, and sort your queries. Being able to work with data will allow you to improve all the projects we've worked on in this book, as well as your future projects, and help make your apps more usable and useful.

Now that we've learned how to work with the Android file system and databases, we are now ready to work with 3D graphics and with linked assets such as objects, materials, and textures.

---

20. http://processing.org/reference/map_.html

Part V

Creating 3D Graphics and Cross-Platform Apps

CHAPTER 11

Introducing 3D Graphics with OpenGL

Rich graphics are the staple of sophisticated mobile games and data visualizations, and recent Android phones are well equipped with the necessary graphics hardware to deliver 2D and 3D graphics rendering without degrading performance. When we play 3D games or interact with complex data visualizations, the geometry that composes such a scene must be redrawn a few dozen times per second on the device screen—ideally sixty times or more—for animations and interactions to appear smooth and fluent. Besides the geometry, which consists of points, lines, and polygons, we typically also work in a 3D scene with textures, lighting, and virtual cameras to control the appearance of shapes and objects and to change our perspective within the scene.

All Android phones and tablets sold today support OpenGL ES,[1] a lightweight implementation of the popular Open Graphics Library for embedded systems—the industry standard for developing interactive 2D and 3D graphics applications across platforms. It's a free application programming interface and graphics pipeline that allows the software applications we create to leverage the graphics hardware built into our desktop computers, game consoles, and mobile devices for better graphics performance.

Processing is a great environment to create sophisticated graphics, and it comes with an OpenGL library that can be used in all modes. On the Android, Processing takes advantage of the graphics processing unit, or GPU, built into the mobile device. Only hardware acceleration makes it possible to animate thousands of data points, text characters, polygons, image textures, and lighting effects while maintaining a sufficiently high frame rate. Despite the multicore CPUs built into the latest Android devices today, we rely on the

---

1. http://www.khronos.org/opengles/

graphics hardware and OpenGL to achieve the smooth animations and special effects we are looking for.

In this chapter we'll create basic 3D shapes, use lights and textures, and manipulate the viewpoint of a virtual camera. We'll create apps that employ 3D cubes and spheres and use different types of lighting. We'll texture a sphere with a NASA image of the Earth at night and superimpose our camera preview as texture onto a 3D box. We'll also render a large amount of text with custom lighting, and we'll position it dynamically on the screen using our familiar touch screen input. We'll continue our investigation into shapes and 3D objects in Chapter 12, *Working with Shapes and 3D Objects*, on page 289, as the second part of our introduction to 3D graphics.

Let's get started by taking a closer look at OpenGL in Processing.

11.1 Introducing 3D Graphics and OpenGL

The Open Graphics Library (OpenGL) is the industry standard API for creating 3D (and 2D) computer graphics and runs on most platforms. It can be used to create complex 3D scenes from graphic primitives such as points, lines, and polygons. One of OpenGL's most important features is that it provides an interface for communicating with the accelerator hardware, or GPU, typically built into computer graphic cards, game consoles, and mobile devices. The GPU is responsible for providing us with the frame rates we need to animate geometry, render complex textures and shades, and calculate lighting effects. If a particular device hardware does not support all of OpenGL's feature sets, the library uses software emulation via the CPU instead, allowing OpenGL to still run the application on most platforms but at a lower frame rate.

Andres Colubri has now integrated his GLGraphics library into Processing 2.0, providing us with a major upgrade to the P2D and P3D graphics renderer in Processing,[2] with exciting new features for creating cutting-edge graphics that make use of OpenGL hardware acceleration. When we use the OpenGL renderer in Processing 2.0, we can gain a high level of control over textures, image filters, 3D models, and GLSL shaders—OpenGL's shading language for rendering effects on graphics hardware.[3] Now we can also create groups of shapes using Processing's createShape() method and retain geometry in the GPU's memory for significantly improved graphics performance. If you'd like to preview your sketch in the emulator using OpenGL hardware acceleration, you need to add

---

2. http://www.processing.org/reference/size_.html
3. http://en.wikipedia.org/wiki/GLSL

the GPU emulation hardware property when you create your Android Virtual Device (AVD).[4]

Let's take a look at the methods we'll use to work with the 3D graphics and OpenGL classes and methods we'll use in this chapter.

size(width, height, MODE)[5] Defines the dimension of the display window in pixels, followed by an optional render mode parameter. By default, the renderer is set to 2D. Use 3D to draw 3D shapes. You should call size() only once in setup() as the first line of code.

P3D and OPENGL[6] Identical render modes defined in the size() method—the OPENGL renderer used to differ from P3D, but it is now an alias pointing to the P3D renderer. P3D allows us to use the z-axis as the third dimension in our sketch, oriented perpendicular to the device screen. Larger z values move objects further into the scene, negative z values toward us. The P3D renderer uses OpenGL hardware.

displayHeight A Processing constant that returns the current height of the device display in pixels

displayWidth[7] A Processing constant that returns the current width of the device display in pixels

Let's get started with basic 3D geometry and lighting.

11.2 Work with 3D Primitives and Lights

For our first 3D app, let's explore simple geometry and lights to get a feel for the 3D coordinate system and learn how to control the position and scale of 3D objects on the device's display. We'll get started with two 3D primitives, the sphere() and the box(), and also define the scene lights using an ambient and a directional light source, as illustrated in Figure 41, *Using 3D primitives and lights*, on page 269.

To create the 3D scene, we use the size() method, which we've used so far only for the desktop applications we've created. The method defines the window width and height, but it can also be used to replace the default Processing 2D (P2D) renderer. For the Android apps we've created so far, we haven't used size(), because if we don't use it, Processing defaults the app to full screen, which is standard for all applications on the Android.

---

4. http://developer.android.com/tools/devices/emulator.html#acceleration

5. http://processing.org/reference/size_.html

6. http://wiki.processing.org/w/Android#Screen.2C_Orientation.2C_and_the_size.28.29_command

7. http://wiki.processing.org/w/Android#Screen.2C_Orientation.2C_and_the_size.28.29_command

For our 3D scene, we need to switch from the default P2D to the P3D renderer. Both Processing renderers are very similar, but the P2D render has optimized smoothing settings to display 2D figures. If we use the size() method with two parameters, our sketch defaults to the P2D renderer. If we provide a third one for the render mode, P3D, we've created a 3D sketch.

Processing also provides us with two constants to retrieve the display width and height of the device we are running our app on. They're called displayWidth and displayHeight, and we can also use those constants to set our app to full screen via the size() method.

Working with Lights

The different types of virtual light sources available in Processing are defined by their direction, amount of falloff, and specular values. *Falloff* defines the falloff rate for lights due to increased distance to the object they illuminate, defined in Processing as a constant, linear, or quadratic parameter using the lightFalloff() method.[8] A specular light is the highlight that appears on shiny objects, defined by the lightSpecular()method,[9] which provides a more realistic 3D impression based on how specular light interacts with material surfaces. The material appearance of objects can be defined via the specular() method as well as via the shininess() and emissive() methods.[10]

lights()[11] Sets the default values for ambient light, directional light, falloff, and specular values, making the 3D objects in the scene appear lit with medium ambient light and look dimensional.

ambientLight()[12] Adds an ambient light to the scene, which is a type typically used in a 3D scene alongside directional light sources—it makes objects appear evenly lit from all sides. The method uses three parameters for the light color and three parameters for the position of the light.

directionalLight()[13] Adds a directional light to the scene coming from a defined direction—it illuminates an object more where the light hits perpendicular to the surface and less so at smaller angles. The method uses three parameters for the light color and three parameters for its direction.

---

8.   http://www.processing.org/reference/lightFalloff_.html
9.   http://www.processing.org/reference/lightSpecular_.html
10. http://www.processing.org/reference/shininess_.html and http://www.processing.org/reference/emissive_.html.
11. http://processing.org/reference/lights_.html
12. http://processing.org/reference/ambientLight_.html
13. http://processing.org/reference/directionalLight_.html

pointLight()[14] Adds a point light to the scene; an omnidirectional light source emitting light from one point—it uses the light color and position within the scene as parameters.

spotLight()[15] Adds a spotlight to the scene, which offers the most control through parameters including the light color, position, direction, angle of the spotlight cone, and the concentration of the spotlight

Create a 3D Scene

We'll use the lights() method for this project, which sets default light values for the scene.[16] The default values for ambient light are then set to ambientLight(128, 128, 128), defining a medium bright white ambient light. In addition, we'll use the touch screen interface to control a directional light, where we translate the finger position on the display into a direction for this directional light, allowing us to change the objects' illumination interactively.

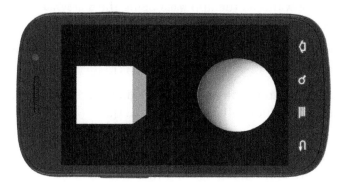

Figure 41—Using 3D primitives and lights. The illustration shows a cube and a sphere illuminated by two light sources, a default ambient light and a directional light source, that you control with your fingertip.

Let's take a look at our program, which is fairly concise for this basic scene.

Mobile3D/PrimitivesLights/PrimitivesLights.pde
```
void setup() {
  size(displayWidth, displayHeight, P3D);
  orientation(LANDSCAPE);
  noStroke();
}
```

---

14. http://processing.org/reference/spotLight_.html
15. http://processing.org/reference/spotLight_.html
16. http://processing.org/reference/lights_.html

```
void draw()
{
  background(0);
  float lightX = map(mouseX, 0, width, 1, -1);
  float lightY = map(mouseY, 0, height, 1, -1);

  lights();
  directionalLight(200, 255, 200, lightX, lightY, -1);

  translate(width/4, height/2, 0);
  box(height/3);
  translate(width/2, 0, 0);
  sphere(height/4);
}
```

Let's take a look at the methods we use to place the 3D primitives and control the directional light.

❶ Turn on the Processing 3D renderer using the size() method. Define the current device width as the app width using the displayWidth constant, and define the app height using the displayHeight constant.

❷ Calculate the horizontal direction of the light source by mapping the width of the screen to values with a range of [-1..1].

❸ Calculate the horizontal direction of the light source by mapping the height of the screen to values with a range of [-1..1].

❹ Call the default lights for the scene using default lighting values. Use the lights() method within draw() to retain the default lights in the scene instead of setup(), where only default lighting values are set.

❺ Use a directional light source with a greenish hue, and direct it based on the horizontal and vertical position of a fingertip on the touch screen.

Let's test the app.

Run the App

Now run the sketch on the device. This time we don't need to set Android permissions or import any libraries because we are not using hardware that requires authorization and it's all part of Processing's core functionality. When the app starts up, move your finger across the screen and see the directional light change direction based on your input.

A greenish halo around the specular highlights comes from our colored directional light source, and because we also have the default ambient light at work through calling the lights() method, the objects in our scene do not appear completely dark on the opposite side of the directional light source.

Now that we've created a 3D scene using basic 3D primitives and lights, we are ready to work with textures that we can superimpose onto 3D geometry.

11.3 Apply an Image Texture

For this next project we'll render a 3D night view of the Earth using a NASA image texture showing the light concentrations that emanate from the urban centers of our planet. We'll use the NASA JPEG image as a texture wrapped around a 3D sphere() shown in Figure 42, *Applying an image texture to a sphere*, on page 271. This time we'll create the 3D primitive using Processing's PShape class so we are able to apply a texture onto that shape. We'll create the sphere with the createShape() method and a SPHERE parameter, and then we'll use the shape() method to display the 3D object on the device screen.

The NASA satellite image of the Earth seen at night is also an equirectangular projection,[17] as we used already in Section 9.8, *Visualize Real-Time Earthquake Data*, on page 232, for visualizing earthquakes. An image texture with such a projection stretches perfectly around our sphere, recompensating for the distortions toward the poles that we observe in the flattened JPEG image.

Figure 42—Applying an image texture to a sphere. The bright spots on the image that covers the sphere show urban centers—such as New York City and Rio de Janeiro—in North and South America.

Let's take a look at the code.

Mobile3D/TexturedSphere/TexturedSphere.pde
```
❶ PShape sphereShape;
❷ PImage sphereTexture;
```

---

17. http://visibleearth.nasa.gov/view.php?id=55167

```
void setup() {
  size(displayWidth,  displayHeight,  P3D);
  orientation(LANDSCAPE);
  noStroke();
  fill(255);

  sphereTexture = loadImage("earth_lights.jpg");
  sphereShape = createShape(SPHERE, height/3);
  sphereShape.texture(sphereTexture);
}

void draw() {
  translate(width/2, height/2, 0);
  rotateY(TWO_PI * frameCount / 600);
  shape(sphereShape);
}
```

Here's what we need to do to apply the image texture.

❶ Create a PShape variable called sphereShape.

❷ Create a PImage variable called sphereTexture.

❸ Load the JPEG image texture using loadImage().

❹ Create the SPHERE PShape object we'll use to render the Earth, with a size of one-third the device's screen height.

❺ Apply the image texture to the shape using the PShape texture() method.

❻ Rotate the sphere slowly on the spot around the y-axis at a rate of one revolution per second. Use the frameCount constant to calculate the rotation.

Now let's run the sketch.

Run the App

Run the sketch on the device and you'll see a sphere covered with our NASA image texture on the screen. It covers one-third the screen height and rotates slowly around its vertical axis. We don't control this scene interactively, but we can watch the Earth rotate and we can observe the bright spots where densely populated cities are located.

Now that we've learned how to use static images as textures for 3D objects, we can move on to a moving image texture, which we'll discuss in the next section.

11.4 Use the Camera Preview as 3D Texture

Let's map a live camera preview of our front-facing Android camera next. When we use images as textures for 3D objects in Processing, we can take advantage of the fact that moving images are handled essentially like static images, displayed as a PImage object but updated every time we receive a new image from the camera. Building on the previous image texture project on page 271, we can use the Android camera previews as textures via the KetaiCamera class we've worked with in Section 5.3, *Display a Back-Facing Camera Full-Screen Preview*, on page 96.

For this project we'll use the BOX 3D primitive instead of the SPHERE, and we'll map the camera preview on every face of the box, as shown in Figure 43, *Use a camera preview as a 3D texture*, on page 273. We are already familiar with the code to instantiate a KetaiCamera object and the methods to start and stop the camera, which we'll reuse from Section 5.3, *Display a Back-Facing Camera Full-Screen Preview*, on page 96.

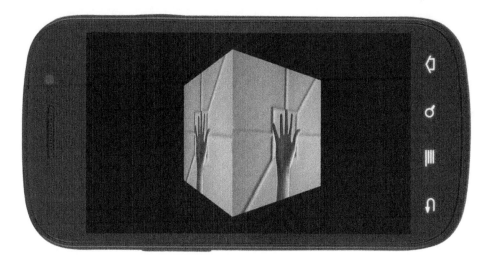

Figure 43—Use a camera preview as a 3D texture. The camera preview image is mapped on every face of the 3D box as an image texture.

Now let's take a look at the parts of the code that deal with the 3D box and camera texture.

Mobile3D/CameraTexture/CameraTexture.pde

```
import ketai.camera.*;
KetaiCamera cam;
```

```
PShape boxShape;
PImage sphereTexture;

void setup() {
  size(displayWidth, displayHeight, P3D);
  orientation(LANDSCAPE);
  noStroke();
  fill(255);

  boxShape = createShape(BOX, height/2);

  cam = new KetaiCamera(this, 320, 240, 30);
  cam.setCameraID(1);
}

void draw() {
  background(0);

  translate(width/2, height/2, 0);
  rotateY(PI * frameCount / 500);
  shape(boxShape);
}

void onCameraPreviewEvent()
{
  cam.read();
}

void mousePressed()
{
  if (cam.isStarted())
  {
    cam.stop();
  }
  else
  {
    cam.start();
    boxShape.texture(cam);
  }
}
```

Here's what we need to do to apply the camera preview as a shape texture.

❶ Create a KetaiCamera object cam with a resolution of 320 by 240 pixels.

❷ Set the camera ID to 1 for the front-facing camera.

❸ Apply the cam image as a texture() for the boxShape.

Let's test the sketch.

Run the App

Run the sketch on your Android device. When the scene starts up, you'll see the 3D box rotate once every ten seconds. Tap the screen now to start up the camera. As soon as a camera preview image is available, we use it as a texture for our box.

Feel free to change the BOX back to a SPHERE 3D primitive and observe how the image wraps around the sphere.

Let's now take a closer look at the different types of light sources we can work with in Processing.

11.5 Work with Spot and Point Lights

Lighting affects the appearance of all the geometry in a scene, which is why we'll take a closer look now at the various lighting options we have in Processing. Let's create a sketch using three colored spotlights, as shown in Figure 44, *Using spotlights*, where we can see how each of the light sources interacts with the surface of the 3D geometry.

Figure 44—Using spotlights. The three colored spotlights introduced to the scene (red, green, blue) add up to white in the additive color space.

We'll use the basic light colors red, green, and blue, because those colors mixed together create white light in the additive color space.[18] We'll keep the geometry simple and continue working with our basic sphere shape. But to get a more accurate sphere geometry, we'll increase the render detail of the sphere using the sphereDetail() method.[19] It defines the number of vertices of

---

18. http://en.wikipedia.org/wiki/Additive_color
19. http://processing.org/reference/sphereDetail_.html

the sphere mesh, set by default to 30 vertices per full 360 circle revolution, and we increase it to 60 vertices per revolution, resulting in one vertex every six degrees (360 degrees divided by 60 vertices).

The spotLight() method we'll use takes eleven parameters and offers the most amount of control compared with other light options in Processing.[20] We can set the light color, position, direction, angle, and concentration using the method. Let's take a look.

```
spotLight(v1, v2, v3, x, y, z, nx, ny, nz, angle, concentration)
```

v1	The red or hue value of the light—red in the default RGB color mode and hue in the HSB color mode
v2	The green or saturation value of the light
v3	The blue or brightness value of the light
x	The horizontal or x position of the light
y	The vertical or y position of the light
z	The depth or z position of the light
nx	The direction of the light along the x-axis
ny	The direction of the light along the y-axis
nz	The direction of the light along the z-axis
angle	The angle of the light cone
concentration	The concentration exponent determining the center bias of the spotlight cone

Every object we draw after calling this or any other lighting method in Processing is affected by that light source; objects drawn before the method call are unfazed by the light source. To retain a light source in the scene, we must call the lighting method within draw(). If we call the lighting method in setup(), the light will only affect the first frame of our app and not the consecutive frames.

We'll place our three colored spotlights slightly off-center while pointing straight ahead at the scene. Each of the lights will hit our sphere object at an individual spot off the sphere's center, and we can observe how the three spotlights interact with the sphere's surface when they mix together. We'll define the spotlight cone angle at 15 degrees, which happens to match a standard lens used in theater lighting, and we'll keep the concentration bias at 0 to achieve the maximum blending effect between the colors for now.

---

20. http://processing.org/reference/spotLight_.html

Once we've tested the spotlights, we'll replace them with point lights and compare the difference. Point lights offer less options and control than spot-lights do, which makes them arguably easier to use as well. Point lights are omnidirectional light sources emanating equally in all directions from one specified point in 3D space. The pointLight() method takes only the light color and position as parameters.

Let's go ahead and write our spotlight program next.

Mobile3D/SpotLights/SpotLights.pde

```
PShape sphereShape;
int sSize;

void setup()
{
  size(displayWidth, displayHeight, P3D);
  orientation(LANDSCAPE);
  noStroke();
  fill(204);
❶  sphereDetail(60);
❷  sSize = height/2;
  sphereShape = createShape(SPHERE, sSize);
}

void draw()
{
  background(0);
  translate(width/2, height/2, 0);

❸  spotLight(255, 0, 0, sSize/4, -sSize/4, 2*sSize, 0, 0, -1, radians(15), 0);
❹  spotLight(0, 255, 0, -sSize/4, -sSize/4, 2*sSize, 0, 0, -1, radians(15), 0);
❺  spotLight(0, 0, 255, 0, sSize/4, 2*sSize, 0, 0, -1, radians(15), 0);

//  pointLight(255, 0, 0, sSize/4, -sSize/4, 2*sSize);
//  pointLight(0, 255, 0, -sSize/4, -sSize/4, 2*sSize);
//  pointLight(0, 0, 255, 0, sSize/4, 2*sSize);

  shape(sphereShape);
}
```

Let's take a look at the methods we use for defining the spotlight and sphere detail.

❶ Increase the number of vertices composing the sphere to 60 for one full 360-degree revolution.

❷ Define a variable for the sphere size called sSize.

❸ Create a red spotlight pointing straight at the scene, slightly offset to the right and up.

❹ Create a green spotlight pointing straight at the scene, slightly offset to the left and up.

❺ Create a blue spotlight pointing straight at the scene, slightly offset to the bottom.

Let's test the sketch.

Run the App

Now run the sketch on the device, and see how the increased sphere detail and the three spotlights produce a high-quality color blending effect on the sphere's surface.

Let's take a look at our current frame rate to see how computationally expensive this operation is. Go ahead and add these two lines of code at the end of draw():

```
if (frameCount%10 == 0)
    println(frameRate);
```

On the Nexus S, the slowest of the devices tested for this book (Figure 1, *Tested Android phones and tablets*, on page xx), we still get minimum frame rates of 60, which is the default Processing uses if we don't determine otherwise via the frameRate() method. This is true despite the fact that we have multiple hundreds of vertices and polygons at work to create our sphere with increased detail and we superimpose multiple light sources onto the sphere surface.

Let's replace the spotlights now with point light sources and see the difference. They are already present in the code, on page 277, but currently commented out. The color and position of the point light is identical to the spotlight we've used.

Rerun the app and take a look at how the three colored light sources cover the sphere—mixing white in the center of the sphere. The lighting seems identical to the spotlights since we've used a fairly wide spotlight cone earlier and we also did not add a concentration bias. Now change back to the spotlights and decrease the current 15-degree cone angle to, let's say, 5, and increase the concentration bias to 1. You'll see how spotlights offer additional controls over the light cone and concentration in our 3D scene.

Now that we've explored the different types of virtual lights in Processing, let's continue our work on geometry, specifically typography in a 3D space.

11.6 Use Custom Fonts and Large Amounts of Text

A typical scenario in a data visualization project is to use text with a custom font alongside graphic elements on the device display. Text labels and large amounts of body text quickly add complexity and a lot of work for our device to render the scene. We can enlist Processing's OpenGL capabilities to help keep the frame rate up. Let's create a sketch where we cover the screen dynamically with text positioned along the z (or depth) axis of the 3D scene, depending on where we touch the screen surface, as shown in Figure 45, *Text rendered in lights*, on page 279. We'll work with custom fonts for this project, both released by Google and available for us to use without restriction.

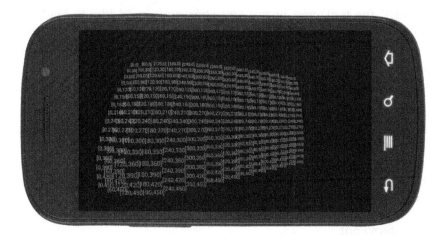

Figure 45—Text rendered in lights. Large amounts of text can be rendered with lighting effects using OpenGL.

Processing uses a default font called Lucida Sans for all its modes because it is available on all platforms. We've come quite far in this book without switching to a custom font for our apps, focusing on the particular chapter topics and keeping any lines of code we don't desperately need away from our sketches. Now it's time we learned how to use a custom font for our app.

Processing provides a PFont class to us for working with custom fonts loaded into our sketch. We can use it in two ways:

- Using Processing's createFont() method,[21] we can load an already installed system font into our app at a defined font size. This way of working with

---

21. http://www.processing.org/reference/createFont_.html

a custom font requires that the font we'd like to use as the createFont() parameter is available on the platform we'll run our app on. To find out what's available on the system, the PFont class provides us with a list() method, which we can use to print a list of all available system fonts to the console.

• Alternatively, we can use the "Create Font..." dialog in the Processing menu, shown in Figure 46, *Use a custom font in Processing*, on page 283, and available under Tools, which allows us to import any font we'd like—and are allowed—to import into our app. Processing opens all the fonts that are installed on our desktop system in a window. We can select the font we'd like, the point size for our import, whether we'd like to "smooth" the font, and how many characters we'd like to load, and it shows a font preview for the selections we've made. For the import, we can give the font a custom name for our sketch, and when we OK the dialog window, the font will be loaded as a Processing font file (.vlw) into the data folder of our sketch. Once we've created the font, we can load it into a PFont object in our sketch using the loadFont() method.[22]

Both methods require that we set the current font used to draw text() in our sketch to the font we've created or loaded using the textFont() method.[23] This is necessary because we could work with two or more fonts in one sketch, and therefore we use the textFont() method like we'd also use fill() or stroke(), this time setting the current text font for all the text we draw after the method call.

Load a System Font

Android has introduced comprehensive typography and app design guidelines with Ice Cream Sandwich to improve the user experience across the myriads of apps available for the OS.[24] The typography guidelines build on a new font family, called Roboto, which we can use without restriction for our apps. If you are running Ice Cream Sandwich or Jelly Bean on your device, you'll have the following Roboto font styles already installed on the system, which we can activate using the createFont() method in Processing.

Use the code snippet below to confirm the font list on your device using the list() method of the PFont class.

```
String[] fontList = PFont.list();
println(fontList);
```

---

22. http://processing.org/reference/loadFont_.html
23. http://processing.org/reference/textFont_.html
24. http://developer.android.com/design/style/typography.html

Printed below is the list() returned to the console on the Nexus S I tested with.

```
[0] "Monospaced-Bold"
[1] "Monospaced"
[2] "SansSerif"
[3] "Serif-Italic"
[4] "SansSerif-Bold"
[5] "SansSerif-BoldItalic"
[6] "Serif-Bold"
[7] "SansSerif-Italic"
[8] "Monospaced-BoldItalic"
[9] "Monospaced-Italic"
[10] "Serif-BoldItalic"
[11] "Serif"
```

We'll first work with Google's current Roboto font and then switch over to an older Google font called *Droid Serif* to learn how to load a custom font that is not currently installed on the system.[25]

We'll use two point lights, a blue one positioned to the left of the screen and an orange one positioned to the right, so we can see how the text reacts to the light sources placed into the scene when they move closer and further away from the virtual camera.

Let's take a look at the code.

Mobile3D/TextLights/TextLights.pde

```
❶ PFont font;

void setup()
{
  size(displayWidth, displayHeight, P3D);
  orientation(LANDSCAPE);
  noStroke();

❷ font = createFont("SansSerif", 18);
❸ textFont(font);
  textAlign(CENTER, CENTER);
}

void draw()
{
  background(0);

❹ pointLight(0, 150, 250, 0, height/2, 200);
❺ pointLight(250, 50, 0, width, height/2, 200);

❻ for (int y = 0; y < height; y+=30) {
```

---

25. http://www.fontsquirrel.com/fonts/Droid-Serif

```
⑦    for (int x = 0; x < width; x+=60) {
⑧      float distance = dist(x, y, mouseX, mouseY);
⑨      float z = map(distance, 0, width, 0, -500);
⑩      text("["+ x +","+ y +"]", x, y, z);
    }

  }

  if (frameCount%10 == 0)
    println(frameRate);
}
```

Here's what we need to do to place the text dynamically.

❶ Define a PFont variable called font.

❷ Create the SansSerif font from the Roboto font family already installed on the Android device in 18-point size and assign it to the font object.

❸ Define font as the current font used to draw all text() that follows.

❹ Place the blue point light to the left edge of the screen, centered vertically.

❺ Place the orange point light to the right edge of the screen, centered vertically.

❻ Use a for() loop to calculate the vertical position y of the text, spread evenly across the screen width.

❼ Use a for() loop to calculate the horizontal position x of the text, spread evenly across the screen height.

❽ Calculate the distance between the fingertip and the text position on the screen.

❾ Map the calculated distance to the z-axis values ranging from -300 to 100, with text close to the fingertip appearing larger and text at the fingertip position placed at z equal to 100.

❿ Draw the text on the screen at the calculated position [x, y, z].

Let's run the sketch.

Run the App

Run the sketch on the device and observe how the screen shows a grid of text labels in the Roboto system font, indicating their individual [x, y] positions on the screen. Because the mouseX and mouseY constants each default to 0 when the app starts up, you'll see how the text labels in the upper left corner appear larger than the ones in the lower right corner.

Move your finger across the touch screen surface and observe how the text closest to the fingertip enlarges and the other text scales proportionally due to their z positions ranging from 0 (close by) to -500 (distant and small).

Using Roboto as the default font for our app adheres to Android's typography guidelines. It's generally a good idea, though, for us to choose the best font for the job, which is why we'll look next at loading custom fonts that are not already available in the Android OS.

Load a Custom Font

Different fonts are good for different things, and the limited pixel real estate that is available to us on a mobile screen poses particular typographic challenges. We want to use the best font for a particular task and scale. When we introduce a font other than Roboto to the equation, we'll need to use Processing's loadFont() method for loading a custom font into our app. Before we can load the font into the app, we first need to create it via the "Create Font..." tool in the Processing IDE. Let's modify our prior sketch (code, on page 281) now to use a custom font and make the text we'll display scalable so we can evaluate the font's particular text details at different text sizes, as shown in Figure 46, *Use a custom font in Processing*, on page 283.

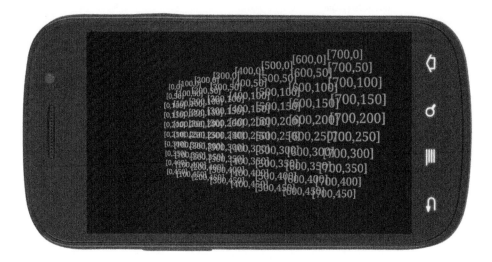

Figure 46—Use a custom font in Processing.   The illustration shows the custom Droid Serif font at different scales, resized based on finger position on the screen.

This sketch is very similar to the previous one. Let's start by making the font we'll use available to our sketch. Let's use Google's Droid Serif font as our custom font for this sketch: it's available for us to use without restriction and has been used on the Android since 2008. Let's download it from the Font Squirrel website, where we can find many other fonts both for free, for personal use, or for purchase.

Download Droid Serif now at http://www.fontsquirrel.com/fonts/Droid-Serif, and extract the file onto your desktop computer. Follow the Displaying Text tutorial on the Processing website to load the font into your system,[26] and then go back to Processing. Now open "Create Font..." from the Tools menu; a window opens as shown in Figure 47, *Create a Processing font*, on page 284. Let's use 48 points for this sketch, and click OK to close the window.

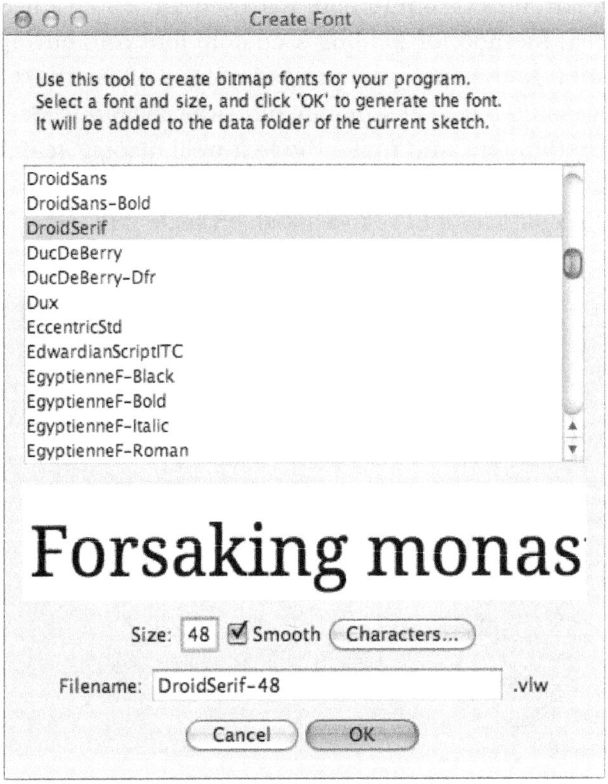

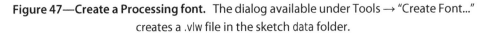

Figure 47—Create a Processing font. The dialog available under Tools → "Create Font..." creates a .vlw file in the sketch data folder.

26. http://processing.org/learning/text/

Processing has just created a custom Droid Serif font for us to use in our sketch, compiling the Processing font file called DroidSerif-48.vlw into our sketch's data folder. It contains all the text characters we need, also called glyphs, as bitmap images that are optimally displayed on the screen at 48 points due to the settings we've chosen when we created the font. Now we are ready to use this custom font in our app.

To display our text at different sizes, let's introduce a variable called scaleFactor to set the individual size for each text box. If we map scaleFactor to values ranging [0..48], we can use the variable as the parameter for textSize() directly. We use 48 points as a maximum, because if we scaled our text beyond that number, we'd quickly see individual characters appear pixelated with jagged edges. After all, we've created the Droid Serif font at 48 points, and because each glyph is rendered as a bitmap image, the same rule applies as for any other pixel image: if you enlarge a pixel image beyond the size and resolution it's optimized for, it appears pixelated and jagged. OpenGL will try to compensate by anti-aliasing, but the quality of the text's appearance will always be highest if rendered at the size it has been created initially.

Let's look at the code.

Mobile3D/LoadFont/LoadFont.pde

```
PFont font;
float scaleFactor = 1;

void setup()
{
  size(displayWidth, displayHeight, P3D);
  orientation(LANDSCAPE);
  noStroke();

❶ font = loadFont("DroidSerif-48.vlw");
  textFont(font);
  textAlign(CENTER, CENTER);
}

void draw()
{
  background(0);

  pointLight(0, 150, 250, 0, height/2, 200);
  pointLight(250, 50, 0, width, height/2, 200);

  for (int y = 0; y < height; y+=50) {
    for (int x = 0; x < width; x+=100) {
      float distance = dist(x, y, mouseX, mouseY);
      float z = map(distance, 0, width, 0, -500);
```

❷
```
        textSize(scaleFactor);
        text("["+ x +","+ y +"]", x, y, z);
    }
  }
}

void mouseDragged()
{
```
❸
```
  scaleFactor = map(mouseY, 0, height, 0, 48);
}
```

Here are the steps we need to take to load the custom font.

❶ Load the font from the font file DroidSerif-48.vlw and assign it to the PFont object font.

❷ Set the textSize() to the size determined by the vertical position of a fingertip on the screen.

❸ Calculate the scaleFactor for the text size we use to draw the text.

Let's test the app next.

Run the App

Run the sketch on your device and move your finger across the screen. You'll now see the Droid Serif font appear on the screen, illuminated by our two point lights. The vertical position of the finger defines the text size of each individual text block, becoming bigger as you move your finger down and smaller as you move up. You can recognize the text serifs better as you move your finger down the screen and increase the text size. The text behaves the same way as our previous one with the scale difference: the z (depth) of each text box remains defined by its distance to the fingertip.

Now that we know how to load and use custom fonts into our apps, we can use the font that's best for a specific task and scale.

11.7 Wrapping Up

You've now learned how to work with geometric shapes, including the 3D primitives sphere and box, and how to illuminate them in a 3D scene. You've applied image textures to these shapes (still and moving) and learned to manipulate the properties of spotlights, ambient lights, and point lights. You've worked with system fonts and loaded a custom font into a Processing sketch using Processing's 3D renderer, which takes advantage of the device's OpenGL hardware acceleration.

If you've mastered this introduction to 3D graphics and OpenGL, you should now be ready to build and control basic 3D scenes and manipulate their elements. There is more to explore, though, when it comes to 3D geometry and interactive 3D apps. Let's dive a little deeper into the subject in the next chapter, where we'll work with Scalable Vector Graphics and 3D Objects and use the Android gyro sensor and the camera as interactive interfaces for controlling a 3D scene.

CHAPTER 12

Working with Shapes and 3D Objects

With the basic understanding we've gained running 3D sketches on the Android in Chapter 11, *Introducing 3D Graphics with OpenGL*, on page 265, we're now ready to tackle some more advanced tasks: working with shapes and objects, generating our own geometric figures, and shifting the point of view of the virtual camera that determines how our scene is rendered. Once we've mastered those tasks, we'll know all we need to create interactive 3D scenes and games and to organize information three-dimensionally.

Processing's features for handling shapes and other figures are quite extraordinary. The PShape class—which we'll use throughout the chapter for much of this work—makes it easy for us to work with Scalable Vector Graphics (SVG) and 3D Object (OBJ) files and to record vertices that define custom shapes and figures algorithmically. PShape leverages the OpenGL hardware acceleration found on most recent Android phones and tablets and is a great example of how we can tackle complex operations with just one class and a few lines of Processing code.

To show the support that PShape provides for handling SVG files, we'll start with a US map saved in that format, and then we'll give users the ability to zoom and pan over its features. Because this format is based on vectors and vertices, users won't lose graphics detail or quality as they zoom the map. We'll also see how to modify the SVG file to highlight typical tossup states during recent presidential elections.

To demonstrate how we can use PShape to manipulate 3D objects, we'll load a model of One World Trade Center from an Object file, including its materials and textures, display it on the touch screen, and then rotate and zoom the figure using multitouch gestures. We'll also create a figure algorithmically and construct a 3D Möbius strip using individual vertices that we record. We'll learn how to store the information we need to draw the figure in the

GPU's memory and thereby radically increase the speed with which it's rendered as well as the number of times per second the image is refreshed.

To give users a way to interact with the Möbius strip, we'll introduce and use the built-in gyro sensor, a component that now ships with the latest Androids. The gyro makes a useful input device, and we'll use it to rotate the figure on the screen by rotating the device itself. We'll conclude the chapter by bringing several of these new features together in a single application that also makes use of Android's ability to recognize faces. We'll use our gaze to control the point of view of the virtual camera. The scene consists of Earth and the Moon—revisiting code from Section 11.3, *Apply an Image Texture*, on page 271, and face recognition features we've explored in Section 5.8, *Detect Faces*, on page 120.

Let's look first at the classes and methods Processing provides to us to work with shapes and 3D objects—we'll use them throughout the chapter.

12.1 Working with the PShape Class

In this chapter, we'll use Processing's PShape features for all the projects we'll create.[1] We can use the class to load 2D vector shape files (.svg) and 3D object files (.obj) and work with 3D vertices generated algorithmically. Let's take a look at the methods we'll use to load and create the 3D scenes in this chapter.

loadShape()[2] A Processing method to load a Scalable Vector Graphic, or .svg, file into a PShape object

beginShape()[3] A Processing method to start recording a shape using vertices—we can connect vertices with the following modes: POINTS, LINES, TRIANGLES, TRIANGLE_FAN, TRIANGLE_STRIP, QUADS, and QUAD_STRIP.

endShape()[4] A Processing method to stop recording a shape using vertices

vertex()[5] A Processing method to add a vertex point to a shape using either *x* and *y* values or *x*, *y*, and *z* values for two and three dimensions, respectively—it takes only two vertices to create a shape, but we can add thousands and are only limited by the memory installed in our device. Vertices are connected with straight lines. To create curves, use the bezierVertex() or curveVertex() instead.[6]

---

1. http://processing.org/reference/PShape.html
2. http://processing.org/reference/loadShape_.html
3. http://processing.org/reference/beginShape_.html
4. http://processing.org/reference/endShape_.html
5. http://processing.org/reference/vertex_.html
6. http://processing.org/reference/bezierVertex_.html or http://processing.org/reference/curveVertex_.html.

create-Shape()[7]	A Processing method to load a 3D primitive or vertices into a PShape—the method can also handle parameters for the 3D primitives BOX and SPHERE. It also mirrors the beginShape() method for recording vertices into a PShape object and is used in conjunction with end()-to-end recording.
camera()[8]	A Processing method to define the camera viewpoint (where the camera is looking and how the camera is facing)—we use it to navigate a 3D scene while keeping an eye on the particular spot we've defined.

In a moment we're going to use these elements to display a map of the United States stored as an SVG graphic. But first let's discuss the SVG format itself and its advantages when it comes to displaying line art such as maps.

12.2 Working with SVG Graphics and Maps

In addition to the fonts that are used to render text, images such as icons, line art, and maps also depend on outlines that remain accurate and legible at different scales. The pixel-based bitmap images that we've worked with so far look best if they are presented with their original size and resolution for a particular device screen.[9] But in scenarios where we'd like to zoom images or graphic elements and we'd like to be independent of the variation in screen resolution found on different devices, we are best served by using vector graphics wherever we can.

A picture taken with a photo camera will never be accurately represented by a vector graphic. However, text, icons, symbols, and maps are good candidates because they typically use outlines and a limited number of colors. SVG is a popular XML-based file format for saving vectors, text, and shapes. It can be displayed on virtually any web browser and handled by most image processing applications.

SVGs are great when we need accurate detail and precise outlines at varying scales. Maps typically contain paths representing geography, city infrastructure, state lines, country borders, nations, or continents. What's more, we understand maps as images at a particular scale, providing overview and a level of detail for this scale, and we expect that we can adjust the scale seamlessly for maps with digital devices. To accomplish this goal, we can

---

7. http://processing.org/reference/createShape_.html
8. http://processing.org/reference/camera_.html
9. http://en.wikipedia.org/wiki/Bitmap

either keep multiple bitmaps in store to adjust for the shifts in scale, or we can use SVG files that do not lose accuracy or quality when they scale.

Maps balance abstraction and detail: we hide a map's details in order to provide a clear overview of an area, but we must add them as a user dives deeper into a particular region of a map. Shifts in scale always present challenges because we can't load everything we need at once, and we can't predict what a user might want to see in more detail at a given moment. So when we work with digital maps, we need to maintain a balance between abstraction and detail and work within the limits of resolution, graphics processing power, and storage of the phones and tablets in the Android universe. With Google Maps and Google Earth, we experience this balance literally as we watch the successive loading process for added detail.

SVG images are not immune to the challenges of rendering large amounts of data. For example, when we work with hundreds of words of text contained in an SVG file, we'll see our frame rate drop quickly because the graphics processor needs to calculate dozens of vector points at different scales for each character. It's the reason why large amounts of text are typically rendered as bitmap images made for one size, and we've explored this approach already in Section 11.6, *Use Custom Fonts and Large Amounts of Text*, on page 279. However, when we work with a headline or a few text labels, we definitely can work with SVG text and change scale, color, or rotation dynamically without sacrificing text legibility or image quality.

Let's turn now to the first project in this chapter, where we'll learn how to display a map of the United States that has been stored in an SVG file.

12.3 Map the United States

For our next project, we'll work with a US map saved as an SVG file, and we'll load it as a file asset into our sketch. The SVG file contains a blank map showing all US states and borders and is available on Wikipedia in the public domain.[10] The XML code in the SVG file contains vertex style definitions to determine how to connect those vertex points, including stroke, thickness, and fill color.

We'll implement this project in two steps. First we load the map using load-Shape(), and then we'll draw it on the Android screen with Processing's shape() method. Second, we'll alter the fill color of states that political poll takers typically consider as swing states during recent presidential elections and draw them as purple shapes on the screen, as shown in Figure 48, *Scalable*

---

10. http://commons.wikimedia.org/wiki/File:Blank_US_map_borders.svg

Vector Graphic map of the United States, on page 293. In both cases, to zoom and pan the map we'll return to the multitouch gestures we learned in Chapter 2, *Working with the Touch Screen Display*, on page 17.

Load the SVG File

Like all file assets we use in Processing, we'll put our SVG file into the sketch's data folder and load it with its file name using our loadShape() method.

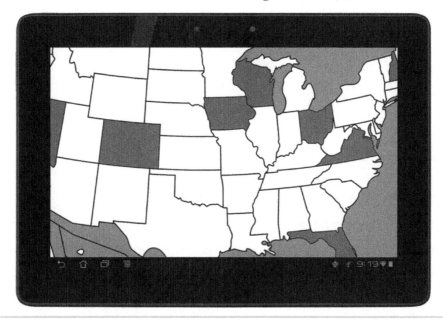

Figure 48—Scalable Vector Graphic map of the United States. The image shows a US map with typical toss-up states. Line detail remains accurate even if we zoom into the map.

Let's take a look at the code for this sketch.

```
ShapesObjects/ScalableVectorGraphics/ScalableVectorGraphics.pde
import ketai.ui.*;

KetaiGesture gesture;

❶ PShape us;
float scaleFactor = 1;

void setup() {
  orientation(LANDSCAPE);
❷ gesture = new KetaiGesture(this);

❸ us = loadShape("Blank_US_map_borders.svg");
```

```
④    shapeMode(CENTER);
    }

    void draw() {
      background(128);

      translate(width/2, height/2);
⑤    scale(scaleFactor);
⑥    shape(us);
    }

    void onPinch(float x, float y, float d)
    {
⑦    scaleFactor += d/100;
⑧    scaleFactor = constrain(scaleFactor, 0.1, 10);
    }

    public boolean surfaceTouchEvent(MotionEvent event) {
      super.surfaceTouchEvent(event);
      return gesture.surfaceTouchEvent(event);
    }
```

Here are the steps we take to load and display the SVG file.

❶ Define a PShape variable called us to store the SVG file.

❷ Create a KetaiGesture class so we can scale the map using a pinch gesture.

❸ Load the Scalable Vector Graphic containing a blank US map.

❹ Set the shapeMode() to center so we can scale the map around its center.

❺ Set the matrix scale() to the current scaleFactor.

❻ Draw the SVG map of the United States.

❼ Integrate the pinch distance d to increase or decrease the scaleFactor.

❽ Constrain the scaleFactor to a minimum of 0.1 of the original map scale and a maximum of 10 times its scale.

Let's test the app.

Run the App

Run the app on the device. You'll see the SVG US map appear centered on the screen due to our call on shapeMode(CENTER). Use the pinch gesture to scale the map, and keep zooming in while observing the line detail of the state borders saved in the file. The image does not become pixelated and the lines remain accurate.

Now that we've learned how to load, display, and scale an SVG file on the Android device, let's take it one step further and modify the properties of the shapes it contains.

Manipulate Shapes Within the SVG File

Now for this second part of our mapping project, we want to take advantage of the fact that SVG files can contain individual shapes that we can work with. In the XML hierarchy of our US map SVG, each state shape is labeled with a two-letter abbreviation, such as "fl" for Florida, which we can call to manipulate the shape's style definitions. To verify, open the SVG map in your favorite photo or vector editor and you'll see that the image consists of individual vector shapes grouped into individual layers and folders that you can edit as you wish.

For this project, we'll highlight the eight states typically considered toss-up states during recent presidential elections.[11] We'll need to single out each of those states in our SVG file, overwrite its style definition, and set its fill to purple before we draw it.

We'll use the getChild() method to find individual state shapes using the two-letter abbreviations saved in the SVG file. We'll store the state abbreviations we are looking for in String array, namely "co" (Colorado), "fl" (Florida), "ia" (Iowa), "nh" (New Hampshire), "nv" (Nevada), "oh" (Ohio), "va" (Virginia), and "wi" (Wisconsin). If we find a matching abbreviation in the SVG file, we'll grab the shape and assign it to a PShape array we'll provide.

To change the shape's color to purple, we'll use disableStyle() to ignore the style definitions included in the file and replace them with our own. We'll also reuse the mouseDragged() method to move the map horizontally and vertically so that we can browse the whole map while being zoomed in at a state level.

Let's take a look at the code we've modified based on earlier code, on page 293.

ShapesObjects/ScalableVectorGraphicsChild/ScalableVectorGraphicsChild.pde
```
import ketai.ui.*;

KetaiGesture gesture;
PShape us;
String tossups[] = {
❶  "co", "fl", "ia", "nh", "nv", "oh", "va", "wi"
};
❷ PShape[] tossup = new PShape[tossups.length];
```

---

11. http://elections.nytimes.com/2012/electoral-map

```
float scaleFactor = 1;
int x, y;

void setup() {
  orientation(LANDSCAPE);
  gesture = new KetaiGesture(this);

  us = loadShape("Blank_US_map_borders.svg");
  shapeMode(CENTER);
  for (int i=0; i<tossups.length; i++)
  {
    tossup[i] = us.getChild(tossups[i]);
    tossup[i].disableStyle();
  }
  x = width/2;
  y = height/2;
}
void draw() {
  background(128);

  translate(x, y);
  scale(scaleFactor);

  shape(us);
  for (int i=0; i<tossups.length; i++)
  {
    fill(128, 0, 128);
    shape(tossup[i]);
  }
}
void onPinch(float x, float y, float d)
{
  scaleFactor += d/100;
  scaleFactor = constrain(scaleFactor, 0.1, 10);
  println(scaleFactor);
}
void mouseDragged()
{
  if (abs(mouseX - pmouseX) < 50)
    x += mouseX - pmouseX;
  if (abs(mouseY - pmouseY) < 50)
    y += mouseY - pmouseY;
}
public boolean surfaceTouchEvent(MotionEvent event) {
  super.surfaceTouchEvent(event);
  return gesture.surfaceTouchEvent(event);
}
```

Here are the additional steps we take to highlight potential toss-up states.

❶ Create a String array containing the two-letter abbreviations of toss-up states.

❷ Create a PShape array called tossup of the same length as the tossups String array.

❸ Assign a child shape in the us map to the tossup PShape array.

❹ Disable the color and opacity style found in the SVG.

❺ Move to the x and y location.

❻ Scale the matrix to our calculated scaleFactor.

❼ Set the new fill() color to purple.

❽ Draw the individual swing states.

❾ Use the KetaiGesture callback method onPinch() to calculate the map scaleFactor.

❿ Use the mouseDragged() callback method to set the horizontal and vertical position of the map on the device screen.

Let's run the app.

Run the App

Run the modified sketch on the device again. This time the app starts up showing "purple states," and we can still zoom into the map and move it horizontally and vertically.

This completes our mapping project and our investigation of Scalable Vector Graphics.

Now that we've learned how to work with shapes and vertices contained in a Scalable Vector Graphic, it's time we looked at another file type comparable to SVG and used for three-dimensional objects—the Object file format.

12.4 Display an Architectural Model Loaded from an Object File

For this project, we'll work with three-dimensional coordinates for vertices that define a figure contained in an Object file, as well as material definitions and image textures linked from that file. We'll use a model of One World Trade Center, also known as Freedom Tower,[12] the lead building of the World Trade Center complex planned by architect Daniel Libeskind and designed by David Childs (to be completed in 2013). The model contains a 3D geometric figure for the main building's architecture and some image textures, shown here:

---

12. http://en.wikipedia.org/wiki/One_World_Trade_Center

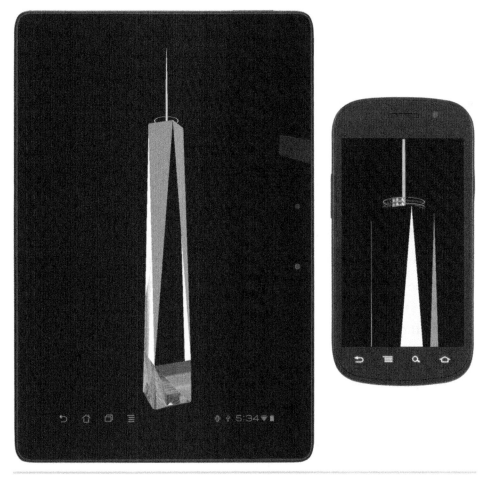

Figure 49—Displaying an Object file. The Object file contains vertices and links to materials and textures for displaying One World Trade Center as a 3D PShape object, shown on the tablet at default scale (left) and zoomed into a roof detail on the phone (right).

Working in 3D, Object (.obj) is a very popular and versatile file format. We can use an OBJ as a self-contained 3D asset and load it into a 3D app on our Android. All the textures for our figure are already predefined in the OBJ file, making it fairly easy to handle in Processing with our familiar PShape class. Yes, it handles OBJ files as well.

Object files are not XML-based in their organizational structure, but they still contain data segments with coordinates for the vertices that define the figure and data segments that link to assets such as materials and textures to the file. The model we'll work with was loaded from Google Sketchup's 3D warehouse and converted into the Object format using Autodesk Maya.[13]

We now have a file called OneWTC.obj, a linked material file of the same name, OneWTC.mtl, and twelve JPEG images named texture0.jpg...texture12.jpg in our sketch data folder.

The code for this project is fairly concise and very similar in structure to our SVG map project on page 293. We'll first load our Object file from the data folder into the sketch and display it using the shape() method. Then we use the onPinch() method to allow for scaling the object and mouseDragged() for rotating the building and moving it up and down vertically.

Here's the code.

```
ShapesObjects/ObjectFiles/ObjectFiles.pde
import ketai.ui.*;

KetaiGesture gesture;

PShape wtc;
int r, y;
float scaleFactor = .02;

void setup() {
  size(displayWidth, displayHeight, P3D);
  orientation(PORTRAIT);
  gesture = new KetaiGesture(this);
  noStroke();

❶  wtc = loadShape("OneWTC.obj");
  y = height/4*3;
}

void draw() {
  background(0);
❷  lights();

❸  translate(width/2, y);
❹  scale(scaleFactor);
❺  rotateX(PI);
❻  rotateY(radians(r));

❼  shape(wtc);
}

❽ void onPinch(float x, float y, float d)
```

---

13. http://sketchup.google.com/3dwarehouse

```
{
  scaleFactor += d/5000;
  scaleFactor = constrain(scaleFactor, 0.01, .3);
  println(scaleFactor);
}

❾ void mouseDragged()
{
  if (abs(mouseX - pmouseX) < 50)
    r += mouseX - pmouseX;
  if (abs(mouseY - pmouseY) < 50)
    y += mouseY - pmouseY;
}

public boolean surfaceTouchEvent(MotionEvent event) {
  super.surfaceTouchEvent(event);
  return gesture.surfaceTouchEvent(event);
}
```

Let's see what steps we need to take to load and display the 3D model.

❶ Load the Object file into a PShape variable called wtc using loadShape().

❷ Switch on the default lights().

❸ Move the matrix horizontally to the center of the screen and vertically to the position y, determined by moving a finger across the screen.

❹ Scale the matrix to the scaleFactor determined by our pinch gesture.

❺ Rotate the building around the x-axis so it appears upright in the PORTRAIT mode and not upside-down.

❻ Rotate the building around the x-axis so we can look at all its sides when we drag one finger horizontally.

❼ Draw the wtc Object file.

❽ Calculate the object's scaleFactor using the onPinch() KetaiGesture callback method.

❾ Determine the vertical position y of the building on the screen and its rotation r using Processing's mousePressed() method.

Let's test the app now.

Run the App

Now run the app on the device. When the 3D scene starts up, the tall One World Trade Center building will appear fullscreen in PORTRAIT mode. Move your finger across the screen horizontally to rotate the building. It's a fairly demanding model for the graphics processor on the Android, so the frame rate is not as high as for most other projects we've worked with so far. Pinch to scale the building, and move your finger across the screen to rotate the building or move it up and down.

Now that we've looked at 3D primitives, Scalable Vector Graphics, and Object files, the missing piece is how to create a figure from scratch using individual vertex points and algorithms.

12.5 Create a Möbius Shape and Control It Using the Gyroscope

In our next project, we'll generate a figure from scratch and use a for loop and a sequence of translations and rotations to create a Möbius strip based on individual vertices that we record. Topologically speaking, the Möbius strip is an interesting example of a 3D figure that does not have a determinable surface area. Practically, it's pretty simple to understand and easy to create using just a piece of paper. If you'd like to try, cut or fold a piece of paper into a strip at least five times as long as it is wide. Hold both ends, and twist one of them 180 degrees while holding the other stationary. Now connect the two ends with a piece of tape and you've got yourself a Möbius strip. It's basically a ring twisted by half a revolution, as shown in Figure 50, *Control a Möbius strip using the gyro*, on page 302.

You can confirm that a Möbius strip has only one side by taking a pen and drawing a continuous line in the center of your paper strip until you've reached the beginning of your line again. You'll need two revolutions to get there, because the Möbius strip is a surface with only one side and only one border.[14] In this project, we'll create this shape using custom vertices. To navigate the 3D scene with our Möbius strip by just rotating our Android device, we'll use a sensor that we haven't yet given the attention it deserves: the gyroscope sensor.

Introducing the Gyroscope Sensor

The Nintendo Wii was the first device to introduce millions of users to gesture-based games, but now similar apps can be purchased for phones and tablets as well. At its heart is an onboard gyroscope sensor. The gyroscope sensor was introduced in 2010 with the iPhone 4 (June 2010), followed by the Samsung Galaxy S (July 2010). Augmented reality (AR) applications are especially able to take advantage of the precise pitch, roll, and yaw angles the sensor provides in real time. The gyro is able to determine the device

---

14. http://en.wikipedia.org/wiki/M%C3%B6bius_strip

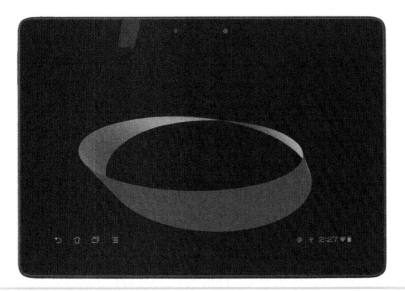

Figure 50—Control a Möbius strip using the gyro. The image shows a PShape object composed of individual vertices that are illuminated by blue ambient light and a white point light source positioned in the center of the strip.

rotation around gravity, for example, when we point the device camera toward the horizon and we rotate it following the horizon line—the accelerometer cannot help us there. Apple's "Synchronized, Interactive Augmented Reality Displays for Multifunction Devices" patent from July 2011 suggests that AR will have an increasing role in the mobile space.

The gyro provides us with information about an Android's rotation, reporting so-called angular rates in degrees for the x-, y-, and z-axes. We can access these readings with the KetaiSensor class and the onGyroscopeEvent(x, y, z) callback method. The angular rate is a positive or negative floating point value reflecting the change for each axis since we last read it. We'll use the standard convention and refer to the rotation around the device's x-axis as *pitch*, around the y-axis as *roll*, and around the z-axis as *yaw*.[15]

Unlike the accelerometer, the gyro is independent of g-force, unfazed by device shakes, and very responsive to device rotation. It's the best sensor for games and 3D scenes that are controlled by moving and rotating the device. The sensor is less ubiquitous than the accelerometer, but it is now found in most Android phones and tablets.

---

15. http://developer.android.com/reference/android/hardware/SensorEvent.html

When a device sits on a table, its gyro reports +-0.000 degrees for pitch, roll, and yaw. To calculate how much a device has rotated, we just need to integrate the values for each of its axes, or in other words, add them all up. Once we've done that we'll know the pitch, roll, and yaw of the device in degrees. The gyro is not aware of how the device is oriented relative to the ground (g-force) or to magnetic north. For that, we'd need to enlist the onboard accelerometer and the magnetic field sensor. But while that information might be critical for a navigation and/or augmented reality app, it's more than we need to know for this one.

A limitation of the gyro is that over time it's susceptible to drift. If we integrate all gyro values while the device is sitting still on the table, we should receive 0.000 degrees for all three axes. However, the values slowly drift after just a few seconds and significantly after a few minutes because we integrate fractions of floating point values many thousands of times per minute, and the sum of all those tiny values won't add up perfectly to 0.000 degrees. For gaming or 3D apps this drift is less relevant, as instantaneous feedback on device rotation outweighs accuracy over extended periods of time. In scenarios where this drift causes problems, the accelerometer can be used to correct the drift.

Record the Vertices for a Möbius Shape

To create the Möbius shape, we'll use an approach that resembles the one we used to create a paper model. To set this up, we'll use a for loop and a series of translations and rotations in three different matrices to determine the individual vertex points we'll use to draw the Möbius shape in three-dimensional space.[16] We've used these methods earlier in Section 2.7, *Detect Multitouch Gestures*, on page 32, and elsewhere.

As with our paper model, we'll choose a center point around which to rotate our band. While we rotate the band one full revolution around the z-axis, we also rotate it by 180 degrees around the y-axis, or half a revolution. Once we've assembled all the vertex points we need to define the two edges of our band in setup(), we can draw the resulting shape in draw() using the beginShape() and endShape() methods.

As the reference for beginShape() points out,[17] "Transformations such as translate(), rotate(), and scale() do not work within beginShape()," so as a workaround, we take each of our vertex points through multiple transformations and look up their final position within our 3D scene, the so-called *model space*. The model space

---

16. http://processing.org/learning/transform2d/

17. http://processing.org/reference/beginShape_.html

x, *y*, and *z* coordinates, which we'll get using modelX(),[18] modelY(), and modelZ(), gives us the final absolute position of our vertex in the scene, and we'll take that position and write it to a PVector array list that we can then use to draw() our shape.

In draw(), we'll use the beginShape(QUAD_STRIP), vertex(), and endShape(CLOSE) methods to assemble the shape, which we draw using the QUAD_STRIP mode, where each of the vertices are connected, and we'll end up with a closed strip surface to which we can assign a fill color.

Using both a blue ambientLight(), as well as a white pointLight() located in the Möbius's center, we'll get a good impression of the three-dimensional shape surface. Because we'll use the device's built-in gyro to rotate the Möbius shape in 3D space around its center point, we'll get to look at all sides by just rotating our Android phone or tablet around its *x*- (pitch), *y*- (roll), and *z*- (yaw) axes.

Let's take a look at the code.

ShapesObjects/Moebius/Moebius.pde

```
import ketai.sensors.*;

KetaiSensor sensor;
float rotationX, rotationY, rotationZ;
float roll, pitch, yaw;

❶ ArrayList<PVector> points = new ArrayList<PVector>();

void setup()
{
  size(displayWidth, displayHeight, P3D);
  orientation(LANDSCAPE);

  sensor = new KetaiSensor(this);
  sensor.start();

  noStroke();
❷ int sections = 360;

❸ for (int i=0; i<=sections; i++)
  {
❹   pushMatrix();
❺   rotateZ(radians(map(i, 0, sections, 0, 360)));
❻   pushMatrix();
❼   translate(height/2, 0, 0);
❽   pushMatrix();
```

---

18. http://processing.org/reference/modelX_.html

```
⑨      rotateY(radians(map(i, 0, sections, 0, 180)));
       points.add(
⑩        new PVector(modelX(0, 0, 50), modelY(0, 0, 50), modelZ(0, 0, 50))
       );
       points.add(
⑪        new PVector(modelX(0, 0, -50), modelY(0, 0, -50), modelZ(0, 0, -50))
       );
       popMatrix();
       popMatrix();
       popMatrix();
     }
   }

   void draw()
   {
     background(0);
⑫   ambientLight(0, 0, 128);
⑬   pointLight(255, 255, 255, 0, 0, 0);

⑭   pitch += rotationX;
⑮   roll += rotationY;
⑯   yaw += rotationZ;

     translate(width/2, height/2, 0);
     rotateX(pitch);
     rotateY(-roll);
     rotateZ(yaw);

⑰   beginShape(QUAD_STRIP);
     for (int i=0; i<points.size(); i++)
     {
⑱     vertex(points.get(i).x, points.get(i).y, points.get(i).z);
     }
     endShape(CLOSE);

     if (frameCount % 10 == 0)
       println(frameRate);
   }

⑲ void onGyroscopeEvent(float x, float y, float z)
   {
     rotationX = radians(x);
     rotationY = radians(y);
     rotationZ = radians(z);
   }

   void mousePressed()
   {
⑳   pitch = roll = yaw = 0;
   }
```

Let's take a look at the steps we take to create the figure and control the scene using the gyro.

❶ Create an ArrayList of type PVector to store all the vertices for our Möbius strip.

❷ Define the number of sections, or quads, used to draw the strip.

❸ Use a for loop to calculate the *x*, *y*, and *z* positions for each vertex used to define the Möbius strip.

❹ Add a new matrix on the matrix stack for our first rotation.

❺ Rotate by one degree around the *z*-axis to complete a full 360-degree revolution after 360 iterations, as defined by sections.

❻ Add a new matrix on the matrix stack for our next transformation.

❼ Move the vertex along the *x*-axis by half the screen height, representing the radius of our Möbius strip.

❽ Add another matrix on the stack for our next rotation.

❾ Rotate around the *y*-axis by 180 degrees for the twist along the Möbius strip.

❿ Set the first vertex point for the current quad element model position in the Möbius strip, displaced by 50 pixels along the *z*-axis with regard to the current matrix's origin.

⓫ Set the first vertex point for the current quad element model position in the Möbius strip, displaced by -50 pixels along the *z*-axis with regard to the current matrix's origin.

⓬ Set a blue ambient light source using the ambientLight() method.

⓭ Set a white point light source in the center of the Möbius strip using pointLight().

⓮ Enumerate the gyroscope x values to calculate the pitch of the device since the app started.

⓯ Enumerate the gyroscope y values to calculate the pitch of the device.

⓰ Enumerate the gyroscope z values to calculate the pitch of the device.

⓱ Begin recording the QUAD_STRIP vertices that make up the Möbius strip.

⓲ End recoding vertices for the strip, and close the connection to the first recorded vertex using CLOSE.

⑲ Receive the gyroscope sensor values for the x-, y-, and z-axes and assign the radians() equivalent of their degree values to rotationX, rotationY, and rotationZ.

⑳ Reset the pitch, roll, and yaw to 0 so we can reset the rotation of the Möbius strip in 3D space by tapping the device screen.

Let's test the app.

Run the App

Run the sketch on the device. The Möbius strip begins lying "flat" in front of our camera. Because the gyro takes care of rotating the Möbius shape, it slowly drifts if we don't do anything. Pick up the Android phone or tablet and rotate it up and down along the x-axis, left and right along the y-axis, and finally flat around the z-axis. The Möbius strip counters this device movement in virtual space, and we are able to take a closer look at the figure. Tap the screen to reset the strip to right where we started.

Now let's take a look at how we are doing on graphics performance for this scene, consisting of 720 vertices, or 360 sections times 2 vertices for the band. I'm using the Google Nexus S phone for this test. Look at the frameRate printed to the Processing console, and you'll see that the sketch is running at a default 60 frames per second, which is good.

Let's multiply the number of sections by 10 and look again. Go ahead and change the sections value in the code from 360 to 3600 and rerun the sketch on the device. On the Nexus S, the frame rate drops to about 14 frames per second.

This drop in the frame rate can be avoided if we take advantage of Processing's OpenGL support for retaining a shape in the GPU's memory. Let's take a look at an alternative method to draw our Möbius shape using the PShape class.

12.6 Use GPU Memory to Improve Frame Rate

Keeping vertices and textures in the GPU's memory becomes very useful when we deal with more complex figures that do not change over time. Processing's PShape object allows us to create a shape from scratch using the createShape() method, which works much like beginShape(). In this modified sketch based on code, on page 304, we create the Möbius strip as a PShape in setup, and then we use the shape() method to draw the shape on the screen. All the transformations remain the same. We keep the QUAD_STRIP drawing mode, and we close the shape we create using the end(CLOSE) method.

Let's examine the changes we've made in the code.

ShapesObjects/MoebiusRetained/MoebiusRetained.pde

```
import ketai.sensors.*;

KetaiSensor sensor;
float rotationX, rotationY, rotationZ;
float roll, pitch, yaw;

PShape moebius;

void setup()
{
  size(displayWidth, displayHeight, P3D);
  orientation(LANDSCAPE);

  sensor = new KetaiSensor(this);
  sensor.start();

  noStroke();
  int sections = 3600;

  moebius = createShape(QUAD_STRIP);
  for (int i=0; i<=sections; i++)
  {
    pushMatrix();
    rotateZ(radians(map(i, 0, sections, 0, 360)));
    pushMatrix();
    translate(height/2, 0, 0);
    pushMatrix();
    rotateY(radians(map(i, 0, sections, 0, 180)));
    moebius.vertex(modelX(0, 0, 50), modelY(0, 0, 50), modelZ(0, 0, 50));
    moebius.vertex(modelX(0, 0, -50), modelY(0, 0, -50), modelZ(0, 0, -50));
    popMatrix();
    popMatrix();
    popMatrix();
  }
  moebius.end(CLOSE);
}

void draw()
{
  background(0);

  ambientLight(0, 0, 128);
  pointLight(255, 255, 255, 0, 0, 0);

  pitch += rotationX;
  roll += rotationY;
  yaw += rotationZ;

  translate(width/2, height/2, 0);
```

```
    rotateX(pitch);
    rotateY(-roll);
    rotateZ(yaw);

❻   shape(moebius);

    if (frameCount % 10 == 0)
      println(frameRate);
  }

  void onGyroscopeEvent(float x, float y, float z)
  {
    rotationX = radians(x);
    rotationY = radians(y);
    rotationZ = radians(z);
  }

  void mousePressed()
  {
    pitch = roll = yaw = 0;
  }
```

Let's take a look at the steps we take to record the shape into a PShape object.

❶ Create a PShape variable called moebius to record vertex points into.

❷ Create the QUAD_STRIP PShape object moebius using the createShape() method.

❸ Add our first strip vertex() to the moebius PShape.

❹ Add the second strip vertex() to the moebius PShape.

❺ CLOSE the PShape object using the end() method

❻ Draw the moebius strip using Processing's shape() method.

Let's test the app.

Run the App

Run the sketch on the device. We've also used 3600 sections as we've done in the code before, but the frame rate is back up to 60 frames per second. The PShape class and its ability to leverage OpenGL is definitely one of the main improvements in Processing 2.0.

You are now able to create figures from scratch by recording the coordinates for the vertices that define the figure. Finally, let's explore how to change the viewpoint of our virtual camera in a 3D scene.

12.7 Control a Virtual Camera with Your Gaze

For this final chapter project, we'll implement an experimental and lesser-known method to interact with a 3D scene—using our gaze to rotate a constellation of planets containing Earth and the Moon. By looking at the scene displayed on our device screen from a specific angle, we can control the rotation of Earth and the Moon around the x- and y-axes, as illustrated in Figure 51, *Control the camera location via gaze detection,* on page 310. Similar to a scenario where we look around a fixed object by moving our head slightly sideways, we cause Earth to rotate and reveal the continents located on its sides accordingly.

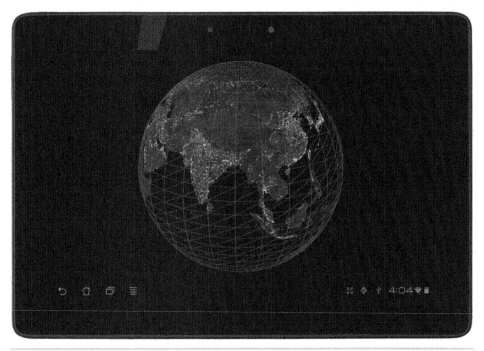

Figure 51—Control the camera location via gaze detection. The 3D scene containing Earth and the Moon is controlled by the relative location of our eyes looking toward the device camera.

We'll place Earth at the center of the scene, since the Moon rotates around Earth in this two-body system. To navigate the 3D scene, we move the camera this time, and not the figure. Earlier, we've rotated the 3D primitives we've worked with around the scene's y-axis and left the virtual camera where it is by default. This time, we are moving the camera() while keeping it continuously pointed at the center of our scene, where we placed Earth—independent of our camera's viewpoint. As a result, we'll always keep an eye on Earth. Compared with the NASA texture image we used in Section 11.3, *Apply an Image Texture*, on page 271, we'll use a higher resolution version of the same image for more accurate detail. We'll use the maximum resolution the PShape can handle—2048 pixels wide or high.

The Moon is about 3.7 times smaller than Earth and located roughly 110 times its diameter from Earth. We'll use these ratios to add a white sphere to our scene and then cause it to revolve around our home planet. Because the Moon is quite far from Earth, both in reality and in our 3D scene, we'll hardly catch it in our camera view. Feel free to place it closer when we test the sketch.

To implement this sketch, we'll translate our coordinate system to the center of the screen located at [width/2, height/2, 0]. Then we place Earth at this new center, [0, 0, 0]. Finally we rotate the Moon around Earth and translate it 110 times its diameter away from Earth.

Our camera is located at [0, 0, height], which means it's also centered horizontally and vertically on the screen but at a *z* distance of height away from the center of Earth's sphere. For example, the height on the Samsung Nexus S device it would be 480 pixels away from the center, and on the Asus Transformer Prime, 800. With a sphere size of Earth set to height/3, both the camera distance and the display size of Earth are defined in relation to the screen height, keeping the scene proportional and independent of the Android device we are using.

To control the scene, we'll use Ketai's KetaiSimpleFace class, which can recognize the midpoint and distance between the eyes of a face detected by the front-facing device camera—as we've done already in Section 5.8, *Detect Faces*, on page 120. We'll assume only one face in the scene less than an arm's length away from the device, which is why we set the maximum number of faces to be recognized to 1. If we find a face, we'll use the x and y location of the face to calculate the position of our camera in the scene. If we don't find a face, we'll fall back to a touch screen input, where we use the mouseX and mouseY position of the fingertip instead.

Let's take a look at the code.

ShapesObjects/LiveFaceDetectionAndroid/LiveFaceDetectionAndroid.pde

```
import ketai.camera.*;
import ketai.cv.facedetector.*;

int MAX_FACES = 1;
KetaiSimpleFace[] faces = new KetaiSimpleFace[MAX_FACES];
KetaiCamera cam;
```

```
① PVector camLocation = new PVector();
  PShape sphereShape;
  PImage sphereTexture;

  void setup() {
    size(displayWidth, displayHeight, P3D);
    orientation(LANDSCAPE);
    stroke(255, 50);
    sphereTexture = loadImage("earth_lights_lrg.jpg");
② sphereDetail(36);
    sphereShape = createShape(SPHERE, height/2);
    sphereShape.texture(sphereTexture);

    cam = new KetaiCamera(this, 320, 240, 24);
    cam.setCameraID(1);
  }

  void draw() {
    if (cam.isStarted())
      background(50);
    else
      background(0);
    translate(width/2, height/2, 0);
③ camera(camLocation.x, camLocation.y, height, // eyeX, eyeY, eyeZ    //
    0.0, 0.0, 0.0, // centerX, centerY, centerZ
    0.0, 1.0, 0.0); // upX, upY, upZ
    noStroke();
④ faces = KetaiFaceDetector.findFaces(cam, MAX_FACES);

    for (int i=0; i < faces.length; i++) {
      //reverse the "face-mapping" correcting mirrored camera image
⑤   camLocation.x = map(faces[i].location.x, 0, cam.width, width/2, -width/2);
⑥   camLocation.y = map(faces[i].location.y, 0, cam.height, -height/2, height/2);
    }

    if (!cam.isStarted()) {
⑦   camLocation.x = map(mouseX, 0, width, -width/2, width/2);
      camLocation.y = map(mouseY, 0, height, -height/2, height/2);
    }
    shape(sphereShape);

    fill(255);
⑧ rotateY(PI * frameCount / 500);
⑨ translate(0, 0, -height/2 / 3.7 * 2 * 110);
⑩ sphere(height/2 / 3.7);
  }

  void onCameraPreviewEvent() {
    cam.read();
  }
```

```
void exit() {
  cam.stop();
}

void keyPressed() {
  if (key == CODED) {
    if (keyCode == MENU) {
      if (cam.isStarted()) {
        cam.stop();
      }
      else
        cam.start();
    }
  }
}
```

Let's take a look at the steps we need to control the scene with our gaze.

❶ Define a PVector camLocation to keep track of the camera position within the scene we'll calculate.

❷ Increase the number of vertices per full 360-degree revolution around the sphere to 36, or one tessellation per 10 degrees longitude.

❸ Set the camera() viewpoint to our calculated location, looking at the exact center of the scene.

❹ Detect up to one face in the camera image.

❺ Map the horizontal position of the PVector camLocation from the cam preview width to the screen width.

❻ Map the vertical position of the PVector camLocation from the cam preview height to the screen height.

❼ Set the camLocation to the fingertip if we are not using gaze control.

❽ Rotate the Moon slowly around Earth, one revolution per 10 seconds at an assumed device frame rate of 60 frames per second.

❾ Place the white Moon sphere at its relative distance to Earth (about 110 times its diameter).

❿ Draw the Moon's sphere.

⓫ Start face detection with the Menu button.

Let's test the app next.

Run the App

Run the sketch on the device. When it starts up, you'll see a sphere drawn on a black background and painted with the NASA-provided image of Earth that we used earlier in this chapter. The camera will not yet have started, and until it is activated, it won't recognize faces.

Move your finger to the center of the screen and observe a view straight ahead at Earth's sphere. Move it left across the screen and you'll move the virtual camera to the left in the scene, move it up and you'll move the camera up, and so on. We get an impression of the movement we can expect when we start the face tracker.

Now press the menu key to start up the camera and begin recognizing faces, indicated by the text printed to the console but also by switching the black background to dark gray. Hold the device comfortably, as you would when you look straight at the screen. Now move your head sideways and see Earth reveal its sides; move your head up and down and see Earth reveal its poles.

Because we are moving the camera and do not rotate Earth, we are getting the side effect that Earth seems to scale—it doesn't. Instead, we are observing what in the motion picture world would be called a tracking shot,[19] where a camera is mounted on a dolly on a track. In our scenario, the track is straight, so we are actually moving further away from Earth as we move left and right, up and down. We could mitigate this effect by putting our camera on a "circular track"; however, it would be a less dynamic "shot" as well.

This completes our exploration of 3D apps in Processing.

12.8 Wrapping Up

You are now able to create 3D apps in Processing using OpenGL's hardware acceleration to render shapes, text, objects, textures, lights, and cameras. Each one of those subjects deserves further exploration. The basic principles of creating or loading shapes and objects, using image textures, working with different types of lights, and animating camera movements also remain the same for more complex 3D apps.

Let's apply our knowledge about hardware-accelerated graphics now in our last chapter, where we'll develop cross-platform apps running in the HTML5 browsers installed on all smart phone devices shipped today.

---

19. http://en.wikipedia.org/wiki/Tracking_shot

CHAPTER 13

Sharing and Publishing Applications

Once you've finished an app, it's only natural to share it with others. You might want to send it to a friend or colleague for testing. Maybe you want to post it on your website so your followers and clients can download it. Or maybe you want to move the app to Eclipse to create a production version using Java and direct calls to the Android SDK. You could decide to publish the app in Google Play or even offer it as a web app that users can run in an HTML5-ready browser regardless of the devices they own. We'll address each of these scenarios in this chapter and discuss their advantages and disadvantages. By the time you finish, you'll have an amazingly diverse set of options available to you for deploying your work.

Let's start with the simplest option: sharing your app as an Android sketch or APK with friends and colleagues.

13.1 Share Your Code

A straightforward way to share an app is to compress and ship off the Processing sketch folder that contains your source code and its resources. Others can then use Processing for Android to run it on their own devices and add their own features. A second option is to provide friends and colleagues with a copy of the Android application package (APK) that Processing creates whenever you run your application in Android mode.

Sharing a Sketch

It's easy to share a Processing sketch with another Processing user. All that's required is for Processing, the Android SDK, and the Ketai library (assuming you're using it) to be installed and available on the user's target machine.

To share a sketch, browse to your sketch folder (Sketch → Show Sketch Folder) and compress the sketch folder and all its assets.

- In OS X, control-click your sketch folder and select Compress. A .zip file will be created for you to share.

- In Windows, right-click your sketch folder and select Add to Archive, creating a .zip file for you to share.

- In Linux, right-click your sketch folder and select Compress → Compress as → sketch.zip.

You can rename the compressed file before sharing it, but you shouldn't rename individual files or folders, because the sketch won't open properly if the sketch directory doesn't include a .pde source file of the same name.

A friend or colleague can then unpack the compressed sketch, open it in Processing's Android mode and run the app. This route works for OS X, Windows, and Linux.

Sharing an Android Application Package

Each time you use Processing to run a sketch on an Android device—as you've done in more than forty projects—Processing first builds an Android application package (APK) on your desktop, copies it onto the Android device, and then launches it. The package is enabled for debugging but is not signed. While it is suitable for use by friends and colleagues, it cannot be published at Google Play. Still, it's an easy way to share an app with friends who may not be running Processing but would still like to use it.

When Processing builds the debug version of the APK, it displays the path to its bin directory inside the Processing console window with the following message.

```
Converting compiled files and external libraries into PATHNAME/bin
```

You can navigate to that bin directory by browsing to the PATHNAME on your file system using a utility like Windows Explorer or MacOS Finder or through a terminal window. You'll find the APK there under the name SKETCHNAME-debug.apk and you can then send it to anyone who wants to load it onto a device and test it out.

Because the APK that Processing creates is meant for debugging, it's not meant for distribution on your blog or website. We'll learn how to disable debugging and sign the app for public release in Section 13.4, *Publish Your App to Google Play*, on page 322.

Once you begin to share your project with others, it's useful to think about branding your app by giving it a recognizable identity. One way to do that is by customizing its icon. We'll take a look at how to do that in the next section.

13.2 Brand Your App

When you run a Processing sketch on an Android device, Processing provides it with a default icon. You're not required to change it, but sticking with the default icon will hardly make your app stand out. An icon is the only visual element—besides a label—that's available to distinguish your app from others.

Although an Android icon is necessarily small, it still needs to stand out. The smallest icon size supported by Android is 36 pixels square—not much real estate to work with. But the Portable Network Graphic (PNG) format in which Android icons are formatted supports color, text, and even transparency, which we can use to alter an icon's shape or translucency. You'll need to make sure, however, that it has enough contrast to show up against any background color.

The design of an icon is a topic beyond the scope of this book, but you can find more information on the design of launcher icons at the Android developer website.[1] Once you've created an icon with your favorite graphics software and exported your work to a PNG file, loading it into your sketch requires the following steps:

1. Create an icon that is 512 pixels square. If we want to offer the app in Google Play, we'll need a high resolution PNG with 512 x 512 pixels in 32-bit color mode.

2. Scale and export four PNG image files in the following sizes: 96, 72, 48, and 36 pixels. Those four files are the ones we'll include in our sketch folder.

3. Name the 96-, 72-, 48-, and 36-pixel icons as follows: icon-96.png, icon-72.png, icon-48.png, and icon-36.png

4. Create a new Android sketch in Processing called CustomIcon and save it without adding any code statements.

5. Place the icons into the root of the CustomIcon folder (click Sketch, then Show Sketch Folder).

6. Run the app on the device and check the icon you've made.

---

1. http://developer.android.com/guide/practices/ui_guidelines/icon_design_launcher.html

Figure 52, *Custom icons added to a sketch as PNG files*, shows the contents of CustomIcons, which we've created solely to test the custom icons we've made.

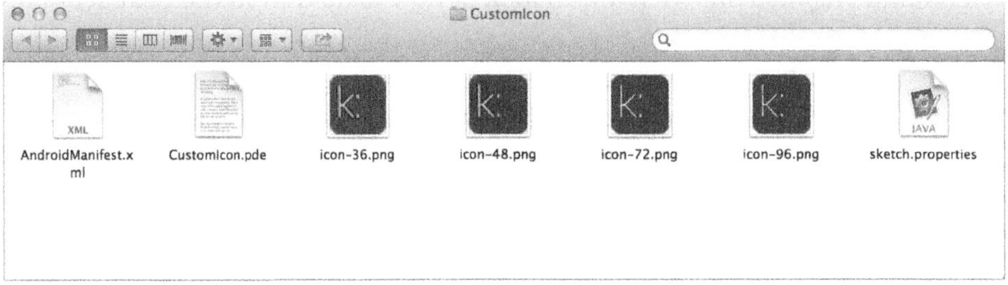

Figure 52—Custom icons added to a sketch as PNG files. Add four PNG custom icons in different sizes to the root of your sketch folder, and Processing will use those instead of the default icon when you run the sketch on your device.

The sketch folder now includes the following files:

AndroidManifest.xml Contains all the properties for our Android app including permissions—Processing always creates this file for us when we run the app or work with the Android Permissions Selector under Android/Sketch Permissions.

CustomIcon.pde Contains no code statements; used to test the icon

icon-36.png A 36-pixel-square PNG image for preview on a low-density screen (120dpi)

icon-48.png A 48-pixel-square PNG image for preview on a medium-density screen (160dpi)

icon-72.png A 72-pixel-square PNG image for preview on a high-density screen (240dpi)

icon-96.png A 96-pixel-square PNG image for preview on an extra-high density screen (320dpi)

sketch.properties Stores the Processing mode in which we've saved the sketch

The Android icon design guidelines discuss many aspects of design consistency and the Android look and feel.[2] Before publishing your app, take a look at this reference. It also offers a template packed with files for your reference.[3]

WebApps/CustomIcon/CustomIcon.pde
```
// Empty sketch for testing icons
```

---

2. http://developer.android.com/guide/practices/ui_guidelines/icon_design.html
3. http://developer.android.com/shareables/icon_templates-v4.0.zip

Run the App

Run the Customicon sketch on your device with the custom icons included in the sketch folder. Once it launches (empty), browse to your apps and find the Customicon app displaying the PNG icon you've just made.

Now that you've seen how to visually brand your app, let's see how to move it into Eclipse.

13.3 Move Your App to Eclipse

There are several reasons you might want to move a sketch to Eclipse. First, it's the only way right now to prepare it for publication at Google Play, as we'll see in Section 13.4, *Publish Your App to Google Play*, on page 322. You'll need to use Eclipse to sign the application and to disable debugging, steps that Google requires and are recommended for any application you plan to release to the public. You'll also want to move to Eclipse if you want to finish up your work by coding in Java code or making direct calls to Android APIs that aren't available through the Ketai library. Or maybe the work you've been doing is a module in a larger Java application being constructed by a team that has chosen Eclipse as its development platform.

Eclipse is the IDE that Google officially endorses for developing Android apps. It's a developer platform that offers an impressive number of features for creating and maintaining a codebase. It's significantly more elaborate than the Processing IDE, which is exactly the reason we've kept it at arm's length until now. It takes a bit more time to download and install and requires a lot more patience to configure and learn.

Eclipse is maintained by a not-for-profit corporation and developer community devoted to building an open source platform for a variety of programming languages. Unlike Processing, Eclipse allows you to examine your code from a number of "perspectives" and provides a variety of inspectors for probing the types and methods you are using. Advanced code highlighting flags errors as you type and makes suggestions on how to fix them. You can also jump directly to the types and methods that we use and see how they're being used. Eclipse offers ways to search your entire workspace, and you can extend the IDE with a variety of plugins. All of these advantages, of course, steepen Eclipse's learning curve.

With more than three dozen Android projects under your belt, there's no reason to shy away from using Eclipse. And if you want to prepare an application for wider distribution, dealing with it is unavoidable. Although the Processing team is at work on an Export Signed Package feature that will eventually let us conduct the complete Android development cycle from within Processing, it remains under construction. Once it's implemented, however, we'll be able to skip Eclipse altogether for many tasks, including *Import and Run a Sketch*, on page 321, and *Sign Your App for Release*, on page 325. But for now we need it.

We'll get started by downloading the Eclipse IDE. Then we'll install the Android Development Tools (ADT) plugin for Eclipse and choose a location for the Android SDK. Finally, we'll walk through the steps to export a sketch from Processing, import it into Eclipse for further work, and export it as a ready-to-run APK. We'll use the earthquake app from Section 9.9, *Add Vibes to the Earthquake App*, on page 239, as our example. A thorough introduction to the Eclipse IDE is beyond the scope of this book. For an in-depth discussion of platform features, please refer to the Eclipse project.[4]

Download Eclipse

You'll find the different flavors of the Eclipse platform on the Eclipse.org website. Google recommends Eclipse Classic or the Java or RCP versions (I used Java for this book). Choose your platform, download it, and follow these steps.[5]

1. Download Eclipse for your operating system at http://www.eclipse.org/downloads/.

2. Start Eclipse and select Help → Install New Software from the Eclipse menu.

3. Select Help → Install New Software from the Eclipse menu to install the ADT plugin.

4. Click "Add..." and paste the following URL into the Location field:

   https://dl-ssl.google.com/android/eclipse/

   You can label this location with a name of your choice.

5. In the list that appears, check the Developer Tools box and finish installing the ADT plugin.

6. Restart Eclipse.

7. In the "Welcome to Android Development" window, select "Use existing SDKs" and browse to the location of your Android SDK.

That completes the installation and configuration of the Eclipse platform for Android development. You're now ready to import a sketch from Processing.

---

4.   http://www.eclipse.org/

5.   http://developer.android.com/sdk/installing/installing-adt.html

Import and Run a Sketch

As our example, we'll use the earthquake sketch we developed earlier in Section 9.9, *Add Vibes to the Earthquake App*, on page 239. We'll first export the sketch from Processing, then import it into Eclipse as an Android project, and finally create an application package that can be emailed or hosted on a web server and installed directly on any Android device.

Let's get started. To create an Android Project to export to Eclipse, follow these instructions:

1. In Processing, open the quake code, on page 240, in Processing Android mode.

2. Choose Export Android Project from the File menu. Processing creates an android directory for us in the sketch folder. Note the path to this directory so you can browse to it from Eclipse in our next step.

Follow these instructions to import the Android Project into Eclipse:

1. In Eclipse, choose File/New/Project... → Android/Android Project from Existing Code. Browse to the android directory, highlight it, and click Open. The Import Projects dialog shows you the path to the project you've selected.

2. Check "Copy projects to workspace" and click Finish.

You've now created an Android project from an existing source, and you'll find it in your Eclipse workspace under the name processing.test.dataearth- quakesshake.DataEarthquakesShake. Without taking any additional steps, we can test our Android app by running it on a device using Eclipse. This will automatically create an Android application package (APK) inside the bin directory of the project, which we can share. Let's try it:

1. Take a look at the bin directory within your Eclipse project before you run the app. You should find that no .apk file has yet been created.

2. Connect your device to your workstation with a USB cable.

3. On the Eclipse main menu, select Run → Run As... → Android Application. The app will launch on your device as shown in Figure 36, *Earthquakes reported worldwide during the last hour*, on page 234.

4. Now look again in the bin directory for the project. You should find that an APK file has been created for the application.

The Android application package (APK) that Eclipse creates is, for all practical purposes, identical to the package described in *Sharing an Android Application Package*, on page 316. Like the APK that Processing creates, the default Eclipse package is unsigned and debugging is enabled, which makes it unsuitable for Google Play or widespread distribution. Still, like the APK that Processing creates, it can be shared. This section would not be complete without a brief look at how to use it.

Share an Eclipse-Generated APK

Take a look at the bin directory for the quake application we ran in *Import and Run a Sketch*, on page 321, and you'll find the APK file there.

You can take this file, upload it to a web server, have your followers or clients download it, and call it a day. If instead you expect users to browse directly to the .apk with their Android web browser, follow the steps given in the dialog to install and launch the app on a phone or tablet. If you have already run the app at least once, you'll be prompted to replace the older version with the latest one.

Run the App

To test this functionality, upload the processing.test.dataearthquakesshake.DataEarth-quakesShake.apk onto a web server and try it. You can also email the APK to yourself or a colleague. As long as you can get to the package from your Android device, you'll be able to install and launch it.

Congratulations, you now have the tools to share apps with your friends, followers, and clients. But if you plan to offer them through the Google Play Store or post it for wider distribution, there's more work to do.

13.4 Publish Your App to Google Play

Now that we've created the Android application package, we are one step away from publishing our app to Google Play.[6] Play is the official marketplace for Android apps, home to over 700,000 apps and games (as many as the Mac App Store). The Play Store is the centralized hub for Android apps, and it can be searched and browsed by categories. App users rate the apps available in the Play Store and provide feedback on app benefits and issues. To reach the broadest group of Android customers, you will want to publish your app to Google Play.

---

6. https://play.google.com/store/apps

To participate in Google Play, you must register as an Android developer and sign your app. You'll also want to disable debugging. You can upload the application to the Play Store for free. Royalties for your app sales will be processed through Google Checkout. Google takes a 30 percent revenue share on your gross revenue from sales when you sell your app through the Play Store. You must also agree to the Developer Distribution Agreement to be able to upload your app to the Play Store,[7] and you should definitely complete the publishing checklist for Google Play before uploading your APK.[8]

Once you've completed your upload to the Play Store, your app will show up there within a couple of hours (compared with a couple of weeks in the Mac App Store).

To publish to Google Play, we've got some preparation and cleaning up to do. First we'll rename our Android package to create a unique name space for our app. Then we'll modify the manifest to adjust the app's label, disable the debugging mode, and sign the app for release. Finally we'll take some representative screenshots required for display at the Play Store.

Create a Unique Namespace

When you submit to Google Play, you need to provide a unique package name for our app, which cannot be changed once you've published it—even if you take it down from the store. Therefore, you need to consider it carefully before you publish. You'll also need to take care of the key you'll use to sign the app for release. If you lose it, you'll need to upload the app with a new package name and key.

To create a unique package name, let's apply standard practice and choose a name space that is patterned uniquely after our company domain. For this demo, I'll use my company name—ai.ket.quakeit—and I'll label my app QuakeIt. You should choose your company name and project label and pattern it the same way—com.yourCompany.projectName.

Here's what to do to define a unique package name in Eclipse.

1. Browse to the src directory within the Android project in your workspace and open it.

2. Right-click the processing.test.dataearthquakesshake package name and choose Refactor → Rename...

---

7. http://play.google.com/about/developer-distribution-agreement.html

8. http://developer.android.com/distribute/googleplay/publish/preparing.html

3. Provide the name space for your company, patterned as com.companyname.
   projectname.

Now that we've changed the package name, we also need to change the Android
manifest.

Prepare the Manifest for Play

Let's open the AndroidManifest.xml file to change the app's label and to disable
debugging. Double-click the manifest file that is located in the root of our
Eclipse project. It opens in the Eclipse editor as shown in Figure 53, *The
Android manifest XML file*, on page 324, providing us with text fields, drop-
down menus, and buttons that we can use to make adjustments to the file.
A number of tabs on the bottom of the editor window are available; the Manifest tab is shown when we initially open the file.

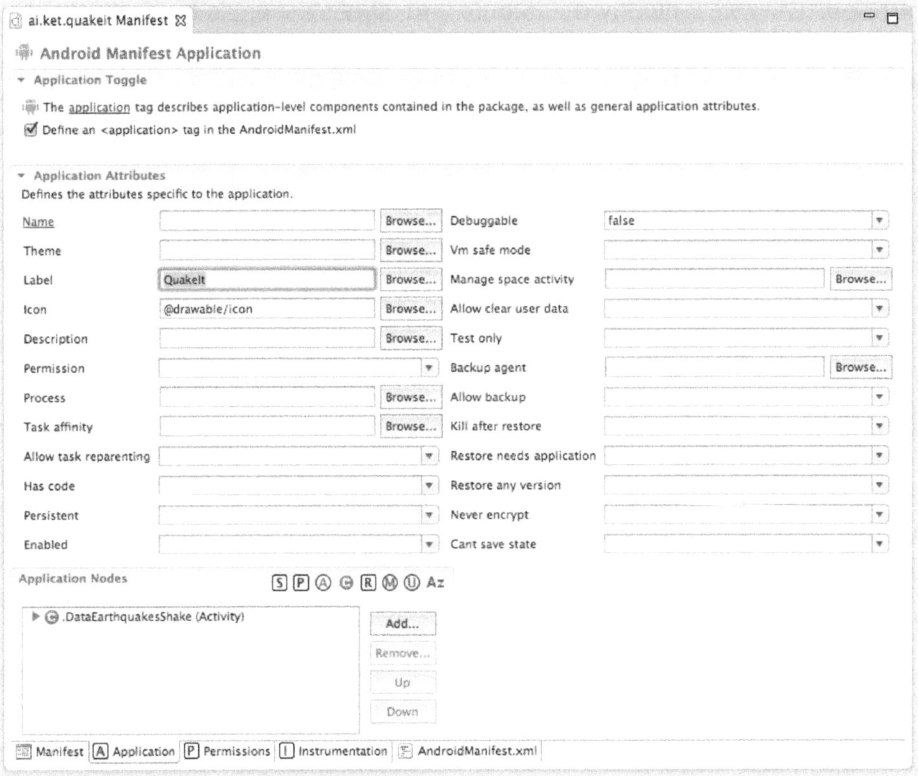

Figure 53—The Android manifest XML file. We create an app's label by typing it into the
Label field of the Android Application Manifest form that Eclipse provides. To disable
debugging, we set Debuggable to "false."

Change the following attributes in the manifest using the text fields and drop-down menus in the Eclipse UI:

1. In the Manifest tab, change Package into the name space you've just used to rename your package—ai.ket.quakeit in my case. Save your change to this field, which then also changes the package name in the gen directory.

2. Rename the app by clicking on the Application tab and changing the text in the Label field. This will change the name of your app once it's installed on the device.

3. Set Debuggable to false using the drop-down menu—we won't need to debug the app any more after we publish.

4. Rename the project so it is consistent with this name space. This step is optional, but it allows us to stay consistent with our naming convention. Right-click our project in the Eclipse workspace and choose Refactor → Rename... from the menu. Rename the project consistently; I'll choose ai.ket.quakeit again.

Save the changes you've made. Let's test the app again and check if the changes we've made still produce an Android application package that we can run on our device.

Run the App

To test if all the changes worked out OK, run the project as an Android application in Eclipse. When the app starts up, check the bin folder in your Eclipse workspace. You'll find an ai.ket.quakeit.apk now based on the change we've made to the project name; yours will be named accordingly.

Now browse to the apps on your device. You'll find the app there with the label you've chosen, which in my case is QuakeIt.

Let's sign the app for release.

Sign Your App for Release

Android requires all apps to be digitally signed with a certificate held by the developer. Up to this point, Processing signed the apps for us using a debug key. For release, we need to sign our app with a private keystore that is available only to us. A debug key will not be sufficient. The private key identifies us as the author of the app.

To release to Google Play, we also need to register with Google as the Android developer for a one-time $25 registration fee. Google asserts that this fee encourages "higher quality products on Google Play (e.g., less spammy products)." You'll also need to register as a merchant with Google Checkout so sales can be processed.[9]

To sign the earthquake app we've created with a private key, let's use Eclipse's Android application wizard. Since we have Eclipse and the Android development tools available, it's the easiest way to generate the private key we'll use to sign the app. Alternatively, we could create the private keystore via the command line.[10]

Here's what we need to do to sign the app.

1. Select the earthquake Android project in your Eclipse workspace and go to File → Export.

2. In the Android folder, select Export Android Application and click Next. The Export Application wizard starts.

3. Check if the earthquake project shows up under Project, otherwise browse to it and click Next. The wizard performs a check to see if the project can be exported.

4. Check "Create new keystore" in the Keystore selection dialog shown in Figure 54, *Use the Export Android Application wizard to create a key*, on page 327, assuming you don't already have an existing keystore available (otherwise browse to your existing keystore. Provide a name for your keystore in the Location field along with a password of your choice. Make sure to take note of this information, as you can reuse this key for your next signed release.) Click Next.

5. Provide your personal information tied to this key and click Next.

6. Select a destination for your signed .apk. Feel free to change the name of the file if you like. It has nothing to do with the application label we've specified earlier. Click Finish.

Congratulations—you've completed the steps to sign the app for release with a private keystore. You can also use this signed app to share with friends, followers, and clients as we've done earlier. However, this signed application package is now ready for Google Play.

If you'd like to further customize and polish your release, try these online resources to help you do that:[11]

---

9.   https://checkout.google.com/sell

10. http://developer.android.com/tools/publishing/app-signing.html#cert

11. http://developer.android.com/tools/publishing/app-signing.html

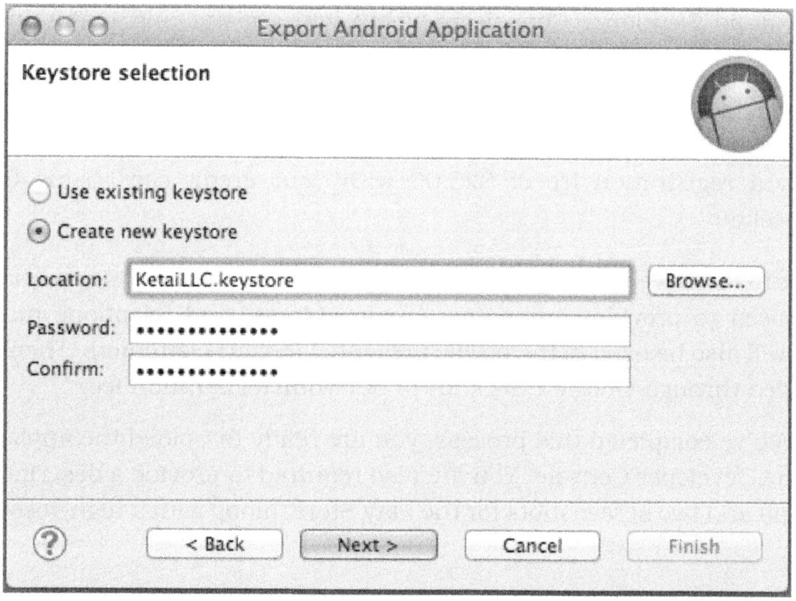

Figure 54—Use the Export Android Application wizard to create a key. We launch the Export Android Application wizard from the File → Export menu.

- To obtain a suitable private key[12]
- To compile the application in release mode[13]
- To sign your application with your private key[14]
- To align the final APK package[15]

With a properly configured manifest and a proper signature, your application is almost ready for release to Google Play. All that remains is for you to complete the Google publishing checklist and upload the application.

Complete the Google Publishing Checklist

You should also consider a number of things before you hit the upload button to Google Play. To make sure you address them all, Google provides a comprehensive publishing checklist. You should read though the checklist online before you release your app.[16]

---

12. http://developer.android.com/tools/publishing/app-signing.html#cert
13. http://developer.android.com/tools/publishing/app-signing.html#releasecompile
14. http://developer.android.com/tools/publishing/app-signing.html#signapp
15. http://developer.android.com/tools/publishing/app-signing.html#align
16. http://developer.android.com/distribute/googleplay/publish/preparing.html

The Android Developer Console is where you register and maintain your developer account. If you are not a developer yet, you need to do the following:

- Create a developer profile.
- Agree to the Developer Distribution Agreement.[17]
- Pay a registration fee of $25.00 with your credit card using Google Checkout.

Browse to the Developer Console and set yourself up by following the dialog.[18] You'll need to provide your name, email address, and telephone number, which will also be used in the profile presented to your customers. Then you'll be guided through Google Checkout to pay your registration fee.

Once you've completed this process, you are ready to upload the application from the Developer Console. You are also required to provide a description of your app and two screenshots for the Play Store, along with a high-resolution icon.

The description requires keywords that your customers can use to find the app. Do some research on the title and keywords before you choose them. Your description should include the app's features and benefits and communicate clearly if you require certain hardware.

You've already made the 512-pixel high-resolution icon earlier in Section 13.2, *Brand Your App*, on page 317. Make your final adjustments, if necessary. Let's learn how to take screenshots next.

Take Screenshots

Eclipse includes a tool that we can use to take screenshots known as the DDMS, or Dalvik Debug Monitor Server.[19] DDMS is an integral component of Eclipse and allows us to also monitor the activities in the device's Dalvik virtual machine. To use it, first make sure your device is connected to your workstation via USB and then start up the DDMS perspective as follows:

1. Select Window → Open Perspective → Other... → DDMS.

2. Click on your Android device listed in the Name window. You'll see in the LogCat window all activity in the Dalvik virtual machine.

3. Click on the icon that looks like a digital camera in the upper right corner of the Devices window. The Device Screen Capture window appears. Click

---

17. http://play.google.com/about/developer-distribution-agreement.html

18. http://developer.android.com/distribute/googleplay/publish/console.html

19. http://developer.android.com/tools/debugging/ddms.html

Rotate to rotate the image orientation as shown in Figure 55, *Using the device screen capture tool*, on page 329.

4. Click Save to save your preferred image format.

You can choose Refresh to capture the best and most representative image for your app.

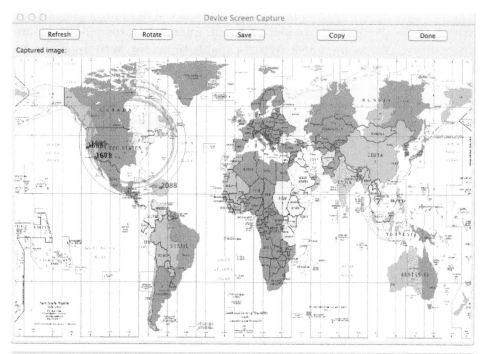

Figure 55—Using the device screen capture tool. In the Eclipse DDMS perspective you can capture screenshots directly from your Android device connected via USB.

Now you've created all the materials we need to submit to Google Play.

Submit Your App to Google Play

Proceed to Upload Application in your Developer Console.[20] When you've completed all the upload forms in Google Play, you are done! You've successfully completed the entire process of native Android app development—from development to distribution.

We're approaching the end of the book, but one question inevitably remains. What if we'd like to run our app on a platform other than Android—an iPhone

---

20. https://play.google.com/apps/publish/

or Windows phone, for example. Can we? Today the short answer is no. But a new mode recently added to the Processing IDE does offer a possible alternative. We'll investigate that option in the final section of this book.

13.5 Package Your App to Run in HTML5-Ready Browsers

When you want to reach the broadest audience and the widest range of devices and platforms, web applications are the way to go. Web apps are commonly written in JavaScript and can deliver a rich, interactive experience to users when they're run in the latest HTML5-capable browsers. Web apps can be integrated within a web page, and they can interact with web services and APIs such as Twitter or Flickr. Best of all, with a web app, you only need to maintain a single code base instead of a separate native application for each platform—iOS, Android, BlackberryOS, or Windows—that you wish to accommodate.

Thanks to the recently introduced JavaScript mode for Processing, you can now translate a Processing sketch into a JavaScript program and distribute it as a web application. As JavaScript, the sketch can, in theory, run in any HTML5-ready browser. However, as they say, some restrictions apply. We cannot, for example, use the same Ketai library that we've used throughout this book to interact with hardware sensors and devices on smartphones and tablets. Instead, we'll need to use web APIs for this task. The W3C's Sensor API Specification and Geolocation API Specification, however, exist today as working drafts and are not yet official.[21] And even when they are, support for the new APIs is unlikely to be consistent across browsers, and we'll need to consider which browser features we can use.[22]

The infamous remark by the CEO of Facebook ("I think the biggest mistake we made as a company is betting too much on HTML5 as opposed to native.") did not help HTML5's cause,[23] and this has contributed to the perception that compared to natively written apps, HTML5 web apps provide an inferior user experience. Many disagree, though, and a web application might be the best approach for your latest Processing project.

For one thing, the new HTML5 standard supports graphical and multimedia features not previously available. These include the new <canvas> element for rendering 2D and 3D graphics, as well as elements to handle audio and video. HTML5 supports SVG for 2D vector graphics, and HTML browsers typically

---

21. http://www.w3.org/TR/geolocation-API/ and http://www.w3.org/TR/geolocation-API/.
22. http://caniuse.com
23. http://www.forbes.com/sites/jjcolao/2012/09/19/facebooks-html5-dilemma-explained/

support the WebGL APIs,[24] which are based on OpenGL ES for 3D graphics. All of these features, and others we haven't mentioned, make it all the easier to translate the rich graphics of a Processing sketch to JavaScript code that can be rendered in the latest HTML5-ready browsers on Apple, Android, and Windows phones and tablets.

The availability of HTML5 support in the latest web browsers is not the only source of improved performance for rich web apps. JavaScript itself has gained a tremendous boost in power thanks to the arrival of more powerful JavaScript engines like SquirrelFish (Safari), V8 (Chrome), SpiderMonkey (Firefox), Futhark (Opera), and Chakra (Internet Explorer). We draw on this power when we use the JavaScript mode in Processing. JavaScript mode invokes Processing.js,[25] which translates our Processing code into JavaScript commands that render directly inside the HTML5 canvas without plugins. Using Processing.js and the OPENGL renderer, we can also take advantage of the WebGL APIs and their ability to interact with the graphics hardware (GPUs) found on current smartphones and tablets.

It's true that web apps have traditionally required an Internet connection at all times, and although native apps tend to require frequent network updates, they remain operational even when a carrier or Wi-Fi connection is unavailable. However, HTML5 now supports Offline Application Caching APIs that can be used to assure that users have access to a web app even when it's offline.[26]

Frequently updated benchmark tests show that improved browser performance has encouraged a steady migration of desktop applications into the Cloud,[27] with the web browser serving as the interface. From search engines to banks, blogs, games, software emulators, and news sites, JavaScript is used to enhance the user experience and make those sites interactive.

Web apps have no built-in revenue model, which is great for users but may or may not fit your intentions. To sell a web app for mobile devices, you can embed it inside a native app as a web view and distribute it via the Play Store or the App Store.[28] Web apps can be searched for and found via standard search engines and don't necessarily require the approval of a vendor.

---

24. http://www.khronos.org/webgl/
25. http://processingjs.org/articles/p5QuickStart.html
26. http://www.w3.org/TR/offline-webapps/
27. http://codehenge.net/blog/2012/08/javascript-performance-rundown-2012/
28. http://developer.android.com/reference/android/webkit/WebView.html or http://developer.apple.com/library/mac/#documentation/Cocoa/Reference/WebKit/Classes/WebView_Class/Reference/Reference.html.

Processing is an especially powerful language for creating visually rich user experiences, and HTML5 makes it possible to duplicate many of those features in a web app. Once our Processing sketch is translated into JavaScript code, it runs in a canvas without the use of browser plugins, and the canvas is not cut off from the other parts of the site. Making the switch is relatively straightforward, as we'll see in the next section.

Run a Sketch as a Web Application

iOS phones, BlackBerry OS, or Windows Mobile phones and tablets—all of these support HTML5 to run our Processing.js applications. We'll test this approach using familiar code, from the previous chapter to focus on the JavaScript mode in Processing without getting sidetracked developing a new project.

Let's get started and implement the 3D sketch as shown in Figure 56, *Run a sketch in a web browser (left)*, on page 332.

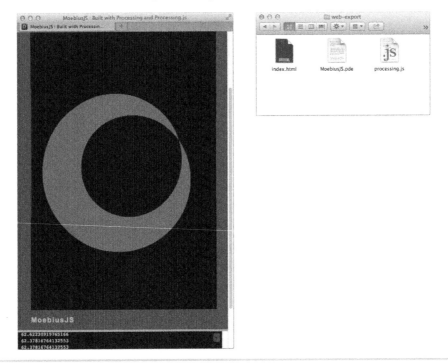

Figure 56—Run a sketch in a web browser (left). The JavaScript mode creates a web-export directory (right) that includes an HTML canvas (index.html), the Processing sketch MoebiusJS.pde, and the processing.js package.

We want to get an idea about the differences, if there are any, and see how the sketch performs compared to the native app in the mobile browser. We'll concentrate first on the 3D graphics and later explore how we can use the device orientation to control the rotation of our figure in 3D space.

The following sketch includes all the code we need to create and render our 3D figure. There is no difference between the code in JavaScript mode and the code, on page 304, we've used in the native Android mode. We've removed the Ketai code to read the gyro sensor because the Ketai library is not operational in the browser.

WebApps/MoebiusJS/MoebiusJS.pde

```
ArrayList<PVector> points = new ArrayList<PVector>();

void setup()
{
  size(480, 800, P3D);

  noStroke();
  int sections = 360;

  for (int i=0; i<=sections; i++)
  {
    pushMatrix();
    rotateZ(radians(map(i, 0, sections, 0, 360)));
    pushMatrix();
    translate(width/2, 0, 0);
    pushMatrix();
    rotateY(radians(map(i, 0, sections, 0, 180)));
    points.add(
      new PVector(modelX(0, 0, 50), modelY(0, 0, 50), modelZ(0, 0, 50))
    );
    points.add(
      new PVector(modelX(0, 0, -50), modelY(0, 0, -50), modelZ(0, 0, -50))
    );
    popMatrix();
    popMatrix();
    popMatrix();
  }
}

void draw()
{
  background(0);
  ambientLight(0, 0, 128);
  pointLight(255, 255, 255, 0, 0, 0);

  translate(width/2, height/2, 0);
```

```
  beginShape(QUAD_STRIP);
  for (int i=0; i<points.size(); i++)
  {
    vertex(points.get(i).x, points.get(i).y, points.get(i).z);
  }
  endShape(CLOSE);

  if (frameCount % 10 == 0)
    println(frameRate);
}
```

We'll use the println(frameRate) method to get feedback on the sketch performance running in the browser. Let's go ahead and test the app in the web browser.

Run the App

Check the JavaScript mode and run the Möbius sketch. Processing will launch your default web browser and start the MöbiusJS sketch in a new window, as shown in Figure 56, *Run a sketch in a web browser (left)*, on page 332.

When we press Run, Processing creates a web-export folder inside the sketch folder that contains an HTML page called index.html, the Processing source file MoebiusJS.pde, and the processing.js JavaScript port of the Processing language.

You'll need to edit the HTML layout of index.html before you publish this web application.

Editing Browser Apps Online

If we're developing sketches that will be rendered in a web browser, we can use the browser itself to live-code them online. This allows us not only to develop sketches on the desktop computer but also to write and preview sketches directly on the Android device. A few online editors can even render Processing code that we write online directly into a canvas preview on the same page.

One editor I recommend is SketchPad, available at http://sketchpad.cc. The name of this editor alludes to the Processing sketch metaphor and the "pad" included in the widely used open-source EtherPad online editor. EtherPad enables collaborative coding in real time—in the words of its sponsors, "much like a live multiplayer online editor."[29]

We can use SketchPad to program directly in the browser and render the Processing sketch inside a canvas. We can also use it to code collaboratively with others. We can share a link to the sketch we are working on with one or

---

29. http://etherpad.org/

more developers. Each contribution to the sketch is updated for everyone in real time and individually color-coded. If we register for an account, we can save the sketch and create private or public groups or classes, which can be used by a number of universities and institutions to teach programming online.

Because SketchPad is based on EtherPad, all contributions are recorded along a time line. Each revision is marked on a time slider and added every time a user previews it in the web canvas, allowing each collaborator to see the evolution of the sketch. Sketchpad's live-coding features are an excellent example of how Processing.js can be integrated into the surrounding web page and APIs, such as EtherPad.

Let's now take a look at some experimental ways to access the device hardware within the browser.

Work with an Accelerometer and a GPS Device

When we'd like to bring the native app user experience to the web, it's useful to take a look at the work W3C is currently doing to allow browsers to access the hardware features of mobile devices, such as those responsible for device orientation and location. For this final project, let's make use of the most recent W3C draft specification and create a sketch that includes JavaScript methods to access orientation and location information available on a mobile device.[30]

Not all HTML5 browsers currently support this draft specification. Also, this feature will only work with mobile devices or laptop computers with built-in hard drives that have moving parts. The restriction comes from the fact that desktop computers and laptop computers with solid state hard drives don't have an accelerometer built in and are therefore not able to detect device orientation.

For this final sketch, let's add the device orientation to the code, on page 333, as an interface to control the rotation of our Möbius figure in 3D space. Also, let's display the current device latitude and longitude, as shown in Figure 57, *Using device orientation and location in a Processing web app*, on page 336, to check if we have access to the browser location feature as well. We'll work with two tabs, one main tab that includes the code to position and display our Möbius figure, and a second one called ketai.js that contains all the JavaScript methods we need to gather the location and orientation data from the browser.

---

30. http://www.w3.org/TR/orientation-event/#deviceorientation/

Figure 57—Using device orientation and location in a Processing web app. The web browser gives us access to the device orientation and location via JavaScript. We print the device latitude and longitude into the console on the bottom of the display.

Using JavaScript, ketai.js takes care of registering the app for deviceorientation events as well as any devicemotion reported to the web browser. We don't want to dive too deep into the JavaScript language, but we'll comment on the significant methods we are using next.

Let's take a look at the code.

WebApps/MoebiusJSOrientationLocation/MoebiusJSOrientationLocation.pde

```
❶ PVector location = new PVector();
❷ PVector orientation = new PVector();

ArrayList<PVector> points = new ArrayList<PVector>();
void setup()
{
  size(480, 800, P3D);

  noStroke();
  int sections = 360;

  for (int i=0; i<=sections; i++)
```

```
    {
      pushMatrix();
      rotateZ(radians(map(i, 0, sections, 0, 360)));
      pushMatrix();
      translate(width/3, 0, 0);
      pushMatrix();
      rotateY(radians(map(i, 0, sections, 0, 180)));
      points.add(
        new PVector(modelX(0, 0, 50), modelY(0, 0, 50), modelZ(0, 0, 50))
      );
      points.add(
        new PVector(modelX(0, 0, -50), modelY(0, 0, -50), modelZ(0, 0, -50))
      );
      popMatrix();
      popMatrix();
      popMatrix();
    }
  }

  void draw()
  {
    background(0);
    ambientLight(0, 0, 128);
    pointLight(255, 255, 255, 0, 0, 0);

    translate(width/2, height/2, 0);
    rotateX(orientation.x);
    rotateY(orientation.y);
    rotateZ(orientation.z);

    beginShape(QUAD_STRIP);
    for (int i=0; i<points.size(); i++)
    {
      vertex(points.get(i).x, points.get(i).y, points.get(i).z);
    }
    endShape(CLOSE);
    if (frameCount%100 == 0)
      println("Latitude: " + location.x + " | Longitude: " + location.y);
  }

③ void orientationEvent ( float ox, float oy, float oz)
  {
④   orientation.set(ox, oy, oz);
  }

⑤ void locationEvent(float lat, float lon)
  {
⑥   location.set(lat, lon);
  }
```

Here are the steps we need to take to add location and orientation features to our sketch.

❶ Define a PVector called location to store incoming latitude and longitude values.

❷ Define a PVector called orientation to store incoming latitude and longitude values.

❸ Include a callback method for returning orientation data called every 200 milliseconds, defined in ketai.js.

❹ Set the orientation vector to the incoming orientation's *x*, *y*, and *z* values.

❺ Include a callback method for returning location data called every 200 milliseconds, defined in ketai.js.

❻ Set the location vector to the incoming latitude and longitude values.

Now let's take a look at the ketai.js tab, which includes all the necessary code to receive callbacks from the browser that report orientation and location data.

WebApps/MoebiusJSOrientationLocation/ketai.js

```
document.addEventListener('DOMContentLoaded', function() {
❶  bindToSketch();
}
, false);

function bindToSketch () {
  var sketch = Processing.getInstanceById('MoebiusJSOrientationLocation');
  if ( sketch == undefined )
❷    return setTimeout(bindToSketch, 200);

  if (window.DeviceOrientationEvent) {
    window.addEventListener('deviceorientation', function(event) {
❸      sketch.orientationEvent(event.beta, event.gamma, event.alpha);
      console.log(event);
    }
    , false);
  }
  else if (window.DeviceMotionEvent) {
❹    window.addEventListener('devicemotion', function(event) {
      sketch.orientationEvent(
        event.acceleration.x, event.acceleration.y, event.acceleration.z
      );
    }
    , true);
  }
```

```
  else {
    window.addEventListener('DeviceOrientationEvent', function(orientation) {
      sketch.orientationEvent(orientation.x, orientation.y, orientation.z);
    }
    , true);
  }

  if (navigator.geolocation)
  {
    navigator.geolocation.watchPosition(
    function success(position) {
      sketch.locationEvent(position.coords.latitude, position.coords.longitude);
    }
    ,
    function error(e) {
      // Ignore and use defaults already set for coords
      console.log('Unable to get geolocation position data: ' + e);
    }
    );
  }
}
```

We are working with the following JavaScript methods to capture orientation and location events.

❶ Call the bindToSketch() method when the web page is loaded.

❷ Set the timeout to the JavaScript method bindToSketch(), calling itself again after 200 milliseconds.

❸ Add an event listener for device orientation as determined by the device accelerometer.

❹ Add an event listener for device motion as determined by the device accelerometer.

❺ Add an event listener for the device location determined by the network IP address or GPS receiver.

Now let's test the sketch.

Run the App

Run the JavaScript sketch in your browser. The browser will prompt you to allow the use of location data for this page. Once you agree, observe the latitude and longitude data printed to the browser console. You can also test the orientation feature using a laptop computer if it is equipped with a standard hard drive (if you have a solid state drive, you typically won't have an accelerometer built in).

The final destination of your web app is a web server so that you can access it on any platform from any smart phone, tablet, or desktop computer. Transfer the contents of your web-export folder to your preferred web server, browse and test the sketch, and then distribute the URL publicly.

13.6 Wrapping Up

This concludes our exploration of the myriad ways you can build Android applications with the Processing language and IDE. In more than forty projects, you've learned how to easy it can be to work with the touch screen panel, device sensors, location devices, cameras, peer-to-peer networking, and OpenGL-accelerated graphics found on the latest Android phones and tablets. You've learned how to share your work with friends and other developers and how to publish it to Google Play. And finally, you've learned how to use the new JavaScript mode to generate applications that run in a browser.

You're now ready to dive into the world of Android app development. With the skills you've learned in this book, you can add multitouch gestures in your applications, write location-based and navigation apps, implement data-visualizations, create camera-based apps, work with peers via Bluetooth and Wi-Fi Direct, and build apps that communicate via near field communications with payment terminals and other mobile devices. And for any of these, you can create rich OpenGL graphics and draw on the power of the trove of hardware sensors and devices found on today's Androids.

It's been a pleasure to be your guide to the world of Processing for Android. Now it's up to you. Have fun!

Appendix

A1.1 Android Version History

Throughout the book we often use the following names to refer to particular Android releases and their software dependencies.

- Jelly Bean (4.1/4.2)
- Ice Cream Sandwich (4.0)
- Honeycomb (3.0/3.1)
- Gingerbread (2.3)
- Froyo (2.2)
- Eclair (2.0/2.1)

You can find a comprehensive version history and feature list at http://en.wikipedia.org/wiki/Android_version_history.

A1.2 The Ketai Library Classes

The Ketai library contains the following main classes, all of which we use in the book:

KetaiGesture[1] A class giving us access to Android's Gesture class, providing us with the basic multitouch gestures typically used with a touch screen interface, including (single) touch, double-tap, long tap, flick, pinch, and rotate[2]

KetaiSensor[3] Contains methods to interact with all of the sensors commonly found on an Android device, listed in Section 3.2, *Introducing Common Android Sensors*, on page 41—we work with this class for the projects in that chapter.

---

1. http://ketai.googlecode.com/svn/trunk/ketai/reference/ketai/ui/KetaiGesture.html
2. http://en.wikipedia.org/wiki/Multi-touch#Multi-touch_gestures
3. http://ketai.googlecode.com/svn/trunk/ketai/reference/ketai/sensors/KetaiSensor.html

KetaiLocation[4] Contains methods to work with the Android Location Manager, calculating estimates for the device's current location using GPS or network localization techniques—we work with this class in Chapter 4, *Using Geolocation and Compass*, on page 69.

KetaiCamera[5] Contains methods to use the front- and back-facing device cameras, including flash and face recognition—we work with this class in Chapter 5, *Using Android Cameras*, on page 93.

KetaiSimpleFace[6] Contains a method to find faces within a Processing image, returning a list of detected faces, including features such as eye positions and distance—since API level 14, Android also offers face detection as a hardware feature on the latest devices that support it, made available through the KetaiFace class in KetaiCamera, which we work with in Chapter 5, *Using Android Cameras*, on page 93.[7]

KetaiBluetooth[8] Contains methods to transfer data between Android devices via Bluetooth—KetaiBluetooth simplifies the process for scanning available Bluetooth devices, querying paired devices, establishing a radio frequency communication channel, and connecting to other Bluetooth devices. We work with this class in Chapter 7, *Peer-to-Peer Networking Using Bluetooth and Wi-Fi Direct*, on page 151.

KetaiWiFiDirect[9] Contains methods to transfer data between Android devices via Wi-Fi Direct, a new peer-to-peer standard available on some devices since Android 4.0 (API level 14)—devices connect directly to each other without a Wi-Fi access point. KetaiWiFiDirect simplifies the process of discovering and connecting to other Wi-Fi Direct–enabled devices. Wi-Fi Direct enables connections across longer distances when compared with Bluetooth. We work with this class in Chapter 7, *Peer-to-Peer Networking Using Bluetooth and Wi-Fi Direct*, on page 151.

KetaiNFC[10] Contains networking classes to exchange data via near field communication (NFC)—we work with this class in Chapter 7, *Peer-to-Peer Networking Using Bluetooth and Wi-Fi Direct*, on page 151.

---

4.   http://ketai.googlecode.com/svn/trunk/ketai/reference/ketai/sensors/KetaiLocation.html

5.   http://ketai.googlecode.com/svn/trunk/ketai/reference/ketai/camera/KetaiCamera.html

6.   http://ketai.googlecode.com/svn/trunk/ketai/reference/ketai/cv/facedetector/KetaiSimpleFace.html

7.   http://ketai.googlecode.com/svn/trunk/ketai/reference/ketai/camera/KetaiFace.html

8.   http://ketai.googlecode.com/svn/trunk/ketai/reference/ketai/net/bluetooth/KetaiBluetooth.html

9.   http://ketai.googlecode.com/svn/trunk/ketai/reference/ketai/net/wifidirect/KetaiWiFiDirect.html

10. http://ketai.googlecode.com/svn/trunk/ketai/reference/ketai/net/nfc/KetaiNFC.html

KetaiList[11] Contains methods and constants to create a UI selection list. KetaiList simplifies the process to create a native Android UI list using a String array. We work with this class in Chapter 7, *Peer-to-Peer Networking Using Bluetooth and Wi-Fi Direct*, on page 151.

KetaiKeyboard[12] A Ketai class giving us access to the native Android software keyboard, providing methods to show, hide, and toggle the keyboard

A1.3 Writing to a Text File on a Web Server

Let's recap. We are not able to exchange information between devices if we do not identify each party involved. One device needs to learn about the other through some kind of identifier. In addition, location information must be stored in such a way that both devices can access it. This is where the web server comes in. It functions as a shared place that can both store and serve information.

The location.php PHP script on the project server (serverURL) is set up in a way that it stores the location info of every identified device in a separate text file. You've already written your location to that server if you ran the sketch earlier. If you'd like to host your PHP script on your own server, you are at the right place here. The idea of keeping personal data close by and secure is comprehensible and advisable. Therefore, let's discuss the steps that need to be taken to install location.php on your server. Then we'll talk about one method to encrypt the location data.

1. Click to download the location.php file below.

2. FTP to your server of choice with your FTP software of choice.

3. Create a folder in your public web directory to host your locations, such as deviceLocator.

4. Check the permissions on the folder so that "owner" is set to "write" 755, which stands for the following: owner—read, write, and execute permissions; group—read and execute permissions; others—read and execute permissions.

5. Modify the device locator sketch variable serverURL to point to the new location.

6. Run the sketch on Android 1.

---

11. http://ketai.googlecode.com/svn/trunk/ketai/reference/ketai/ui/KetaiList.html

12. http://ketai.googlecode.com/svn/trunk/ketai/reference/ketai/ui/KetaiKeyboard.html

7. Swap the myName and deviceTracked identifiers and run the sketch on Android 2.

8. Go find!

Now that you are running your device finder app on two Android devices that are connected to the web server, let's take a closer look at the PHP script that reads and writes our data. It's a very concise script that works as a hub between the app on the device and the text files that contain location data. What makes one locations.php script perform different tasks is based on the basic principle that data can be attached to the requested URL using the so-called GET method.[13] PHP makes GET data automatically available to the script. In our case we tell the script whether we request a location from the other device or update our location info. The actual location data is submitted to the script with the same GET method. Let's take a look.

Geolocation/DeviceLocator/location.php

```php
<?
        // Geolocation Device Locator PHP Script
        // Writing to a text file on a web server
❶       if(isset($_GET['get']))
        {
❷               $filename = $_GET['get'].".txt";
❸               if(file_exists($filename))
                {
❹                       $file = file_get_contents($filename);
❺                       echo $file;
                } else
                        echo "ERROR! No location found for " . $_GET['get'];
        }
        //if the request is an update, we dump the location into a file
        // named after the device making the request
❻       else if(isset($_GET['update']) && isset($_GET['location']))
        {
❼               $fh =fopen($_GET['update'].".txt", "w");
                if($fh == FALSE)
                {
                        echo "ERROR.  Cannot open file on server.";
                        return;
                }
❽               if(fwrite($fh, $_GET['location']."\n") == FALSE)
                        echo "ERROR. Writing to file.";
❾               if(fclose($fh) == FALSE)
                    echo "ERROR. Closing file,";
        }
?>
```

13. http://www.php.net/manual/en/language.variables.external.php

OK, what's going on here? Let's recap what we sent to the PHP script. If we are getting the location of the other device, we are sending this message:

```
serverURL + "?get="+deviceTracked
```

This translates into the following:

```
http://www.ketaiProject.com/rad/location.php?get=yourNexus
```

If we are writing an update to our own location, then we send this:

```
serverURL+"?update="+myName+"&amp;location="+latitude+","+longitude+","+altitude
```

In the end it looks like this:

```
http://www.ketaiProject.com/rad/location.php
        ?update=myNexus&amp;location=41.824698,-87.658777,0.0
```

Hence, our location.php script received either a variable named get with an assigned string value yourNexus, if we are requesting the location of the other device, or the script received a variable named update set to myNexus and a variable named location set to the latitude, longitude, and altitude, separated by ",". PHP makes these $_GET[] variables automatically available to the script, handling this as follows:

❶ Check to see if we received a get request via the GET method.[14]

❷ Point to the text file named, like the string, as a KetaiLocation-type variable, updated when our device detects a location update.

❸ Check if we got a file with this name on the server.

❹ Get the contents of the file;[15] fail gracefully if doesn't contain content.

❺ Check whether we got an update request and location info via GET.

❼ Open the file for writing.[16]

❽ Write the location to a text file.[17]

❾ Close up the file—all done.[18]

PHP is great at making information submitted via GET (and POST) available to the script. Our script checks whether we've received a get request or an update, causing it to either look up a text file on the server or to write one.

---

14. http://www.php.net/manual/en/reserved.variables.get.php

15. http://us2.php.net/manual/en/function.file-get-contents.php

16. http://us2.php.net/manual/en/function.fopen.php

17. http://us2.php.net/manual/en/function.fwrite.php

18. http://us2.php.net/manual/en/function.fclose.php

Again, we don't have to dive into PHP to make this work, since it does its job on any server if the folder permissions are set to "write" (chmod 755). It's good to have an idea, though, of what the script is actually doing.

Introducing PHP

PHP is a very versatile server-side scripting language. It's the most popular server-side module and is installed on more than one million web servers. As a general purpose scripting language, it is used for dynamic web pages, where content is rendered at runtime. In the web industry, LAMP architecture has become widely popular (LAMP is an abbreviation for Linux, Apache, MySQL, and PHP services provided by an Internet service provider). Examples for web content management systems written in PHP include WordPress, MediaWiki, and Drupal. PHP is used as a server-side programming language on more than 75 percent of all web servers.

A1.4 Troubleshooting

Generally, check if you have the correct permission for your sketch under Android → Permissions.

Device killed or disconnected. Log: Failure [INSTALL_PARSE_FAILED_INCONSISTENT_CERTIFICATES] A Processing .apk with the same name has been installed on the device from another PC, resulting in inconsistent certificates.

Failed to open camera for camera ID: 0:Fail to connect to camera service Make sure your sketch has the appropriate permissions to use the camera, located under Android → Permissions. Alternatively, another app might be using the camera and have it locked.

Failed to open camera for camera ID: 0:Fail to connect to camera service The camera is locked down by another sketch or has not been released properly. Restart your device and rerun the sketch.

java.lang.SecurityException Make sure your sketch has the appropriate permissions in the Android Permission Selector you'll find in Processing 2.0 (Android mode) under Android → Permissions.

If you get an error, please double-check whether you have the Android SDK components installed as shown in Figure 58, *Minimum software required for Android*, on page 347. You should start the Android → Android SDK & AVD Manager from the Android menu in Processing and take a look. Make sure you also have the correct device drivers if you are developing on Windows or Linux.[19]

---

19. http://wiki.processing.org/w/Android#Instructions

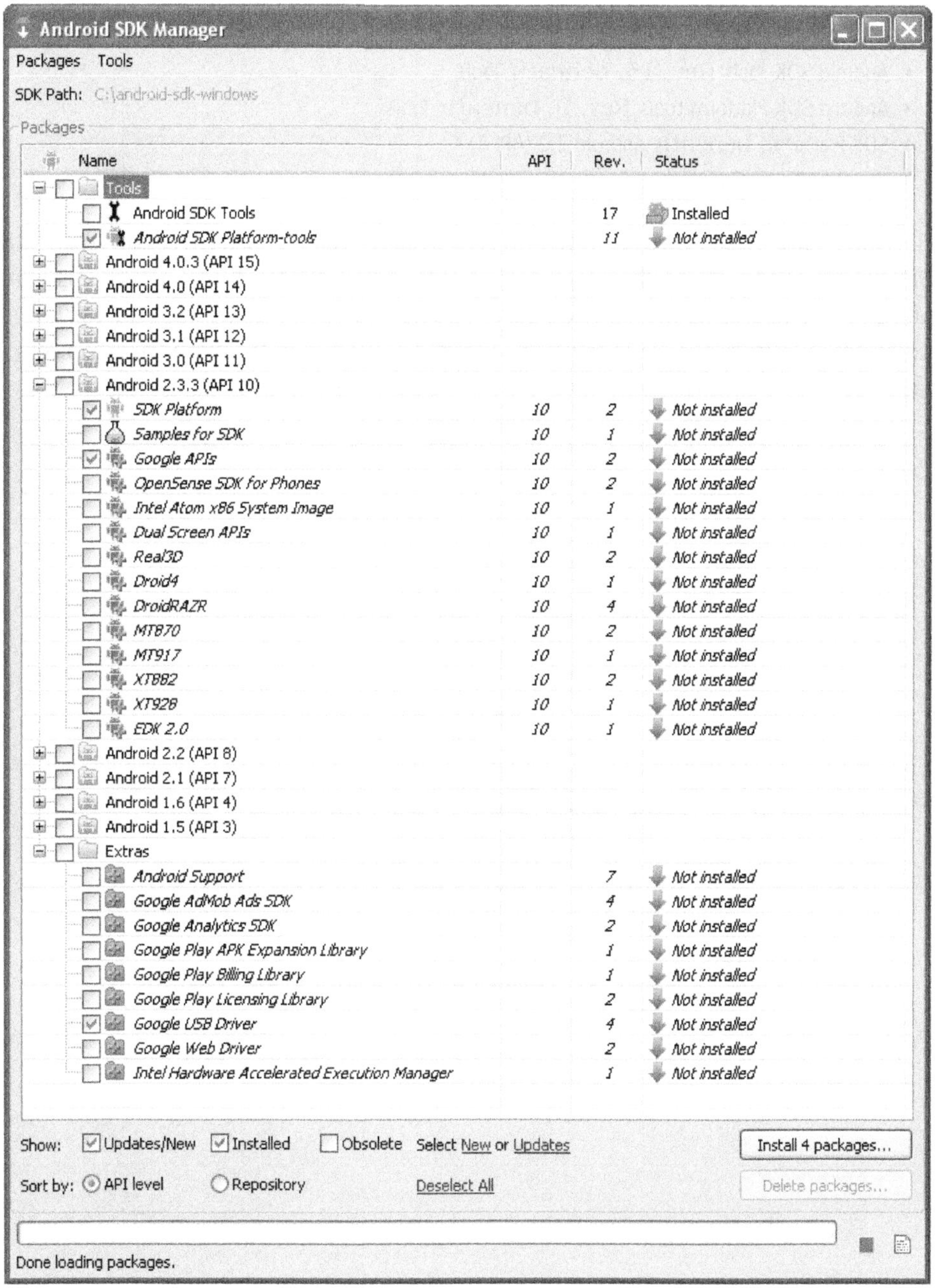

Figure 58—Minimum software required for Android. To run a Processing sketch in the Android emulator or on an Android device, you need the additional packages shown as "Installed" in this screenshot of the Android SDK Manager.

Here's a checklist for what you need:

- Android SDK Tools Rev. 15, beneath Tools
- Android SDK Platform-tools Rev. 9, beneath Tools
- SDK Platform, beneath Android 2.2 (API 8)
- Google APIs by Google Inc., beneath Android 2.2 (API 8)

Because both the Android SDK and API update very frequently, the Android SDK & AVD Manager is the place to check for future updates. You can perform all updates directly from the manager—no need to browse the web for updates anymore. Every time you launch the manager it checks for available updates, and you can select the revisions you might need or are interested in.

Bibliography

[Fry08]   Ben Fry. *Visualizing Data*. O'Reilly & Associates, Inc., Sebastopol, CA, 2008.

[RF10]   Casey Reas and Ben Fry. *Getting Started with Processing*. O'Reilly & Associates, Inc., Sebastopol, CA, 2010.

[RF11]   Casey Reas and Ben Fry. *Processing: A Programming Handbook for Visual Designers and Artists*. MIT Press, Cambridge, MA, Second, 2011.

Index

Long live the command line!

Use tmux for incredible mouse-free productivity, and learn how to create professional command-line apps.

Your mouse is slowing you down. The time you spend context switching between your editor and your consoles eats away at your productivity. Take control of your environment with tmux, a terminal multiplexer that you can tailor to your workflow. Learn how to customize, script, and leverage tmux's unique abilities and keep your fingers on your keyboard's home row.

Brian P. Hogan
(88 pages) ISBN: 9781934356968. $11.00
http://pragprog.com/book/bhtmux

Speak directly to your system. With its simple commands, flags, and parameters, a well-formed command-line application is the quickest way to automate a backup, a build, or a deployment and simplify your life.

David Bryant Copeland
(200 pages) ISBN: 9781934356913. $33
http://pragprog.com/book/dccar

Welcome to the New Web

You need a better JavaScript and better recipes that professional web developers use every day. Start here.

CoffeeScript is JavaScript done right. It provides all of JavaScript's functionality wrapped in a cleaner, more succinct syntax. In the first book on this exciting new language, CoffeeScript guru Trevor Burnham shows you how to hold onto all the power and flexibility of JavaScript while writing clearer, cleaner, and safer code.

Trevor Burnham
(160 pages) ISBN: 9781934356784. $29
http://pragprog.com/book/tbcoffee

Modern web development takes more than just HTML and CSS with a little JavaScript mixed in. Clients want more responsive sites with faster interfaces that work on multiple devices, and you need the latest tools and techniques to make that happen. This book gives you more than 40 concise, tried-and-true solutions to today's web development problems, and introduces new workflows that will expand your skillset.

Brian P. Hogan, Chris Warren, Mike Weber, Chris Johnson, Aaron Godin
(344 pages) ISBN: 9781934356838. $35
http://pragprog.com/book/wbdev

Seven Databases, Seven Languages

There's so much new to learn with the latest crop of NoSQL databases. And instead of learning a language a year, how about seven?

Data is getting bigger and more complex by the day, and so are your choices in handling it. From traditional RDBMS to newer NoSQL approaches, *Seven Databases in Seven Weeks* takes you on a tour of some of the hottest open source databases today. In the tradition of Bruce A. Tate's *Seven Languages in Seven Weeks*, this book goes beyond a basic tutorial to explore the essential concepts at the core of each technology.

Eric Redmond and Jim Wilson
(330 pages) ISBN: 9781934356920. $35
http://pragprog.com/book/rwdata

You should learn a programming language every year, as recommended by *The Pragmatic Programmer*. But if one per year is good, how about *Seven Languages in Seven Weeks*? In this book you'll get a hands-on tour of Clojure, Haskell, Io, Prolog, Scala, Erlang, and Ruby. Whether or not your favorite language is on that list, you'll broaden your perspective of programming by examining these languages side-by-side. You'll learn something new from each, and best of all, you'll learn how to learn a language quickly.

Bruce A. Tate
(328 pages) ISBN: 9781934356593. $34.95
http://pragprog.com/book/btlang

Pragmatic Guide Series

Get started quickly, with a minimum of fuss and hand-holding. The Pragmatic Guide Series features convenient, task-oriented two-page spreads. You'll find what you need fast, and get on with your work.

Need to learn how to wrap your head around Git, but don't need a lot of hand holding? Grab this book if you're new to Git, not to the world of programming. Git tasks displayed on two-page spreads provide all the context you need, without the extra fluff.

Travis Swicegood
(160 pages) ISBN: 9781934356722. $25
http://pragprog.com/book/pg_git

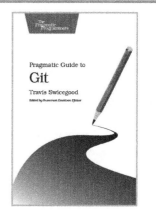

JavaScript is everywhere. It's a key component of to-day's Web—a powerful, dynamic language with a rich ecosystem of professional-grade development tools, infrastructures, frameworks, and toolkits. This book will get you up to speed quickly and painlessly with the 35 key JavaScript tasks you need to know.

Christophe Porteneuve
(160 pages) ISBN: 9781934356678. $25
http://pragprog.com/book/pg_js

Career++

Ready to kick your career up to the next level? Start by growing a significant online presence, and then reinvigorate your job itself.

Technical Blogging is the first book to specifically teach programmers, technical people, and technically-oriented entrepreneurs how to become successful bloggers. There is no magic to successful blogging; with this book you'll learn the techniques to attract and keep a large audience of loyal, regular readers and leverage this popularity to achieve your goals.

Antonio Cangiano
(304 pages) ISBN: 9781934356883. $33
http://pragprog.com/book/actb

You're already a great coder, but awesome coding chops aren't always enough to get you through your toughest projects. You need these 50+ nuggets of wisdom. Veteran programmers: reinvigorate your passion for developing web applications. New programmers: here's the guidance you need to get started. With this book, you'll think about your job in new and enlightened ways.

Ka Wai Cheung
(250 pages) ISBN: 9781934356791. $29
http://pragprog.com/book/kcdc

Be Agile

Don't just "do" agile; you want to *be* agile. We'll show you how.

The best agile book isn't a book: *Agile in a Flash* is a unique deck of index cards that fit neatly in your pocket. You can tape them to the wall. Spread them out on your project table. Get stains on them over lunch. These cards are meant to be used, not just read.

Jeff Langr and Tim Ottinger
(110 pages) ISBN: 9781934356715. $15
http://pragprog.com/book/olag

You know the Agile and Lean development buzzwords, you've read the books. But when systems need a serious overhaul, you need to see how it works in real life, with real situations and people. *Lean from the Trenches* is all about actual practice. Every key point is illustrated with a photo or diagram, and anecdotes bring you inside the project as you discover why and how one organization modernized its workplace in record time.

Henrik Kniberg
(176 pages) ISBN: 9781934356852. $30
http://pragprog.com/book/hklean

The Pragmatic Bookshelf

The Pragmatic Bookshelf features books written by developers for developers. The titles continue the well-known Pragmatic Programmer style and continue to garner awards and rave reviews. As development gets more and more difficult, the Pragmatic Programmers will be there with more titles and products to help you stay on top of your game.

Visit Us Online

This Book's Home Page
http://pragprog.com/book/dsproc
Source code from this book, errata, and other resources. Come give us feedback, too!

Register for Updates
http://pragprog.com/updates
Be notified when updates and new books become available.

Join the Community
http://pragprog.com/community
Read our weblogs, join our online discussions, participate in our mailing list, interact with our wiki, and benefit from the experience of other Pragmatic Programmers.

New and Noteworthy
http://pragprog.com/news
Check out the latest pragmatic developments, new titles and other offerings.

Save on the eBook

Save on the eBook versions of this title. Owning the paper version of this book entitles you to purchase the electronic versions at a terrific discount.

PDFs are great for carrying around on your laptop—they are hyperlinked, have color, and are fully searchable. Most titles are also available for the iPhone and iPod touch, Amazon Kindle, and other popular e-book readers.

Buy now at *http://pragprog.com/coupon*

Contact Us

Online Orders:	*http://pragprog.com/catalog*
Customer Service:	*support@pragprog.com*
International Rights:	*translations@pragprog.com*
Academic Use:	*academic@pragprog.com*
Write for Us:	*http://pragprog.com/write-for-us*
Or Call:	+1 800-699-7764

CPSIA information can be obtained at www.ICGtesting.com
Printed in the USA
LVOW03s1454130114

369228LV00033B/252/P